Simon Stephens

Plays: 1

Bluebird: 'as accomplished, comic and revealing about the people who litter London's streets as anything I've ever seen on stage or screen' *The Times*

Christmas: 'displays a sharp ear for the surface absurdities and dark undercurrents of everyday conversation, a touchingly compassionate attitude towards those down on their luck' *Daily Telegraph*

Herons: 'What is remarkable about Simon Stephens's play is that, while graphically acknowledging the nihilistic cruelty of east end school kids, it is also filled with a sense of life's miraculous potential. It deals with damaged characters yet is imbued with a poetic lyricism' *Guardian*

Port: 'the drama undoubtedly grips . . . Stephens is superb at capturing the cruelties of childhood and adolescence. But he is also blessed with compassion and a gift for dark humour' *Daily Telegraph*

Simon Stephens' play *Bring Me Sunshine* was staged at the Assembly Rooms at the 1997 Edinburgh Fringe Festival, transferring to the Riverside Studios in London the same year (revived in 2000 at the Manchester Royal Exchange). *Bluebird* was produced by the Royal Court in London in 1998. He was the Arts Council Resident Dramatist at the Royal Court in 2000 and the Pearson Playwright at the Royal Exchange in 2000–01. His next play, *Herons* (Royal Court, 2001), was nominated for the Olivier Award for Most Promising Playwright. His radio play *Five Letters to Elizabeth* was broadcast on BBC Radio 4 in 2001, and *Digging* on Radio 4 in 2003. His next stage play, *Port* (Royal Exchange, 2002), was awarded the Pearson Award for Best New Play in 2001/2. *One Minute* was produced by the Actors Touring Company in June 2003; *Christmas* premiered at the Pavilion Theatre, Brighton, before transferring to the Bush Theatre, London, in January 2004, and *Country Music* was produced by the Royal Court in 2004. In 2005 *On the Shore of the Wide World* was co-produced by the Royal Exchange and the National Theatre, opening in Manchester in April and transferring to London in May.

D1343852

also by Simon Stephens

Country Music
Christmas
Harper Regan
Motortown
On the Shore of the Wide World
One Minute
Pornography
Port
Punk Rock

Stephens Plays: 2

SIMON STEPHENS

Plays: 1

Bluebird
Christmas
Herons
Port

with an introduction by the author

Methuen Drama

Published by Methuen Drama

5 7 9 10 8 6 4

First published in 2005 by
Methuen Publishing Limited

Methuen Drama
A & C Black Publishers Ltd
36 Soho Square
London W1D 3QY
www.methuendrama.com

Christmas first published 2003, this revised edition 2005; *Herons* first published
2001, this revised edition 2005; *Port* first published 2002, this revised edition 2005

Simon Stephens has asserted his right under the Copyright, Designs and Patents
Act, 1988, to be identified as the author of this work.

A CIP catalogue record for this book is available from the British Library

ISBN 978 0 413 77547 4

Typeset by SX Composing DTP, Rayleigh, Essex
Printed and bound in Great Britian by
Good News Digital Books, Ongar

Contents

Simon Stephens:
A Chronology

1997   *Bring Me Sunshine* (Assembly Rooms, Edinburgh, and Riverside Studio, London)

1998   *Bluebird* (Royal Court, London)

2001   *Herons* (Royal Court): nominated for the Olivier Award for Most Promising Playwright
        Five Letters to Elizabeth (radio play, broadcast on BBC Radio 4)

2002   *Port* (Royal Exchange, Manchester): Pearson Award for Best New Play in 2001/2

2003   *Digging* (radio play, broadcast on BBC Radio 4)
        One Minute (produced by the Actors Touring Company, Crucible Theatre, Sheffield)

2003/4 *Christmas* (Pavilion Theatre, Brighton, and Bush Theatre, London)

2004   *Country Music* (Royal Court)

2005   *On the Shore of the Wide World* (Royal Exchange, Manchester, and National Theatre, London)

Introduction

It is something of a crass simplification but it strikes me nevertheless as true that playwrights come to playwriting through one of two routes. Some are frustrated actors who decide to write themselves a cracking role. In fact, most of Britain's best playwrights could be described like that. Others are writers who somehow stumble upon the theatre as the medium that best articulates what they want to say. I would feel more comfortable being described in this second way.

I've always written. Ever since I was about six. I've often felt happier writing than doing almost anything else. It's thrilling to me that I make a fair chunk of my living by writing, because it's something that I've always wanted to do. It's rather odd to me in retrospect, however, that I should do it by writing for the theatre.

I was born in 1971 and raised in Stockport, a suburb to the south of Manchester. Before I was eighteen, I reckon I went to the theatre seven times, at most. If it's true that I wanted from a young age to be a writer, I think it is also fair to say that I always wanted to be a songwriter. I wanted to write lyrics like Elvis Costello or Tom Waits or Mark Eitzel. My biggest disappointment was that I only ever really sang like a drain. My adolescence was graced and charged by the TV dramas of Dennis Potter and Alan Bleasdale and the films of David Lynch and Martin Scorsese. It was their work, much more than it was the work of any playwright, that introduced me to the notion of dramatic writing.

I decided to do a degree in History rather than English because I loved literature too much to want to dissect it. It was at York University that I found my way to the theatre (more often than not out of some attempt to chat up some Home Counties English student), a dank little place, on the peripheries of the campus, called the Drama Barn.

While watching plays here, I was struck with quite a simple notion: What if it were possible to create the same sense of toughness and compassion, comedy and brutality that I found in the dramatic work of Bleasdale and Potter, of

Lynch and Scorsese, in a dramatic medium that allowed
you to lock the doors? What if you were in the same room as
Frank Booth or Yosser Hughes and you couldn't get out?
What if other people were in there with you? It was a notion
that led me to write for theatre.

It was a notion that has sustained me ever since.

It is important to say that *Bluebird* is not the first play I
ever wrote. In fact, it is the ninth. At York, for two years in
Edinburgh, and then for three years in London after that, I
wrote a series of terrible plays. I don't even know where half
of the scripts for these plays are any more. Some of them
were produced in fringe venues in those cities. A couple of
them were, rightly, never produced at all. I learned
something from all of them. Too much is made out of
blazing accidental amateurism in new-writing theatre
nowadays. It puts an awful burden on genuinely first-time
playwrights. I am glad I had the chance to fuck up and fuck
up again and again.

It's also important for me to say that I never formally
studied playwriting, and certainly never at university. The
necessary subject of all plays is humanity. Playwrights
explore, artistically, what it is to be a human being, with
more rigour and detail than the practitioners of any other
art. In that sense I learned more about my subject from
managing a bar or from working in cafés, and travelling on
night buses and working for a mobile disco company and as
a *Betterware Homecare Catalogue* delivery man than I ever
would have done on any playwriting course. While I
passionately believe that it *is* possible to teach playwriting, at
least that it is possible to learn and develop many of the
elements of a playwright's craft, I equally believe that
academic study alone will not suffice for anybody. You need
to have lived a bit.

I wrote *Bluebird* in 1997. I was living in north London with
Polly, the woman who was to become my wife. After the
decision to have a baby, I decided to write about the worst
possible thing that I could imagine ever happening to a
father. I wrote about a taxi driver who has failed as a father

in the most appalling way; about a taxi driver and about London at night, because as a barman I'd come to meet a lot of taxi drivers and travel a lot through London at night. The characters that populate the play are nearly all based on people I've served drinks to at one time or another. I sent it to the Royal Court. They produced it in their 1998 Young Writers Festival. It was my first professional production.

Bluebird was directed by Gordon Anderson at the Ambassadors Theatre when the Court was residing in the West End. It was a complete revelation for me. Not only did it get me reviewed in 'grown-up' papers, but it also got me working with actors of the highest calibre. It got me a friendship and collaboration with Gordon that is still ongoing. A series of meetings with TV and film producers followed, the like of which continue to bewilder me to this day. It also got me an agent: Mel Kenyon. I have continued to learn more from her than I have from most other people working in theatre.

Ian Rickson, the Court's artistic director, commissioned a new play from me shortly before *Bluebird* opened. This play would go on to become *Christmas*, which came out of reading and rereading *The Cherry Orchard*. And out of drinking and playing pool in the pub next door to our house. This pub, called the Eclipse, was closing down because it was refusing to adapt to the massive cultural shifts in north London. It was refusing to do food, to allow children, to ban smoking. It was losing money hand over fist. It was a pub that had fallen out of time. It struck me that it worked accidentally as some kind of metaphor for the disappearance of the traditional working-class man. A sector of society that, like Chekhov's aristocracy, had become redundant without even realising it.

The writing process behind *Christmas* was rather erratic and the first draft was rather ropy. At the time of working on the play I was earning my living as a schoolteacher in Dagenham. It was also the time that my first son, Oscar, was born. Also, because I had neither the money nor the time to go to the theatre much, I had no idea that the Royal Court had already produced a play about working-class men spending a night in a pub together, and that the play (Conor McPherson's *The Weir* for fucksake!) was rather fucking brilliant and had done rather well. So when Ian rejected my play I was crestfallen, but not completely surprised.

On the other hand, when Ian rang me a week later to ask me to be Resident Dramatist at the Court for the year 2000, I was staggered. This would allow me to quit my teaching job and to write full-time and spend more time with Oscar. It was an extraordinary gesture of genuine generosity. It changed my career.

The play I wrote at the end of my residency, a year in which I learned a massive amount (including the meaning of the word 'playwright'), was *Herons*. I wanted to write (or 'wrought', as I might have had it for a short time) a play that dramatised the kind of life that surrounded me while I was working in Dagenham and living in the East End. I wanted to dramatise working-class teenagers with all of the honesty, cruelty and insight they could display. I wanted to capture their vibrant, violent language. I wanted to write a play about the British poor that was as hopeful and poetic as it was tough.

Herons was produced at the Theatre Upstairs in 2001. *Port*, the last play in this collection, was produced by the Royal Exchange, Manchester, in 2002, after twelve months there as a Resident Dramatist. It was in writing these two plays that I really began to feel, for the first time, any kind of confidence in my capacity to make drama. *Port* was the first play I'd ever written about Stockport. It was the first play I'd ever written with a female central character. Unlike any play I'd ever written before, *Port* took place over the course of years rather than days. Like *Herons*, teenage characters dominated. Unlike *Herons*, in *Port* they grew up; in *Port* they became adults.

Also in 2002 the actress Jo McInnes, who had played Clare Macneil in *Bluebird*, asked me if I had any plays I'd never had produced. She was looking for plays for her theatre company APE. I gave her a copy of *Christmas*, and in 2003 and 2004, nearly five years after it was first written,

APE produced *Christmas* at the Brighton Pavilion and the Bush Theatre, London.

It makes sense to me that these plays are clustered together. They mark a period in my career that bridges the gap from wanting to make money out of my writing to starting to make that money. They span the period of wanting to have children to becoming the father of two (my second son Stanley was born in February 2002). They also span the period of my dad's illness from alcoholism to his eventual death from cancer in January 2001. They also mark a shift in my work. There is a sense in the first two or three plays in this collection that dramaturgically, technically, I don't really know what I'm doing. It's a sense I'm quite proud of. By the time I wrote *Port*, I was at least starting to plan the structure of my plays a little bit and to figure out how stages work.

I recently reread these four plays in one sitting. It felt like an oddly self-indulgent way to spend an evening. It felt kind of weird. It was like looking at old photographs, or listening to old audiotapes of yourself speaking, or to old records you once loved. I liked all the plays, which was a relief. I liked all of their dramaturgical mistakes and oddness, and so decided not to change anything about them for republication.

I was heartened and dismayed at one and the same time to find that these plays reinvestigate the same themes again and again. My response to the plays was rather impressionistic. It is the work of other people to decipher what the plays mean or what their impressions suggest. I realised, though, that these are all city plays. Specifically they are plays driven by the relationship between Manchester and London. They are plays more about drinkers than about drug users, and more about the drunk than the sober. All four of the plays sit under the terrified possibility of acts of random violence. Fathers dominate the action more than mothers do. There are characters in all of them that are burdened by the weight of their past and hanker after flight of some kind. They are characters that strive to see or to sense with some kind of clarity, who use stories to explore their world, and some live in the face of death. The characters often try not to cry, and just as often try to speak with some kind of truth. There are also some good jokes in these plays, and one or two magic tricks.

I think these plays that could be loosely described as naturalistic. I'm uncertain about using that adjective myself. I am happier to acknowledge what is important to me theatrically than to describe my plays with any kind of unifying terminology. I am suspicious of any kind of surfeit of visual experiment or visceral sensation in theatre because all too often that experiment seems to me to lack emotional or psychological substance. I am, on the other hand, nervous about current trends for verbatim theatre, because the writers of many verbatim plays seem to place too high a value on questionable notions of authenticity and undervalue the power of metaphorical truth. I am also suspicious of any play that champions a political idea with unquestioned coherence, or with any lack of doubt. My plays tell stories about people. In that sense they are riddled with contradiction and confusion and behaviour that is odd, misguided and illogical. In that sense, too, they are fuelled with a spirit that to put the human form and the human voice on a stage with any kind of simplicity is theatrical enough.

These four plays were written to explore rather than to persuade. They were written to exclaim rather than to decry. I wrote them to try to make sense of that which frightened or aroused or saddened or elated me over the five-year period between 1997 and 2002. In writing them I tried make sense of what it is to be raised in Stockport and to live in London. Or to be the son of an alcoholic who died before he was sixty. Or the father of two sons. Or to be a schoolteacher or a barman, a DJ in the suburbs of Edinburgh, or a husband.

In that spirit they are, and this book is absolutely and unreservedly dedicated to my wife.

I've been blessed in my career to work with actors and directors and designers and literary managers and artistic directors of real muscle and to meet and befriend and learn from playwrights of the highest calibre. Some of them I've worked with more than once. The best of them have felt like allies. Many of them have become mates. Without them I would have written much worse plays than I have done so far.

Some of the people who I helped me while I was writing these plays are: Gordon Anderson, Leo Butler, Dominic Cooke, David Eldridge, Marianne Elliot, Siobhan Finneran, Sarah Frankcom, Jane Hazlegrove, Robert Holman, Stephen Jeffreys, Anthony Lamble, Emma Lowndes, Jo McInnes, Stuart Morris, Chloe Moss, Mark Ravenhill, Ian Rickson, Fred Ridgeway, Paul Ritter, Lee Ross, Billy Seymour, Andrew Sheridan, Nick Siddi, Rae Smith, Nick Tennant, Simon Usher, Che Walker, Graham Whybrow, Ryan Winsley, Michael Wynne. I have learned from every single writer who I've taught at the Young Writers Programme at the Royal Court, and from all of the staff members in that department and in that theatre.

Simon Stephens
July 2005

Bluebird

Bluebird was first performed at the Royal Court Theatre Upstairs, London, on 1 December 1998. The cast, in order of appearance, was as follows:

Jimmy Macneill	Chris Gascoyne
Guvnor	Danny Webb
Robert Greenwood	Christopher Ettridge
Young Man	Fraser Ayres
Angela Davies	Angela Lonsdale
Girl	Laura Sadler
Clare Macneill	Jo McInnes
Richard Wright	Ewan Stewart
Woman	Gina Aris
Man	Paul Chequer
Andy Green	Andrew Dennis
Billy Lee	Paul Ritter
Janine Williams	Jane Gurnett

Directed by Gordon Anderson
Designed by Keith Khan
Lighting by Johanna Town
Sound by Rich Walsh

Characters

Jimmy Macneill
Guvnor
Robert Greenwood
Young Man
Angela Davies
Girl
Clare Macneill
Richard Wright
Woman
Man
Andy Green
Billy Lee
Janine Williams

Spotlight on **Jimmy Macneill**. *Aged thirty-two. Strong, short, dishevelled. Unshaven. He is a taxi driver. Manchester-born. Hunched in a red phone box at the rear of the stage. Speaking on the phone.*

Jimmy   Hello. I'm sorry for bothering you. I wonder if you could help me. I'm trying to get in touch with somebody. Somebody who used to live at this number. She's called Clare Macneell. Macneill. Yes. (*Disappointed.*) Really? I don't suppose you have any kind of forwarding number for her? No idea at all? OK. Sorry for bothering you. G'night.

Headlights of a taxicab fill the stage. Urban jungle-jazz music plays loud. Mixed in with sounds of a taxi-firm radio. After a short while the music fades. It should return in between each scene to provide a rhythm to the night and the driving. Lighting becomes full but moody, neon, night-time.

A thin man, maybe wearing shorts and a Hawaiian shirt and sucking a can of Special Brew through a straw is **Jimmy**'s *next passenger. He is* **Guvnor**. *He addresses* **Jimmy** *who responds to nothing. Just continues driving.*

Guvnor   I was working on a case last week. (*No response.*) I couldn't afford a desk. (*Pause.*) I got up. There was a tap on the door. (*Pause.*) Which was an odd place for a tap I thought. (*No response.*) Yesterday morning I was at my local off-licence. I went to buy some cigarettes. There was this guy in there buying a four-pack of Guinness. Scouser. With an unusually high-pitched voice. A very ugly-looking man. Turns to me. Says to me, 'That's cheap, eh? Ninety-nine pee? That's pretty cheap. They fluctuate the prices, y'know? Up and down. Sometimes they can be one twenty-nine. But nah, that's pretty cheap right enough. The only thing that annoys me about the Guinness,' he says to me, 'the only thing that annoys me about the Guinness is that every fucker always says about how it's Irish and that. It's not fucking Irish. It's not a fucking Irish drink. It's a Russian drink. Specifically. It's specifically a Russian drink. Invented by Joseph Stalin and Leon Trotsky. Y'know? It's not fucking Irish. I should know and all,' he says, 'I should know and all. I am a communist!' (*No response.*) He says this and he grins and he walks out of the door of the shop. He was quite a happy guy. Which matters, I suppose. Honestly, though. It's bloody mad. Do you not reckon? Does it not get to the point where you're just thinking, 'This is fucking mental'? Y'know what I mean. It was a very hot morning this morning, for example. You probably noticed that. I went to work on the bus this morning and just as I was getting off the bus this guy got on who was almost entirely spherical and he had this big red round face and he was completely bald. Gets on the bus as I'm getting off and stops me. Says to me, 'Now then, young man. What are you going to do when winter comes?' He gets on. Pays his fare and I get off and go to work. I mean winter. That's like seven months away. I hadn't even thought about it. (*Pauses for a response. Gets none.*) Do you not reckon? Do you not reckon that things have started to get just a little bit out of hand? (*No response. Getting more frantic.*) Earlier on tonight I'm riding the Victoria Line into the West End. I get on at Brixton. All the way there there's this guy. Jamaican guy. About sixty years old. And he's standing on the tube rearranging all the discarded flyers that had fallen out of the day's newspapers. All the book club and the record club and life insurance offers. Tearing them exactly into two halves and lying them face up so that everybody can see them. He was taking it very seriously. He was very meticulous. I mean, what does it all mean? Eh? Do you have any idea what it all means? At all?

Jimmy   That's four pounds seventy.

Lights fall.

Lights rise on **Robert Greenwood** *in the back of* **Jimmy**'s *cab. A balding, drunken, upper-middle-class, fat man of fifty.*

Robert   They say it's going to be hot. This summer. I heard it on the radio. They say it's going to be the hottest summer we've had in years. I can barely believe it.

Jimmy   The Queen Caroline Estate. This all right for you?

Robert   I'm not getting out here. I just wanted to look at it. It's very beautiful in many ways. Don't you think?

Jimmy   I like the lighting.

Robert   The footlights? Very theatrical. And its colour. It could do with a touch of paint. But still, its colour is quite startling. Do you know how many people get mugged here every year?

Jimmy   I have no idea.

Robert   Thirty-eight. Now that doesn't sound like very many, does it? Does it?

Jimmy   I don't know.

Robert   It doesn't. It doesn't sound like very many. It's one every eight days. When you think about that it grows rather black. Would you not agree?

Jimmy   It's very sad.

Robert   Sad? I don't know whether it's what I would call sad. My daughter lived here for a while.

Jimmy   Oh yeah?

Robert   She had a flat here.

Jimmy   They're not bad. The flats in this place. There are many worse.

Robert   I cried today for the first time since I was a boy.

Jimmy   Why were you crying?

Robert   It's not a crime, you know.

Jimmy   I know that.

Robert   I cried for almost an hour.

Jimmy   What happened to you?

Robert   Do you believe in ghosts?

Jimmy   In ghosts?

Robert   I do. You can sense them.

Jimmy Maybe.

Robert There's no maybe about it, my friend. Do you know what the distinguishing factor of the ageing process is?

Jimmy There are a lot of things.

Robert No. The main distinguishing factor of the ageing process is the overwhelming sense of regret.

Jimmy That's a very sad idea.

Robert It's the truth, my friend.

Jimmy What do you regret?

Robert Too many things to count.

Jimmy I don't want to be funny but this is adding up. I don't want you to regret the size of the fare.

Robert You must excuse me, my friend. I am very drunk.

Jimmy That's all right. Do you want me to take you home?

Robert She was very proud of this place, you know? Moved here after she left home. Bought all her own furniture. Made a little nest for herself. She was seventeen. When she left home she was only seventeen. Too young, you understand. Far too young. I told her. At the time I remember telling her. Told her to wait a couple of years. She would hear nothing of it. She was a very independent girl and she did well for herself. Used to cook for us occasionally. Cook for myself and my wife. One night. She woke up in the middle of the night. Heard somebody in her kitchen. Small kitchen adjoining the bedroom and three o'clock in the morning she wakes up and it was, 'Hold on a second, I'm being burgled.' That's was what she must have thought. Of course. She's eighteen now. She's an adult now. She's grown up. She thinks, 'Nobody's going to burgle my flat. No little fucker's going to burgle my flat.' Gets up in the middle of the night to go and investigate. Now. I ask you. Imagine yourself a burglar. You're a professional, let us say. This is maybe the third, the fourth flat you've broken into in a month. Grab the video. Grab the television. Bugger off and flog the lot of them and think nothing of it. Somebody catches you and, well, that's very unfortunate but as soon as you are interrupted you scarper. Run like the bloody clappers. Drop the goods and leg it. You understand what I mean?

Jimmy   Yes.

Robert   No but seriously. That's what you do, isn't it? Of course that's what you do. It makes perfect bloody sense. Not this little shit though. She walks in on him. Says to him, 'What the bloody hell do you think you're doing?' Do you know what he does? Do you?

Jimmy   I have no idea.

Robert   Have a bloody guess for God's sake.

Jimmy   Tells her he's from pest control.

Robert   Picks up a kitchen knife and stabs her in the tit.

Jimmy   Christ.

Robert   He stabs her in the tit. Eight times. Leaves her. And this is the punchline. He leaves the bloody video. Leaves all her cash. Leaves everything. Just leaves. She's bleeding to death on her own kitchen floor and he just leaves. I mean, Christ. What can you say? Eh? Answer me that.

Jimmy   I'm sorry.

Robert   Sorry? You're sorry? My friend, you can have no possible idea.

Jimmy   I know that.

Robert   I like to come here. Night-times. Drive around. Look at the place where she used to live. She'd be twenty-seven now. They actually caught the guy. Daniel Washington. Twenty-four years old. Drug addict. Gave him fourteen years. And I've been keeping my eyes peeled. For

developments. He had his sentence cut. For good
behaviour. Do you have any children?

Jimmy   No I don't.

Robert   Well, believe me. If you had children. If you
knew how I felt. It is enough to almost kill me.

Jimmy   I can imagine.

Robert   And then last week we had a young lady round to
visit us. From the victim support agency. Smart lady. Pretty
young thing. I must admit they have been quite good to us.
She came round last week to let us know that, for reasons of
good behaviour and a regular attendance to a drug-
rehabilitation programme that had apparently proven quite
successful, Mr Washington was due for release. This
afternoon. After eight years. Now. You seem like a rational
and reasonable man. Eight years? Is that enough time to
come to terms with something like that?

Jimmy   I would say not.

Robert   It is no time at all, my friend. It is no time at all.
It took me a matter of minutes.

Jimmy   To do what?

Robert   I decided that I would go and welcome Mr
Washington back into the world.

Jimmy   I see.

Robert   It was surprising to me just how easy it was to get
hold of a knife. It took me merely a couple of phone calls.
And cost me fifty pounds to get hold of a most fearsome
weapon. Can you believe that?

Jimmy   I don't know.

Robert   Everything was so bloody simple. I knew that he
was in Pentonville Prison. I telephoned to find out the exact
time of his release. And this afternoon I took off work. Took
the train to Caledonian Road. Two o'clock in the afternoon.
Traffic was actually starting to pick up. I made my way to

the entrance of the prison. Waiting outside I asked the guard on the door when he was going to be released. He told me that it wouldn't be too long. That he was out of his cell and gathering his things. He said that he didn't know that somebody had arranged to come and see him. Said that he would be glad.

Jimmy   What happened?

Robert   About fifteen minutes I was waiting. Holding the knife that I had brought beneath my coat. Touching the edge of the blade. And thinking about her. And what he'd done to her. After about fifteen minutes the guard comes to ask me if I wanted to go inside and meet him.

Jimmy   What did you say?

Robert   I told him that it didn't matter. That I would be all right. He asked me what my name was. Asked me twice. I didn't know what to say. I had this picture in my head of him collecting his things. Of what he would look like now. After eight years. Collecting his things. Changing into his civilian clothes. And the guard asked me if I was all right. He had very blue eyes. The guard. A very clear, quite startling blueness. And I turn around. And walk away.

Jimmy   Christ.

Robert   I am very drunk.

Jimmy   I'm sorry.

Robert   I've been sitting in a pub on the Caledonian Road for four hours. I have never felt so numb.

Jimmy   I'm sorry.

Robert   What's your name?

Jimmy   Jimmy.

Robert   What's going to happen to us, Jimmy? Have you any idea?

Jimmy   I don't know.

Robert   What's going to happen to us all?

Jimmy   Would you like me to drive you home?

Robert   Yes. I think so. Please. I think you better had.

Lights fade.

Lights rise on an energetic **Young Man** *of some thirty years. He is dressed casually. Not smart.*

Young Man   I like your shirt.

Jimmy   Thank you.

Young Man   Where did you get that then?

Jimmy   Marks and Spencer's.

Young Man   Marks and Spencer's, eh? Great. (*Beat.*) Where's that then?

Jimmy (*bewildered*)   They're a very big chain store. They're all over the place.

Young Man   Are they really?

Jimmy   Yeah.

Young Man (*very enthusiastic*)   That's brilliant.

Lights fade.

Lights rise. **Jimmy** *has returned to the phone box. He is speaking to* **Clare**'s *sister. He talks urgently and quickly. He is edgy and anxious not to allow her time to think about what is actually going on.*

Jimmy   Sarah? Sarah, this is Jimmy. Ah, don't get angry, Sarah. No, Sarah, don't hang up. Don't! Just! Hear me out. Listen. I'm trying to get in touch with Clare, Sarah. I was wondering if you could give me her phone number.

Lights fall quickly.

Jungle music. Lights rise. **Jimmy** *addresses* **Angela Davies**, *a prostitute of indistinguishable age. Haunted, hollow beauty chewed away by years of self-hatred, self-abuse, cold, etc. The cab is obviously parked and the two of them are sharing takeaway coffees.* **Jimmy** *is a* *little awkward and bewildered by this strange situation. She is a wide girl. Hard, independent, sexy and defiant. She flirts, taunts and takes no shit. Below this she is damaged.*

Angela   My foot hurts.

Jimmy   Your foot?

Angela   These bleeding shoes.

Jimmy   Where you going?

Angela   West End.

Jimmy   You want a plaster?

Angela   You what?

Jimmy   A plaster. For your foot?

Angela   What are you talking about you, eh?

Jimmy   It's all right. It's just that I keep plasters in my car. If you wanted a plaster for your foot you could have one.

Angela   I've been walking for nine hours.

Jimmy (*finding a plaster for her*)   You ought to get yourself a more sturdy set of footwear if that's the kind of walking you're doing. Get some Timberland. Or Caterpillar. Fine shoes.

Angela   I come here all the time. They have the best coffee in King's Cross.

Jimmy   This is a very unusual situation.

Angela   I'm a very unusual person.

Jimmy   I don't often find myself sharing cups of coffee with the fares.

Angela   Is that what you call them?

Jimmy   What?

Angela   People who you give lifts to? You call them a 'fare'?

Jimmy   Yeah.

Angela   That's very impersonal.

Jimmy   Don't take it the wrong way. I meet a lot of people.

Angela   Do you know any card tricks?

Jimmy   No. I can eat fire but card tricks I know nothing about.

Angela   Would you like to see a card trick?

Jimmy   Only if I can be your beautiful assistant.

Angela (*placing a pack of cards on the dashboard between them*) I'll bet you the fare you can't work out how I do it.

Jimmy   Get to fuck.

Angela   All right. I'll bet you half the fare.

Jimmy   Do you do this with every taxi driver you get?

Angela   Pick a card.

Jimmy (*picking a card*)   Because if you do you mustn't get very far.

Angela   Don't tell me what it is.

Jimmy   'Cause, I mean, you'll be stopping and starting every five minutes.

Angela   Now put it back in the pack and shuffle it. Don't let me see what it is.

Jimmy (*following her instructions*)   I'm not ordinarily a gambling man, you understand.

Angela   Now cut. (*He does.*) And turn over the top card. That was your card. The queen of hearts. Am I right?

Jimmy   Yeah. You're right.

Angela   Is that half the fare then?

Jimmy   Go on.

Angela   Funny.

Jimmy   What?

Angela   Most people normally lie.

Jimmy   I'm a disarmingly honest person.

Angela   You're Mancunian, aren't you?

Jimmy   As drizzle.

Angela   I like Mancunians.

Jimmy   All of them?

Angela   Mancunians are very sensitive.

Jimmy   Jesus.

Angela   I had a Mancunian boyfriend once.

Jimmy   What happened to him?

Angela   He killed himself.

Jimmy   Fucking hell.

Angela   Jumped off a bridge over the M25.

Jimmy   Christ.

Angela   He was eighteen.

Jimmy   Where are you from, darlin'?

Angela   I'm not your darling.

Jimmy   Sorry.

Angela   Don't call us that. I'm nobody's fucking darling.
It's very fucking patronising.

Jimmy   I meant it as a term of endearment. Not a
declaration of ownership.

Angela   Yeah, well. I hate it when people call us that. I'm
from Sunderland.

Jimmy   What a marvellous town Sunderland is.

Angela   It's a dump of pissy shite.

Jimmy   Pissy shite. That's an odd idea.

Angela   I left when I was fourteen.

Jimmy   And came to London.

Angela   No. To Dorset.

Jimmy   Dorset?

Angela   Aye.

Jimmy   Well, I'm sorry to tell you this, my friend, but this isn't fucking Dorset. I think you've been misinformed.

Angela   Tell us about it. I went to stay with my uncle.

Jimmy   What happened?

Angela (*matter-of-fact*)   He raped me and beat my face to shit.

Jimmy (*unfazed*)   You were obviously very close.

Angela   I came to London when I was fifteen.

Jimmy   How old are you now?

Angela   How old do I look?

Jimmy   I have no idea.

Angela   Have a guess.

Jimmy   Twenty-nine.

Angela   Twenty-nine?

Jimmy   Yeah.

Angela   I'm nineteen.

Jimmy   Fuck off.

Angela   Where do you live?

Jimmy   Bluebird Towers. By the Goldhawk Road Arches. Hammersmith.

Angela   'Cause I'm looking to move house. Is it nice there?

Jimmy   Bloody wonderful.

Angela   I don't like Hammersmith.

Jimmy   Hammersmith's all right.

Angela   Full of Irish. I hate the Irish.

Jimmy   What do you hate the Irish for?

Angela   Tight-arsed smelly-faced bastard drunks. My uncle was Irish.

Jimmy   That's fairly unequivocal.

Angela   You use a lot of long words.

Jimmy   Don't worry about it. I can't spell them.

Angela   You see that hotel?

Jimmy   Across the road?

Angela   The Great Northern.

Jimmy   Sounds like a hospital.

Angela   That's where I stay.

Jimmy   What a desirable residence.

Angela   It looks very beautiful from the outside, don't you think?

Jimmy   Yes I do.

Angela   You should see the rooms.

Jimmy   Why?

Angela   They're terrifying.

Jimmy   Terrifying?

Angela   It gets very hot in there.

Jimmy   I see.

Angela   Especially these past few weeks. It's been killing us.

Jimmy   Where do you want to move to?

Angela   I'm going to live in America.

Jimmy (*doubtful*)   America?

Angela (*defiant*)   Yeah.

Jimmy (*singing the Leonard Bernstein tune*)   La la la la la la.

Angela   You what?

Jimmy (*quoting from the same*)   You can have fun in America.

Angela   I'm going to live in Santa Barbara.

Jimmy   What the fuck do you want to live in Santa fucking Barbara for?

Angela   My favourite telly programme's *Santa Barbara*.

Jimmy   Good reason.

Angela   What's your favourite telly programme?

Jimmy   I don't own a television.

Angela (*staggered*)   God. What's your favourite song?

Jimmy   Have you ever heard of Otis Redding?

Angela   No.

Jimmy (*realising the relevance of Otis Redding's nationality*)   He's American. My favourite song is a song by Otis Redding called 'My Girl'.

Angela   I could have been a singer.

Jimmy   What happened?

Angela   Nothing. Nothing happened. That's the point.

Jimmy   Those marks. On your face. How did you get them?

Angela   Fucking hell.

Jimmy   What?

Angela   Are you a social worker?

Jimmy   No. I'm a taxi driver.

Angela   I walked into a wall.

Jimmy   You must have been walking very quickly.

Angela   Running. And I fell down some stairs.

Jimmy   That was very clumsy.

Angela   I'm a very clumsy person.

Jimmy   Tell me to fuck off if it's none of my business but should I be worried about you?

Long pause. Good three seconds.

Angela   It's very good the coffee here, isn't it?

Jimmy   You didn't answer my question.

Angela   Best fucking coffee in King's Cross.

Jimmy   What are you going to the West End for?

Angela   I've got a meeting.

Jimmy   Are you not going to be late? Sitting here drinking pissy coffee, doing fucking card tricks and talking shit about America?

Angela   I wasn't talking shit. I mean it.

Jimmy   Would you like another one?

Angela   I wasn't talking shit.

Jimmy   OK. Would you like another coffee?

Angela   No thank you. I don't have time. (*Beat. Maybe she examines herself in the passenger-seat mirror.*) There was a time, you know, when I thought I was going to be a film star.

Jimmy   Really?

Angela   No shit. What do you reckon of that? Do you think I could have done it?

Jimmy   It's a distinct possibility. You have a certain charisma.

Angela   I've lost my looks. I know that. You don't have to be polite about it.

Jimmy   I wouldn't say that.

Angela   No?

Jimmy   You have very striking eyes. They're very blue.

Angela   This guy wanted to put me in one of his films. Gave me his card. Told me to give him a ring sometime.

Jimmy   Did you ring him?

Angela   I lost the card. I don't want to go.

Jimmy   Go where?

Angela   To this meeting.

Jimmy   I see.

Angela   I'm very tired.

Jimmy (*challenging, he knows that it is a pickup*)   What is this meeting?

Angela (*not fazed, challenging him back*)   What do you think it is?

Jimmy   I wouldn't like to guess.

Angela   That's probably very wise. You really don't want to know.

Jimmy   That's a shame.

Angela   Thanks for having a coffee with us.

Jimmy   That's my pleasure. Are you going to be all right?

Angela (*flirting with him*)   Are you married?

Jimmy   Yes I am.

Angela (*pulling a can of Coke from her pocket*)   Never mind. I come here all the time.

Jimmy   You said. Are you going to be all right?

Angela   So if you ever wanted to buy me another coffee you could probably find me here.

Jimmy I'll bear that in mind. Are you going to be all right?

Angela I'll show you how to do that card trick.

Jimmy I can hardly wait. You look after yourself.

Angela I always do. What's your name?

Jimmy Jimmy.

Angela Jimmy what?

Jimmy Jimmy Cagney.

Angela Good name.

Jimmy I made it up myself.

Angela More people should do that.

Jimmy What's your name?

Angela Maria.

Jimmy Maria?

Angela Maria Callas.

Jimmy Nice to meet you, Maria.

Angela Nice to meet you too, Jimmy.

Lights fall.

Lights rise. A **Girl** *has entered* **Jimmy**'s *cab. She is fifteen. Dressed in the bright and vivid clothes and make-up of late-rave culture. Sexy and vibrant and young. Wearing shades. Chewing conspicuous bubble gum. The two do not talk for a while. She is humming. Looking out of the window.*

Girl (*quietly, suddenly, whispered*)
    What shall I do with this absurdity –
    O heart, O troubled heart – this caricature,
    Decrepit age that has been tied to me
    As to a dog's tail?

Jimmy *doesn't respond. He is, however, evidently surprised, moved.*

Girl   This is where I get out.

Jimmy   That's five pounds eighty.

Lights fall.

*Lights rise on **Jimmy** again in phone box. We hear **Clare**'s voice on the other side of the line.*

Clare   Hello? (*Pause.*) Look, is anybody there?

Jimmy   Clare?

Clare   Speaking.

Jimmy   It's Jimmy.

*The line falls dead as **Clare** hangs up. Lights fall.*

*Lights rise on **Jimmy** and **Richard Wright**. A Scottish engineer on the London Underground. Dressed in the Underground engineers' blue-and-orange overalls. Bone-tired with a cigarette.*

Richard   This city. It's full of music, did you ever notice that?

Jimmy   Music?

Richard   Everywhere you turn. Radios. Shopfronts. Pubs. Cafés. Cars. Fucking everywhere. Everybody with their own little personalised packed compacted discs of love songs and soundtracks.

Jimmy   Fuck.

Richard   One time. Long ago. There must have been a silence here.

Jimmy   What are you talking about?

Richard   This place is never totally quiet. Even when you think it is it's only because you're so accustomed to the noise that you've stopped noticing any more.

Jimmy   You never stop noticing.

Richard   That's what I yearn for sometimes. That's what I could kill for. For there to be no noise. No noise at all. How's business, Jimmy?

Jimmy   Fair to middling. Yourself?

Richard   Shite. Desperate.

Jimmy   What do you do?

Richard   I'm an engineer.

Jimmy   I see.

Richard   On the Underground.

Jimmy   Hard work?

Richard   Repair work. Every night I go to offer one sorry fucking attempt at securing some kind of engineering solidity on the living breathing mother that is our capital's tube system.

Jimmy   So which particular subterranean anomaly and public safety hazard are you doctoring tonight?

Richard   Light bulbs.

Jimmy   I see.

Richard   Checking the transformers on the forty-eight trackside light bulbs each side of the track between Clapham North and Stockwell.

Jimmy   Forty-eight?

Richard   Each side.

Jimmy   Fuck me.

Richard   Thank you. No. Each one of them shagged. Every single fucking light bulb and every single fucking transformer between the two stations on each side of the track.

Jimmy   That's terrible.

Richard   It fucking is terrible, Jimmy. (*Pause.*) With the weather like it's been these past two weeks it gets so fucking hot down there it is just fucking mental. I'm getting out of here.

Jimmy   I know that ambition particularly well. Not always easy though, eh?

Richard   There are two defining factors about most people in this city as far as I can tell.

Jimmy   What are they?

Richard   They come from somewhere else. And they want to leave. Take it from me, Jimmy. You see all these people on the fucking trains. Last thing at night. When you're going to work. Good, healthy, normal people with legs, hair, eyes, bowels, bollocks, hopes, hungers, all manner of normal human faculties. You see them on that last train and they've grown totally fucking empty. I'm not going to let that happen to me.

Jimmy   I never travel on the train.

Richard   I don't blame you, pal. Scares the fuck out of me sometimes, Jimmy. I catch myself staring at them. Just end up wanting to fucking shake them. Kick them. I recognise myself in them too much. Y'know what I mean?

Jimmy   I think so.

Richard   I smoke too much. I'm getting through fifty a day at the moment.

Jimmy   No shit?

Richard   Fifty fags a day.

Jimmy   That's quite a handful.

Richard   Spend all my money on my fags and my family.

Jimmy   You can't take it with you.

Richard   At least I get to see the fucking fags. You married, Jimmy?

Jimmy   Yes I am.

Richard   How long have you been married?

Jimmy   Eleven years.

Richard   That's good. Your wife. Does she not mind you driving at night.

Jimmy   I wouldn't know. I never asked her. I haven't seen my wife in five years.

Richard   What did you do before you drove a cab?

Jimmy   If I told you wouldn't believe me.

Richard   Why not?

Jimmy   Nobody ever does.

Richard   I'd believe you.

Jimmy   I was a writer.

Richard   A writer?

Jimmy   Yeah.

Richard   Lying bastard. What did you write?

Jimmy   I was a novelist.

Richard   Why did you stop writing?

Jimmy   I didn't have anything left to say.

Richard   Do you not regret it?

Jimmy   I regret many things, big man. But that isn't one of them.

Richard   How long have you been driving for?

Jimmy   Five years.

Richard   Do you ever get scared?

Jimmy   Scared?

Richard   Driving. Letting a total stranger into the back of your cab. Does it never scare you?

Jimmy   No.

Richard   They could rob you.

Jimmy   They wouldn't.

Richard   How do you know that?

Jimmy   I'd break their fucking arms.

Richard   They could rob you. Shoot you. Kill you. Rape you. And you'd be utterly powerless to stop it.

Jimmy   I've got a baseball bat.

Richard   Big fucking deal. What's the worst thing that ever happened to you? In your job?

Jimmy   That's an odd question.

Richard   Come on, Jimmy, man. Think. Bit of the old grey stuff. Put it to work.

Jimmy   Somebody tried to mug me once.

Richard   What happened?

Jimmy   Couple of smacked-up fuckheads jump in the back of the cab. Said to us, 'Give us your fucking money, you thick Northern Bastard, or we'll fucking kill you.'

Richard   What did you do?

Jimmy   Beat the crap out of the two of them with a baseball bat.

Richard   No shit.

Jimmy   Told you. Always keep a baseball bat underneath the driver's seat. It helps.

Richard   You really beat them up?

Jimmy   Too fucking right I did.

Richard   Jimmy.

Jimmy   Yes, mate.

Richard   Do us a favour.

Jimmy   What's that, mate?

Richard   Next time. Give 'em your money.

Jimmy   Fuck off. They were just a couple of jumped-up pricks.

Richard   Do you know what the worst thing that ever happened to me is?

Jimmy   Tell me.

Richard   One time I had to cut a corpse from the wiring in the tracks. Had an old boy throw himself under one of the work trains. Punter. Southbound platform on the Northern Line at Kentish Town. Just as it was pulling in. Throws himself in front of it.

Jimmy   Christ.

Richard   It was a mess.

Jimmy   I bet.

Richard   Died on impact. Train carried him maybe ten feet. Runs him over. Ambulance gets there. Needs some help negotiating the cables and the wires to get him off the tracks. We were doing the escalators there. Fucking hell, Jimmy. They called us down. Station master gives us a call over the blower. Can the engineers make their way to the southbound platform. What a fucking state. We helped the paramedics down on to the track. Helped lift the boy up on to the stretcher on the platform. You could feel the place where his neck had snapped. And all the blood clinging to his clothes and to the track. And his eyes were open and they were as grey as stone. He was just staring. His skin had turned a sick cold blue. And his face was contorted and solid. Dead. He had the most terrifying expression of fear in his eyes that I swear I have ever seen. You try to look away. Avert the old eyes. Try not to look. It's not always possible. You know what I mean.

Jimmy   I hope they pay you well.

Richard   I live like a king.

Jimmy   I hope so.

Richard   We get paid so much fucking money, Jimmy, we can barely even move for it. But I think I'm going to jack it in.

Jimmy   What are you going to do?

Richard   I've been offered some work.

Jimmy   Oh yeah. What kind of work's that, mate?

Richard   The kind of work that pays a shitbag of money in cash. In a very short space of time. A driving job. For an acquaintance of mine. The kind of work that only a desperately scared man would tell a fucking taxi driver about.

Jimmy   I see.

Richard   It's actually remarkably easy. It merely involves parking a car at a certain time in a certain space. Collecting a package in a car park. Driving the package about five hundred miles to the north-west of England and delivering it to another man that I have never met before in another car park at a motorway service station. Not the kind of job prospect that I took my Open University degree in philosophy with a view to securing. But lucrative, Jimmy, and very motherfucking scary. This is where I get out, mate.

Jimmy   You don't sound too convinced.

Richard   This is where I get out.

Jimmy   I know that. You don't sound too convinced.

Richard   I don't have any choice.

Jimmy   That's not true.

Richard   Of course it's fucking true, Jimmy. You know it's fucking true.

Jimmy   I know nothing of the sort, pal.

Richard   Do you believe in the intransience of love?

Jimmy   You what?

Richard   What about the communicability of the human spirit?

Jimmy   Those are very odd questions.

Richard   They're about the most important questions in the whole fucking world, Jimmy. Give me an answer.

Jimmy   Yes. I do.

Richard   You believe in both of them.

Jimmy   Unquestionably.

Richard   You see, the thing is, Jimmy, I'm starting to fucking wonder. I'm starting to lose faith in those things. You lose faith. And then what are you meant to do?

Jimmy   You want to know something quite funny?

Richard   What's that, pal?

Jimmy   That's actually my name. Jimmy. It's actually my fucking name an all. That's seven pound, mate.

Lights fall.

Lights rise on a young couple sat in the back of **Jimmy**'s *car. Pointedly not talking. Staring out of their own windows.* **Jimmy** *concentrates on his driving. The* **Woman** *sighs. She is apparently angry. After a short while the* **Man** *looks up. He strokes the back of her neck.*

Woman (*exaggerated whisper*)   I love you.

Man (*ditto*)   I love you too.

Jimmy *smiles. Lights fall.*

Lights rise on **Jimmy** *again in the phone box. We hear* **Clare**'s *voice on the other end of the line.*

Clare   Hello?

Jimmy   Clare. It's Jimmy. (*Long pause. Five seconds.*) It's Jimmy, Clare. Are you there?

Clare   What do you want?

Jimmy   I want to see you. (*Pause again.*) Can I see you?
Clare? Look. You don't have to say anything. I would just
like to see you tonight. I have something that I want to give
you. (*No response.*) I promise. Just tonight. I can pick you up.
If you tell me where to meet you.

Clare   OK.

Jimmy   I'm going to be very late. I have to work tonight.

Clare   Do you know what night it is tonight?

Lights fades.

Lights rise. **Andy Green** *enters. Six-four, brick-shithouse-built
bouncer in a bouncer's black jacket and dicky bow.*

Andy   Hackney.

Jimmy   Right you are.

Andy   You know Hackney?

Jimmy   Yes. I know Hackney.

Andy   Y'know Goldbourne House. On the Beauvoir
Estate.

Jimmy   Side of the canal?

Andy   S'right.

Jimmy   You been working?

Andy   What?

Jimmy   You been working tonight?

Andy   I don't like taxi drivers.

Jimmy   All taxi drivers?

Andy   All of 'em.

Jimmy (*taking the piss*)   How do you know?

Andy   Are you being funny, mate?

Jimmy   No.

Andy   Then shut up.

Jimmy   I had somebody in the cab tonight. Tried to convince me that the art of polite and civilised conversation was actually dead. I told him to fuck himself in the mouth. I mean, you're a perfect example.

Andy   You what?

Jimmy   There is always hope, my friend.

Andy   I've been working.

Jimmy   Nightclub?

Andy   Yeah.

Jimmy   Busy night?

Andy   Mad busy.

Jimmy   Good money?

Andy   I don't know. It doesn't affect me. I get paid shit whatever happens.

Jimmy   I know that feeling.

Andy   You ever been a bouncer?

Jimmy   No. I haven't.

Andy   Then how the fuck could you know that feeling?

Jimmy   I was just saying –

Andy   Heh? How the fuck could you possibly know what I mean?

Jimmy   Is it true that all bouncers are gay?

Andy   Fuck you.

Jimmy   Is it true that bouncers don't have a sense of humour?

Andy   Do you want your arms breaking, mate?

Jimmy   Do you want a cigarette?

Andy   You what?

Jimmy   Do you want a cigarette?

Andy   Yeah.

Jimmy   Here, take one.

Andy   Thank you.

Jimmy   I'm a sarcastic cunt.

Andy   You are that.

Jimmy   Just ignore me.

Andy   I was trying to.

Jimmy   So. What's it like then?

Andy   What?

Jimmy   Being a bouncer?

Andy   You don't want to know.

Jimmy   You know what I do want to know?

Andy   What's that?

Jimmy   Like bouncers, yeah? Why the fuck are they called bouncers? Do you ever wonder that?

Andy   Are you a Scouser?

Jimmy   Manc. I mean, you don't exactly look very bouncy. If you'll excuse the observation. And most people, yeah, when you punch them in the mouth or smash their fucking heads on the ground they don't exactly fucking bounce.

Andy   I hate fucking Mancs.

Jimmy   Thank you.

Andy   We had a boy sent to hospital tonight. Seventeen years old.

Jimmy   What did he do?

Andy   Two pints of piss lager shandy and he thinks he's a fucking hard bastard. Tries to start kicking off.

Jimmy   Why's that then?

Andy   We caught him trying to push the fucking Es.

Jimmy   Oooh. Bad boy.

Andy   Trying to push them on to fucking teenage girls.

Jimmy   Oooh. Very bad boy.

Andy   I mean, that is so fucking stupid. You just don't do that. You do not go to a club like the club we work at and try pushing the fucking shite. We have surveillance cameras pointing at every single fucking corner of the building. We can see every fucker pick their nose, scratch their arse, grab a bit of tit. Fucking anything. You do it in our place and we fucking see you.

Jimmy   I believe you.

Andy   So we goes up to him and politely suggest that he might think about collecting his coat. And he's giving it all the fucking gangster shite. You know what I hate?

Jimmy   I can imagine that you hate many things.

Andy   If there is one thing I cannot fucking stand it is your white boy trying the fucking patois. That reeks of so much bullshit. So there's three of us, yeah, and he's giving it all this Jamaica crap. We put our arm around him. Suggest he makes a fucking move. You know what he does?

Jimmy   Thrill me.

Andy   Pulls out a fucking blade.

Jimmy   Prick.

Andy   It is out of his hand and he is on the floor before you can say Bob fucking Marley. Headlock. Up and down on the floor. Up and down on the floor. Up and down on the floor. Three times. Blood coming out of his fucking eyes and the knife in the pocket and he is out of the door. And by the time he's hit the fucking pavement the paramedics are waiting for him picking their noses and reading the papers and he's off and he's away.

Jimmy   You work quickly.

Andy   You got any kids?

Jimmy   Used to. Not any more. What about yourself?

Andy   I've got two boys and a girl.

Jimmy   How old?

Andy   Boys're eleven and thirteen. Girl's twelve.

Jimmy   Good ages.

Andy   I tell you, if any cunt tried to push any of that shite on my girl I would fucking kill them.

Jimmy   I believe you.

Andy   And if I ever caught any of my kids with any of it I don't know what I'd do.

Jimmy   Breaks your heart, eh?

Andy   Some of the kids we have down there. I can see my lot in them. And the girls are wearing nothing. Not a fucking stitch half of them. You feel like stopping them. Feel like saying to them, do you know what you are doing? Have you thought about what you are doing? About where you are going? Have you even thought about it? It was hot in there tonight. Leaves you breathless. These past few weeks it's been fucking crazy. You get so thirsty you end up drinking yourself to the ground.

Jimmy   It's frightening, eh?

Andy   I'm sorry. If I was rude to you before. I'm tired.

Jimmy   That's not a problem.

Andy   Takes me a bit of time to relax. To remember that not every cunt is going to try to bottle you.

Jimmy   I can believe that.

Andy   I've seen people in this line of work getting screwed up by it. There is a point when you just have to turn off. Enjoy a bit of sunshine. Hang out in the park with the kids.

Have a lie-in with the wife. I know some boys come back from work go home and use their wife as a heavy bag. You just can't do that. It is just not on.

Jimmy It's not easy sometimes, eh?

Andy You married?

Jimmy Yes I am.

Andy I hope you treat her right, my friend.

Jimmy I try to.

Andy I am a big man. I am a big man, and when the moment calls for it I can be a hard bastard. But I have never so much as laid a finger on my wife, in my life.

Jimmy That's always a good approach to a marriage.

Andy I have never hit my wife and I have never hit my kids.

Jimmy Good man.

Andy One boy. One of our boys. Banged away for fourteen years.

Jimmy Fuck me.

Andy GBH. Cut some fucker's face to shit. Got banged up.

Jimmy That's bad.

Andy This is the only place he can get work.

Jimmy I see.

Andy He is a nasty malevolent motherfucker and I hate him more than I ever believed could be possible. And everybody hates him. The customers hate him. The other bouncers hate him. The bar staff. The managers. Every cunt in that whole fucking building hates that shit. And we are all, every last one of us, too fucking scared to even talk about it to one another. So we laugh at his jokes and we buy him drinks and we admire his car and we tell him that he could pull any one of the girls in the club any time he liked.

Jimmy   That's a wee bit dishonest.

Andy   And when he does we laugh with him. And we offer him our respect. And I tell you, my friend, the next time he does it I am going to kick the fucking crap right out of his arse.

Jimmy   You seem pretty determined.

Andy   You ever see anybody get killed?

Jimmy   One time.

Andy   Who was it?

Jimmy   It was my daughter.

Andy   Christ.

Jimmy   I saw my daughter get run over.

Andy   Fucking hell.

Jimmy   I don't remember very much about it. I try not to think about it.

Andy   I saw a lad get killed once.

Jimmy   Oh aye?

Andy   Outside the club.

Jimmy   What happened?

Andy   He was giving one of the old boys a little bit of aggro. Mouthing off. He was coked up or E'd up or something and he was mouthing off. Our boy gives him a clip round the earhole and he goes absolutely ballistic. Comes at him with a bottle. It's been a bad night for our boy already and he just fucking snaps.

Jimmy   Christ.

Andy   We're trained, most of us, to deal with situations. This boy is just one of the gym boys. Bit of casual work.

He's not been trained at all. Young lad comes at him with a
bottle and he goes absolutely fucking mental. Drags him to
the ground. Starts smacking his head against the pavement.
Over and over. Blood starts running out on to the road.
Before we can do anything. Just takes a couple of seconds is
all. Takes three of us to drag him off and calm him down
and even when I'm dragging him up I'm thinking, 'This is
bad. This is really bad, Andy old son.' And when we get him
up, y'know what I notice most of all?

Jimmy   What's that?

Andy   Is how blue the boy's eyes were. They were such a
still blue. I won't ever forget that, (*Long pause.*) It gets hard
sometimes. Y'know what I mean?

Jimmy   I know exactly what you mean.

Andy   I'm trying. So hard. Trying to raise the boys.
Trying to look after the daughter. Trying to make the wife
happy. Trying to save a bit of money. Trying to get us out
of this shithole. This place. It isn't anywhere to raise a
family. The things that go on here. They break your heart.

Jimmy   I wish you luck, my friend.

Andy   How old was your daughter?

Jimmy   She was seven.

Andy   I'm really sorry.

Jimmy   Don't worry, Andy. You couldn't have known.

Andy   You working all night?

Jimmy   No. I'm going to meet somebody.

Andy   At this time?

Jimmy   I'm going to meet the wife.

Andy   You give her my love, mate.

Lights falls.

Lights rise on **Billy Lee**, *a broken fascist with his wrist in plaster, in* **Jimmy***'s cab. He addresses* **Jimmy***.*

Billy Lee   Everybody asks me if I've broken my wrist. It's enough to fucking drive you mad. A broken wrist takes six weeks to mend. Three snapped tendons and maybe you get some movement back in your hand after twelve months if you're fucking lucky. I've been trying to draw with my left hand but it's just shit and it just makes me fucking so fucking angry. I've been drunk for a week now. I'm going into hospital tomorrow for the operation and y'know why I'm drinking? Do you? Oy?

Jimmy   I have no idea.

Billy Lee   I'm just desperate to blank out the pain. And I'm going in tomorrow and I'm just a fucking guinea pig. Ninety-six stitches. Right around my fucking wrist. I might get some compensation. I better fucking had. But honestly, eh? What do you think about this operation? Am I just a fucking guinea pig or what?

Jimmy   You'll be all right.

Billy Lee   Fucking bastards though. They told me that with an injury like mine there was a possibility that within twelve months I might start to get some movement back in my right hand. It's fucking hopeless though. I'm telling you. It's fucking hopeless. (*Long pause.*) You want to hear a story?

Jimmy   You what?

Billy Lee   You want to hear a story? Do you like stories?

Jimmy   Sure.

Billy Lee   There are a lot of pigeons on Ladbroke Grove.

Jimmy   I'm sorry?

Billy Lee   There are a lot of pigeons on Ladbroke Grove. With it getting so hot they've been rebuilding their nests. Making cooler nests. Accommodating to the heat. You understand?

Jimmy   I think so.

Billy Lee   You know what they do to their young?

Jimmy   Their young?

Billy Lee   Yeah. Those motherfucking pigeons. You know what they do to their young while they're rebuilding their fucking nests to accommodate themselves to the fucking heat?

Jimmy   I have no idea.

Billy Lee   Kick them out.

Jimmy   I see.

Billy Lee   Bastards. They just kick them out. Can you believe that? Monday morning I'm walking down Portobello Road. Look down. There's a tiny naked featherless pigeon hopping down the road. Buggers belief, mate. Absolutely buggers belief.

Jimmy   What did you do?

Billy Lee   What did I do?

Jimmy   To the pigeon.

Billy Lee   I left it. You should never disturb baby birds. Do you want to see my tattoos?

Jimmy   Your tattoos?

Billy Lee   Aye. I've got tattoos. On my good arm. Do you want to see them?

Jimmy   It'd be an honour.

Awkwardly but eventually **Billy Lee** *manages to roll up his sleeve, maybe with his teeth, and shows* **Jimmy** *his good arm.*

Billy Lee   Do you know what that means? Can you read it?

Jimmy   Combat 18.

Billy Lee   Do you know what that means?

Jimmy Of course I know what that means.

Billy Lee (*turning his arm to show* **Jimmy** *the back of his fist*)
What about this? These blue dots, do you know what they
mean?

Jimmy I have no idea.

Billy Lee I ain't never going to get involved in any of that
shit any more. This is where I get out.

Jimmy What do the five blue dots mean?

Billy Lee You don't want to even know.

Jimmy That's six fifty.

Lights fall.

Lights rise on **Janine Williams**, *a smartly dressed, middle-aged,
manic depressive former teacher. She addresses* **Jimmy**.

Janine You know what I think?

Jimmy What's that?

Janine I sometimes think that there is so much confusion
and sadness and hatred and everything. Just everything.
Broken. Horrible. It would just be better. It could just be
simpler. If people said things.

Jimmy I think you're right.

Janine We never, do we?

Jimmy Not very often.

Janine Nobody reads any more.

Jimmy Nobody has time.

Janine Have time for drinking. Have time for smashing
things up. For killing people. Have time for shopping and
mad and stupid crazy things. Bicycles. Hundreds and
hundreds of cars. We have time. If you knew you were
going to die and had time to read one more book before you
died, what book would you read?

Jimmy   I don't know.

Janine   I'd read a pornographic magazine.

Jimmy   Why?

Janine   I can relate to the women in pornographic magazines. Have you ever been in love?

Jimmy   Yes. I have.

Janine   I'm a teacher.

Jimmy   What do you teach?

Janine   Or rather I was a teacher. I don't do much of anything any more.

Jimmy   What did you teach?

Janine   I visit gardens a lot of the time. Sometimes I imagine that it would be nice to be a gardener. (*She has started to cry.*)

Jimmy   Are you all right, darling? Are you crying?

Janine   No.

Jimmy   Here. I've got a handkerchief.

Janine   I'm not crying. All right? Can you not hear me?

Jimmy   I just thought –

Janine (*interrupting*)   They told me they were going to have to make some changes.

Jimmy   Who?

Janine   They told me they were going to have to make some changes and there was nothing they could do for me any more.

Jimmy   Who told you that?

Janine   Who were you in love with? (*No response. Pause.*) Please tell me. I promise I won't tell anyone.

Jimmy   I was in love with a London girl. Called Clare. (**Janine** *is silent so he continues.*) And we got married. And had one child. A baby girl. (*Ditto.*) And I haven't seen her for five years.

Janine (*responding very quickly*)   Why not?

Jimmy   I left her. Or she left me. Somehow. One or the other left.

Janine   Why?

Jimmy   I don't often talk about it.

Janine (*almost angry*)   Look. I just want to hear a story. I've been having a very hard time.

Jimmy   I drank too much.

Janine   I drink too. Sometimes.

Jimmy   I started to do crazy things.

Janine   What happened to your girl?

Jimmy   The girl died.

Janine   I'm sorry.

Jimmy   Why are you having a hard time?

Janine   Things.

Jimmy   What things?

Janine   Just things. Teacups sit for weeks. I don't even wash them any more.

Jimmy   I hate it when that happens.

Janine   Shoelaces.

Jimmy   Shoelaces?

Janine   Do you never get upset by shoelaces? I hate shoes without laces. But sometimes. I could just cry. I'm sorry. I shouldn't be talking about this.

Jimmy   Why not?

Janine   You don't want to hear about it.

Jimmy   I don't mind listening. I like stories.

Janine   I can't have children.

Jimmy   I'm sorry.

Janine   My insides are all wrong. I went to the doctor this afternoon. He said there was nothing he could do.

Jimmy   That's sad.

Janine   And I don't want to adopt. I don't know what I would do.

Jimmy   What do you mean?

Janine   I don't even know how to love a child.

Jimmy   Are you married?

Janine   Of course I'm not married.

Jimmy   Why 'of course'?

Janine   Just. Look at me.

Jimmy   You aren't bad-looking.

Janine   For a long time. I slept with men.

Jimmy   Oh yeah?

Janine   Men I met on trains. In cafés. In pubs. I'd go to pubs to meet men there. I wanted children so badly. I let them do anything to me.

Jimmy   I see.

Janine   One man hurt me. He really humiliated me. Some of the things he said. I was very drunk. But I remember. The things he said.

Jimmy   You should be careful.

Janine   And every month. Like a hammer. Nothing ever happened.

Jimmy   I'm sorry.

Janine   It's very hot in here. People should get, you should get better air conditioning. We can't cope. Will you see your wife again?

Jimmy   I phoned her.

Janine   When?

Jimmy   Tonight.

Janine   What did she say?

Jimmy   I'm going to see her.

Janine   When?

Jimmy   Tonight.

Janine   Good.

Jimmy   What's your name?

Janine   Janine.

Jimmy   That's a nice name.

Janine   It's a stupid name.

Jimmy   No it's not.

Janine   It's a stupid name for a stupid whore.

Jimmy   You're not a –

Janine (*interrupting*)   I should know. I don't have any money.

Jimmy   What?

Janine   I don't have any money. I can't pay the fare.

Jimmy   What did you stop me for then?

Janine   I don't even know.

Jimmy   What did you stop me for if you don't have any money?

Janine   Would you like to go to bed with me?

Jimmy   No.

Janine   You can stop here if you want to.

Jimmy   No. I'll take you home.

Janine   But I don't have any money.

Jimmy   I don't care about that. It's all right.

Janine   What would you do if every customer refused to pay you?

Jimmy   I don't think I'd last very long.

Janine   What will you say to your wife?

Jimmy   I've got a present for her.

Janine   That's nice. How did your daughter die?

Jimmy   She was run over.

Janine   I wouldn't have let that happen. If I'd been her mother.

Jimmy   Sometimes you can't stop these things.

Janine   I wouldn't have let her leave the house without me. I wouldn't have let her out of my sight.

Jimmy   She was seven years old. You can't stop children from having their freedom, Janine.

Janine   You could do. If you wanted to. I could have done.

Jimmy (*has lit a cigarette*)   No. That's not always possible.

Janine   It kills you. It kills me. I have to sit in these rooms and sometimes I can't even breathe.

Jimmy   It's my car.

Janine   I like the colour of the smoke. That blueness. Are you scared of seeing your wife again?

Jimmy   No.

Janine   What do you think she'll be like?

Jimmy   I have no idea.

Janine   No.

Jimmy   I remember her being very beautiful.

Janine   That's good.

Jimmy   She might have changed. She'll be older now.

Janine   Yes, she will.

Jimmy   It's the anniversary.

Janine   What anniversary?

Jimmy   Tonight, five years ago, was the night our daughter was killed.

Janine   I see.

Jimmy   This is where you get out.

Janine   I know that. I don't have any money.

Jimmy   Don't worry about it.

Janine   I'm very scared.

Jimmy   There's no reason to be.

Janine   I probably won't sleep tonight.

Jimmy   Read a book.

Janine   That's quite funny.

Jimmy   You'll be all right, darling.

Janine   Do you think so?

Jimmy   You'll be all right.

Janine   I don't know.

Jimmy   You will be.

Janine   You have very kind eyes.

Jimmy   Thank you.

Janine   You look very tired. But you have very kind eyes.

Lights fall.

Lights rise on **Jimmy** *and* **Clare Macneill**. *The two are alone together standing in confrontation on opposite sides of the cab. Their* *conversation is initially at least hostile and awkward. He is trying harder than her.*

Jimmy   You're looking good.

Clare (*cold*)   Thank you.

Jimmy   You're looking really well. You've cut your hair. Since the last time I saw you.

Clare   That was five years ago. Of course I've bloody cut my hair.

Jimmy   It looks nice. It suits your face. Your bone structure. You have a very classical bone structure.

Clare   When you told me you'd pick me up I didn't expect you to arrive in a bloody taxi.

Jimmy   Do you like it?

Clare   Why did you want to see me?

Jimmy   I had something I wanted to give you.

Clare   Why tonight?

Jimmy   You know why. You know why tonight. You don't need to ask me that.

Clare   I can't stay long.

Jimmy   There's something I want to say to you.

Clare   I shouldn't even be here. This is madness. I don't even know what I'm doing here. I don't even know why I'm talking to you. Maybe I should go.

Jimmy   Wait. Just for a while.

Pause.

Clare   It scared the shit out of me to hear your voice. (*Smiling coldly.*) I was actually almost sick.

Jimmy   Woh. (*Pause.*) Would you like to go somewhere?

Clare   What are you talking about?

Jimmy   Well, I was wondering if you wanted to go somewhere. I mean, we could sit here all night if you wanted to but I thought you might want to go for a drive.

Clare   I don't know, James.

Jimmy   Look. I like driving. I can talk more easily when I'm driving. I can listen with more accuracy. I don't get claustrophobic. I think driving is very intimate. I'd like to drive for a bit. I was wondering if you wanted to join me.

Clare   I see you've retained your enormous sense of self-interest, James.

Jimmy   Did you ever notice how people never talk loudly to one another in cars?

Clare   No.

Jimmy   Well, take it from me. It's fucking true. (*Pause.*) This is an extraordinary city, Clare. It's a city that you should see primarily in the night-time. It becomes more concentrated in the night-time. We could have a look at it for a while.

Clare   Concentrated?

Jimmy   Yeah.

Clare   I'm not going to stay all night.

Jimmy   I'm not asking you to.

Clare (*agreeing*)   OK.

Jimmy (*desperately relieved*)   Thank fuck for that. Where do you want to go?

Clare   I don't know.

Jimmy   I'll take you anywhere you want.

Clare   Is the meter off?

Jimmy (*grinning*)   It's a minicab. It doesn't have a meter.

Long pause.

Clare   You know what I mean.

Jimmy *continues to grin.*

Clare   We could go back.

Jimmy   Back?

Clare   Back to the old house.

Jimmy   That's where I thought you'd want to go.

Lights fall, save for a wash of deep blue. Gentle sound of a quiet backstreet.

Clare   Have you been back here before?

Jimmy   Almost every night.

Clare   Jesus.

Jimmy   Every night. Right in the middle of the night I come back. Just drive past. Down the street. Sometimes sit here for a while.

Clare   Have you got a light?

Jimmy   When did you start smoking?

Clare   Three years ago.

Jimmy   You're an idiot. What do you want to bloody smoke for? As if you start smoking when you're twenty-six. Christ, Clare.

Clare   Have you got a light?

Jimmy   Of course I've got a bloody light. I've been smoking all my life. But you're not having it. I'm not going to encourage this flagrant idiocy.

Clare (*very angry*)   Fuck off.

Jimmy (*passing her a lighter*)   Don't you tell me to fuck off.

Long pause.

Clare   This is the first time I've been back. Since I left.

Jimmy   It's changed a lot, eh?

Clare   It's not changed that much.

Jimmy   They've built a porch. You can't see it too well in the dark but it's really fucking horrible.

Clare   If we sat here. All night. With the lights off. Do you think anybody would notice?

Jimmy   I've done it before.

Clare   What happened?

Jimmy   Nothing. Never does.

There is a pause. As **Jimmy** *talks he grows increasingly conscious that* **Clare** *isn't really listening to him. She is lost in her own thoughts. His words become more urgent in order to compensate.*

First few times I came here I thought the neighbours might have recognised me. Phoned the police. Invited me in for a cup of fucking tea. They were always inviting people in for cups of tea. It used to do my head in. Invite all these people round and nobody used to ever go. I can't even remember their names. (*Pause.*) Funny going back to a place though, eh?

Clare   Funny?

Jimmy   Like listening to a record that you used to love. Used to know as well as the sound of your own breathing. Listening to it after you've put it away for a while. So that it manages to sound as new and as fresh as it ever did but it's still loaded with all of these intangible fucking memories. It's funny.

Clare   It's very sad.

Jimmy   I've been back here so many times now that it's like it's become part of my body. It's as though this place is a physical extension of myself. I come back here. Try to make sense of things. I can sit here for hours sometimes. I know every crack and pebble and cut in every paving stone and every strip of paint down this whole street. I never thought I'd actually develop a physical relationship with a street before.

Clare   Where have you been?

Jimmy   What do you mean?

Clare   All this time, James. Where the hell have you been? You just disappeared.

Jimmy   I didn't disappear. I've been around.

Clare   You didn't phone. You didn't write. Five years and I didn't get a single sodding word from you and then all of a sudden you turn up and you tell me that you want to see me.

Jimmy   I'm sorry.

Clare   You should be. You should be sorry.

Jimmy   I think about you all the time.

Clare (*angry*)   Oh fuck, James.

Jimmy   What?

Clare   Just oh fuck. That's all. Just. Oh fuck.

Long pause.

Jimmy   Do you believe in ghosts?

Clare   What?

Jimmy   It's just something somebody asked me. Earlier on tonight.

Clare   No.

Jimmy   No. Neither do I. (*Pause.*) Can I ask you another question? (*No response.*) This one's a touch more involved. Do you believe in the intransience of love, Clare?

Clare   What are you talking about?

Jimmy   What about the communicability of the human spirit?

Clare   I tried contacting you. At the address you gave me. They told me you'd moved out.

Jimmy   I did.

Clare   Where did you go?

Jimmy   I brought a cab.

Clare   That wasn't what I was getting at. Whereabouts did you move to?

Jimmy   I didn't move anywhere.

Clare   But you only left that address . . .

Jimmy   Yeah, but . . .

Clare   Where did you live? Where do you live now?

Jimmy   There's no point telling you.

Clare   James.

Jimmy   You wouldn't believe me.

Clare   Oh for fuck's sake.

Jimmy   I live in my cab. I sleep in my cab. I've slept in my cab for four and a half years.

Clare   You what?

Jimmy   Park it down beneath the Goldhawk Road Arches, fold down the passenger seat and sleep. Shave in the toilets of the garage there. They have showers there too. So I clean myself up there. Never did understand why they had showers in the garage.

His talk is relentless almost to himself. He has sensed he may be losing this one. She tries to interrupt him.

Clare   James.

Jimmy   There must be more people doing this than I thought there was. It's a good life, Clare. I own two bags which I keep in the boot of my car. One is full of clean clothes. The other is full of dirty clothes. I own an Otis Redding cassette, a very fucking damn good copy of the *A-Z* of London and a dog-eared edition of *Lord Jim* by Joseph Conrad that Alice bought me one year for my birthday.

Clare   Alice didn't buy it for you. I bought it for you and gave it her to give to you. She was six years old, James.

Jimmy   My diet consists entirely of pre-packed pork pies, sweets, canned drinks, machine coffee and those microwaved burgers that some of the garages have. I am very happy.

Clare   James.

Jimmy   I am as happy as I have ever been in my life. I am as happy as a pig in fucking shit. Nobody would believe me but it's true actually.

Clare   Does anybody else know that you do this?

Jimmy   No.

Clare   Did you never think of telling anybody where you are?

Jimmy   No.

Clare   Somebody might miss you, James.

Jimmy   They wouldn't.

Clare   They might.

Jimmy   Did anybody phone for me? Try to get in touch with me? Write to me? Wonder where the fuck I was?

Clare   No.

Jimmy   I told you. Nobody misses me, Clare. There's nobody to miss me.

Clare   Did it not occur to you for one second that I might have liked to know where you were?

Jimmy   The last time I saw you, you said . . .

Clare   I know what I said.

Jimmy   Well then.

Clare   It's very ugly here now. Maybe I should go.

Jimmy   Don't. Not yet. (*Long pause.*) Do you know how many lights there are on each side of the tube track between Clapham North and Stockwell?

Clare   What?

Jimmy   Never mind.

Long pause.

Clare   What about your agent? Did you never want to tell your agent?

Jimmy   I hated them. Screw-faced little pimply-arsed jumped-up fucking shites. I always hated them.

Clare   Do you not write any more?

Jimmy   No.

Clare   Why not?

Jimmy   I can't.

Clare   Of course you can.

Jimmy   No, honestly. I can't even pick up a pen any more. I can barely write receipts. If anybody asks me for a receipt it can get quite embarrassing. I can't even sign my own name any more.

Clare   Funny.

Jimmy   What is?

Clare   That is actually the only real thing I still liked about you. Even now. I always liked your writing.

Jimmy   Thank you.

Clare   I read one of your books again. A few months back. It was good. It actually made me laugh.

Jimmy   That's good. I always thought everybody underestimated the comedy in my books which can be frankly quite devastating.

Pause.

Clare   What are the people like?

Jimmy   The fares. We don't call them people. We call them fares.

Clare   What are the fares like?

Jimmy   I like them.

Clare   Why?

Jimmy   I like the arbitrary nature of that social interaction. It's very random. I find that an endless source of inspiration.

Clare   I don't like the smell of these cars.

Jimmy   The smell?

Clare   They smell of dead people.

Jimmy   Fucking hell.

Clare   Well, not actually dead people. More the dead smell of people still alive.

Jimmy   There you are, you see. The communicability of the human bloody spirit. You knew exactly what I was talking about.

Clare   Why are you doing this, James?

Jimmy   Doing what?

Clare   Living like this. Living in a Nissan bloody Bluebird for God's sake. It's not even a particularly nice car.

Jimmy   I like living in a car.

Clare   Are you a particularly bad taxi driver?

Jimmy   On the contrary. I'm a particularly good taxi driver.

Clare   Do you not make any money?

Jimmy   I make a fine amount of money.

Clare   Why don't you get somewhere to live then?

Jimmy   Money's got nothing to do with it.

Clare   What has it got anything to do with then because I'm fucked if I understand it?

Jimmy   Do you never just get sick of houses?

Clare   No.

Jimmy   I do. I did. I'd be happy if I never saw the inside of another bloody house again.

Clare   I think your rebellion is a touch misguided, James.

Jimmy   I'm not being rebellious. In the fucking least. Clare. I'm just being honest.

Clare   What do you tell people who you meet? If they ask where you live?

Jimmy   I tell them I live in Bluebird Towers. Off the Goldhawk Road.

Clare   That's very good. What if they want to go home with you?

Jimmy   They don't.

Clare   Don't they?

Jimmy   Nobody's wanted to come home with me in five years.

Clare   That's sad, James.

Jimmy   It's not in the least bit sad.

Clare   When was the last time you slept with somebody, James?

Jimmy   It was five years ago, Clare. I slept with you.

Pause.

Clare (*still angry*)   After what happened. I never wanted to see you again but that didn't mean . . . (*New thought.*) I actually wasn't going to show up, you know.

Jimmy   I wouldn't have blamed you. I'm glad you did.

Clare   What is it that you've got for me?

Jimmy   I'll show you later.

Clare   James, don't piss me about.

Jimmy (*trying to maintain civility*)   How have *you* been?

Clare   Is that any of your business?

Jimmy   You're making this very fucking difficult actually, Clare, you know that?

Clare (*sarcastic*)   Oh, you poor bastard. I can't stay much longer.

Jimmy   I'm just trying to . . . Look. I'm sorry. I just want to know. How've you been?

Clare   That's a very difficult question to answer.

Jimmy   Is it?

Clare   I met someone.

Jimmy   I meet a lot of people.

Clare   I've lived with him for the past three years.

Jimmy   You liked him then?

Clare   I still do.

Jimmy   That's always a good thing in a flatmate.

Clare   He's not my flatmate.

Jimmy   I see. What's he called?

Clare   Andrew.

Increasing tension. He grows more terrier-like. She more defiant.

Jimmy   Good name. Nice and religious. I like that in a name. What does he do?

Clare   He's a doctor.

Jimmy   What kind of doctor is he?

Clare   He's a heart surgeon.

Jimmy   Fuck me. A fucking heart surgeon. He must be loaded.

Clare   James.

Jimmy   Is he good?

Clare   What do you mean?

Jimmy   Is he a good heart surgeon?

Clare   He's very good.

Jimmy   Is he?

Clare   Yes.

Jimmy   And is he very rich?

Clare   Incalculably.

Jimmy (*vicious*)   Good on yer, girl.

Clare   Thank you.

Jimmy   What else does he do?

Clare   Apart from heart surgery you mean?

Jimmy   Yeah.

Clare   He collects butterflies.

Jimmy   No he doesn't.

Clare   Yes he does.

Jimmy   Clare, nobody collects butterflies any more. Everybody knows that.

Clare   Andrew does.

Jimmy   Does he not get very lonely? Being the last remaining butterfly collector in the world?

Clare   He's not the last one. He's in a club.

Jimmy (*relentless*)   Christ alive. What football team does he support?

Clare   He doesn't follow football.

Jimmy   What music does he listen to?

Clare   He plays the piano.

Jimmy   What kind of clothes does he wear?

Clare   Jimmy.

Jimmy   Say that again.

Clare   What?

Jimmy   Say that again. Call me Jimmy again.

Clare   Why?

Jimmy   That's the first time you've called me Jimmy all night.

Clare   He wears all kinds of clothes. He likes piano music. And he likes seafood and he reads a lot of history books and he collects butterflies. He doesn't watch football or cricket or rugby or any sport. But he exercises. He swims and he runs and –

Jimmy   Does he work out?

Clare   No. He doesn't work out.

Jimmy   Thank fuck for that.

Clare   What do you want, Jimmy?

Jimmy   I wanted to see you. I have something I want to give to you. I'm also generally interested in how you're getting on having not seen you for such a long time.

Clare (*interrupting*)   We're going to buy a house. In the country. A cottage and we're going to take weekends there and walk and have open fires and we're going to go on holidays to France and also to Germany because that was where his mother was born.

Jimmy   Bloody hell. It's peachy fucking creamy all the way, darlin'.

Clare   I didn't tell you.

Jimmy   What?

Clare   I'm pregnant. I'm going to have a baby. At the start of the year.

This has utterly knocked the wind out of his attack.

Well. Don't you have anything to say?

Jimmy   How do you feel?

Clare   I feel good.

Jimmy   That's good.

Clare   What do you mean by that?

Jimmy   I mean what I said. That's good. It's good news. I'm glad for you.

Clare   How do you feel about it?

Jimmy   What's it got to do with me?

Clare   It has nothing to do with you at all. I just want to know.

Jimmy   How do you expect me to feel?

Clare   I have no expectations.

Jimmy (*honestly, not pathetic*)   It breaks my heart, Clare.

Clare   I'm sorry.

Jimmy   Don't be.

Clare   I didn't want to upset you.

Jimmy   Don't apologise to me. Nobody should apologise to me. I am beneath all apology. No matter what anybody ever does to me it could never be as bad as what I did to you.

Clare   That's not true.

Jimmy   Of course it's true Clare. You know it's true. (*Considerable beat.*) How pregnant are you?

Clare   Two months.

Jimmy   So it'll be a new-year baby.

Clare   That's right.

Jimmy   That's good.

Clare   Is it?

Jimmy   I've started thinking recently that the time of a child's birth in relation to the birth of the natural cycle of the year is enormously important.

Clare   That's bullshit, Jimmy.

Jimmy   Maybe. It's just something I thought.

Clare   I hope you're right, you know, but –

Jimmy   So do I. (*He is attempting to recover his spirit.*) Are you still teaching?

Clare   Yes I am.

Jimmy   Do you still enjoy it?

Clare   Yes I do.

Jimmy   I met a teacher earlier on tonight.

Clare   No you didn't.

Jimmy   I did as well. Mind you. She didn't seem to be taking it too well. All the paperwork. Seemed to have got to her a bit.

Clare   I know that feeling.

Jimmy   How are the kids?

Clare   They're the same. You know. They never change from year to year. Not really.

Jimmy   Have you noticed that marked deterioration in their moral fortitude that I'm always fucking reading about?

Clare   No. Kids have never had any moral fortitude.

Jimmy   That's what I always thought. That's what I always liked about them. So what else have you been up to?

*His thoughts change direction with no pause, breath or consideration.
Almost manic. As though he senses a decreased hostility on her part and
is very anxious to make the most of it.* **Clare**, *surprised slightly by the
mania, pauses to think.*

Clare   I went to painting classes for a while.

Jimmy   Bloody hell.

Clare   It was good.

Jimmy   What kind of painting were you doing?

Clare   Just painting. You know. Still lifes. Watercolours.

Jimmy   Were you any good?

Clare   I don't know. I don't think so.

Jimmy   You always did that.

Clare   What?

Jimmy   Always put yourself down. You shouldn't. I bet
you were a great painter.

Clare   One time. We had to paint a portrait. From a
photograph. I painted a picture of Alice.

Jimmy   Which photograph?

Clare   One of her in Brittany.

Jimmy   What did she look like?

Clare   She was wearing that fisherman's hat. Do you
remember?

Jimmy   Of course I remember.

Clare   And she had an ice cream. And she was smiling a
big ice-cream-smeared smile.

Jimmy   I wish I could see it.

Clare   I'll show it to you one day.

Jimmy   Yeah, maybe. (*Long pause.*) Do you know what
pigeons do to their young when they have to rebuild their
nests to acclimatise to the heat?

Clare   I have no idea.

Jimmy   They just hoof them out. That's pretty bad eh?

Clare   Terrible. (*Long pause.*) Do you realise this is going to be the hottest summer we've had in fourteen years?

Jimmy   Yeah. Everybody keeps telling me that. (*Long pause.*) I was working on a case last week. I couldn't afford a desk. I got up. There was a tap on the door. Which was an odd place for a tap I thought. You laughed! I saw you laugh!

Clare   Do you ever think about her? (*No response.*) Jimmy.

Jimmy   Maybe we should go?

Clare   Jimmy, answer my question.

Jimmy   I'm getting cold. Are you not getting cold?

Clare   Jimmy, for God's sake.

Jimmy   I think about her all the time.

Clare   Do you know how old she'd be now?

Jimmy   Twelve.

Clare   Twelve years. Three months and fourteen days.

Jimmy   I know.

Clare   I celebrate her birthday.

Jimmy   How?

Clare   I pour myself a drink. And then I pour myself another one. And then I hate you more than anybody has ever hated anybody else.

There is a pause. They gather themselves. Her for a fight.

Jimmy   Should we go?

Clare (*pursuing him*)   What do you remember about her, Jimmy? Most of all? Which moment? Which thing that she did?

Jimmy (*matter-of-fact*)   I remember watching her dance. At one of her friend's parties. She danced just like you did. She was mad.

Clare   I know.

Jimmy   Do you still dance?

Clare   Why did you want to see me, Jimmy?

Jimmy   I told you. I have something for you. I used to love to watch you dance.

Clare   What have you got for me?

Jimmy   I'll tell you later. I used to love to dance with you.

Clare   What have you got for me?

Jimmy   I was always a fucking terrible dancer but I still used to enjoy dancing with you. I've got a present for you. What do you remember most of all?

Clare   I remember everything.

Jimmy   It's hard, isn't it?

Clare   I remember everything, Jimmy. Every moment. Every breath. Every utterance. Every touch. Everything. I remember it physically. As though I could feel her. The memories are tangible. Does that make any sense to you?

Jimmy   It makes perfect sense to me.

Clare   But do you know what I remember most of all? Out of everything?

Jimmy   What?

Clare   I remember that I never said goodbye to her. I just buttoned up her coat and kissed her on her head. And told her that her dinner would be ready before too long so that she shouldn't go too far. That's what I remember most of all, Jimmy. I won't ever forget that.

Jimmy   I'm sorry.

Clare   It was very cowardly of you to leave like that.

Jimmy   I know that.

Clare   I had to deal with everything, Jimmy. On my own. I had to deal with packing her clothes away. I had to throw some of her stuff out. I wanted to keep it all. But some of it was just ridiculous. I wanted to keep her library cards. Letters from her school. But I had to face up to the fact that it couldn't happen. On my own. I got all of her things that I couldn't keep or sell into a box and I took them to a skip and I threw them away and you weren't there. You weren't there, Jimmy, and I find it hard to forgive you for that.

Jimmy   I know.

Clare   And I had to deal with the letters, from her school friends. And their visits and cards and gifts and I had to thank them and not break down and kiss their faces or scream at them, 'Why couldn't it have been you?' Because they were seven years old and that would have been irrational and unfair and stupid. I had to face their parents and everybody. Her teachers. Her swimming teacher. I had to go and tell her swimming teacher that she wouldn't be coming to her classes any more because she was dead, Jimmy. She was dead and I had to do it all on my own. And it was hard. And it wasn't fair.

Jimmy   Do you want to know what I had to deal with?

Clare   I don't care. I don't care what you had to fucking deal with.

Jimmy   This is what I wanted to tell you, Clare. I just want you to know.

Clare   I packed away all of her things and saw her buried properly and I went back to my work. And I carried on, Jimmy. I met Andrew and he looked after me so gently. The kind of gentleness that you couldn't understand. And you expect to come back into my life and that everything will be all right and –

Jimmy   I never expected that.

Clare   – I'll hear you out and forgive you so that you can carry on with a clear fucking conscience. Well, you're wrong, Jimmy. You are so bloody wrong you couldn't even believe it.

Very long pause. **Clare** *is exhausted.*

Jimmy (*very lightly, quiet, matter-of-fact, as one telling a story*) There's this guy. And one night he's driving back home from a meeting. And the meeting had gone very badly. Somebody had told him that he didn't have work for him any more. And on the way back home from the meeting in order to numb his disappointment and brace himself for the consequences of this unexpected news he had stopped in a pub. And in the pub he'd drunk three pints of beer. And on the way home from the pub he'd got scared because he had to tell his wife about the way he couldn't pay the mortgage any more. Or for the holiday they'd already booked. Or for any food that week. And he had no idea what he was going to say. He didn't know what he was going to do. So he stopped off at an off-licence. On the way home. And he bought a quarter-bottle of very cheap whisky that he didn't even like but he bought it so that he would have the courage to tell her and he sat in his car outside the off-licence and drank the whole bottle. And drove home. And it's a very warm night. And the sun is coming out. It's a very still night at the beginning of the summer exactly five years ago from tonight. But you knew that anyway, didn't you?

Clare   Jimmy.

Jimmy   And he knows as he's driving that he is drunk. But he doesn't stop. He's very near his home and he's driving very quickly. He doesn't stop. And the sun is getting in his eyes and he's quite surprised because he notices that he's started to sweat and that the sweat is running over his face and into his eyes and his mouth and his nose and it smells very bad. And he turns into his road. Where he has driven many times. And all the houses look the same. And the sun is still out. And he understands that he's driving too quickly. And he doesn't even recognise the houses hardly.

And just then, at the point where he's arriving at his house, he notices that his daughter, who is seven years old, is playing outside his house.

Clare   Don't.

Jimmy   And she looks very beautiful in the sunshine. She has this curly red hair that reminds him of her mother. And she looks up from the game where she has been playing. Sees her dad coming home.

Clare   Don't, Jimmy. For God's sake.

Jimmy   And he even thinks. It only takes half a second. But in that half a second he even thinks. Oh God. Don't let me see her. Don't let her be there. Don't let this happen to me. And he tries. But he can't slow down.

Clare   Jimmy.

Jimmy   It was an accident.

Clare   Jimmy.

Jimmy   I am so sorry.

Clare   Jimmy.

Jimmy   I don't even know how to sleep any more.

Clare   I know.

Pause.

Jimmy   I went to stay at the Great Northern Hotel in King's Cross. Spent my days watching television with the curtains closed. Drinking. I just wanted to die then. I found myself talking to Alice. Telling her not to worry. That I was coming. (*Half-laugh, disbelieving.*) One time I drank so much that I actually almost blinded myself. I still talk to her. Even now.

Clare   What do you tell her?

Jimmy   I tell her about the people that I drive. Some of them are extraordinary. I tell her that I'm sorry.

Clare   Does she talk back?

Jimmy   Sometimes.

Clare   What does she say when you tell her that you're
sorry?

Jimmy   She tells me that she forgives me.

Clare (*finding this difficult to believe*)   Does she?

Jimmy   Sometimes. Sometimes she doesn't say anything.
Do you ever talk to her?

Clare   I talk to her all the time.

Jimmy   I knew you would.

Clare   Of course I do.

Jimmy   I'm glad. What do you say to her?

Clare   Mainly I tell her that I miss her.

Jimmy (*remembering suddenly*)   Oh yeah. I tell her that as
well. (*Pause.*) This afternoon, before I phoned you, I was
working down on the South Bank. Do you remember when
we went there? Just after we were married. We were late for
the theatre. Both of us running over Waterloo Bridge. As
the sun set. I come here sometimes and remember that
night so clearly. You looked very beautiful.

Clare   It was a long time ago.

Jimmy   I remember looking back at you running after
me. Waiting to let you catch up. You had to run more
slowly than me because you were wearing high-heeled
shoes. And you took the shoes off and ran on the pavement
in your bare feet. I remember thinking to myself that I was
so lucky because you were so beautiful.

Clare   It was a long time ago, Jimmy.

Jimmy   Do you think you'll be happy? With Andrew?

Clare   He's a good man. He's a kind man. He's very
attentive to what I need. We look after each other. We're a
good team.

Jimmy   You deserve to be happy.

Clare   I know.

Jimmy   I'd like to meet him.

Clare   I'm not sure that you'd like each other.

Jimmy   Should we go?

Clare   Go?

Jimmy   We could drive for a while.

Clare   I want to go home soon.

Jimmy   I thought we could go to the cemetery.

Clare   Yeah. Yes. OK.

Lights fall, then rise again to the light blue, quiet wash.

Clare   I don't know what to say to her.

Jimmy   No. Neither do I.

Clare   Do you think it's possible to forgive somebody for
something that you can never forget?

Jimmy   No.

Clare   No. Neither do I.

Jimmy   I see.

Clare   But I am glad we came here, y'know.

Jimmy   Me too.

Clare   I won't ever be able to forget what you did. I'm not
sure that I'll ever be able to forgive you. Jimmy.

Jimmy   I know that.

Clare   But in spite of everything, y'know, I do think that it
was important that we came here together. Just one time. I

think I was angry that we never did that before. Does that make any sense to you?

Jimmy (*joking*)   No sense whatsoever.

She laughs. He is going to say something. She stops him.

Clare   Don't.

Jimmy   What?

Clare   It's all right. I know.

Jimmy   Good.

Clare   It's warm.

Jimmy   I know. It might rain.

Clare   Strange, isn't it?

Jimmy   Will you hold my hand?

Clare   Why?

Jimmy   I like holding your hand.

Clare (*holding his hand*)   You have very good hands. I always liked that about you. They're very big. Very hard. Very well defined.

Jimmy   Well defined? I have well-defined hands?

Clare   Yeah.

Jimmy   Well, I never knew that.

Clare   Well, you do.

Jimmy   I was always amazed by how small your hands were.

Clare   Really?

Jimmy   Do you want to know something stupid?

Clare   What's that?

Jimmy   That was when I always understood most clearly that I was a man and that you were a woman. When I looked at your hands. Because your hands are so small.

You've got very small hands and I've got very big hands and I always used to enjoy that.

Clare   You're very strange.

Jimmy (*moving his hands away*)   Yeah. I know.

Clare   I'm hungry.

Jimmy   Do you want to get something to eat? There's a twenty-four-hour garage on the Harrow Road. They do these great pork pies.

Clare   No. I should go. We should have brought some flowers.

Jimmy   Yeah. I know.

Clare   You told me you had something to give me.

Jimmy   I do.

Clare   What is it?

Jimmy   It's quite embarrassing.

Clare   Christ.

Jimmy   You have to promise me that you won't be embarrassed.

Clare   I'm not sure.

Jimmy   Promise me.

Clare   OK. OK. I promise.

Jimmy   I have to go back to the car. Wait here.

He goes back to the car. She lights a cigarette. He returns with a suitcase. Hands it to her.

Here. Here you are. Open it.

Clare   What's in it?

Jimmy   Have a look.

She opens it. Inside is £100,000. She is visibly shaken.

Are you embarrassed?

Clare   I can't take this.

Jimmy   Of course you can.

Clare   I can't.

Jimmy   Clare. There's over a hundred thousand pounds there. Please, take it, Clare.

Clare   Where did you get all this?

Jimmy   I earned it.

Clare   You what?

Jimmy   I've been driving for four and a half years. Every day. I drive for twelve hours a day. Minimum. It gets quite lucrative after a while.

Clare   But.

Jimmy   I don't want it. I don't need it. It means nothing to me.

Clare   How can it mean nothing?

Jimmy   I have no need for it. It is about as useful to me as a suitcase full of drawing pins. Or envelopes. Or shoelaces.

Clare   Jimmy.

Jimmy   This isn't an apology. It's not a bribe. It's not any kind of attempt to compensate or make up for what I did. I want you to know that. I absolutely understand that there is no way I could ever do that.

Clare   Jimmy.

Jimmy   I don't know anybody else. I have no other friends. It is simply that I have something in my possession that I don't want and I thought that I would get in touch with you so that I could let you have it. I wanted to see you, Clare. I'm so glad that you came.

Clare   I don't know what to say.

Jimmy   Please. Just take it.

Clare   I hated you. I hated you. I hated you. I hated you so much.

Jimmy   I know.

Clare (*starting to cry*)   Oh fuck. Oh fuck, Jimmy.

Jimmy   Don't.

Clare   Whatever happened? Jimmy? What happened? It's not fair.

Jimmy   I know.

Clare   I don't understand it.

Jimmy   I know.

Clare   She was so young.

Jimmy   Yes. She was.

Lights fall.

Lights rise on **Jimmy** *and* **Clare** *back in the car. The tone has the air of conclusion.*

Clare   What will you do now?

Jimmy   I'm going to carry on.

Clare   Carry on?

Jimmy   I'm going to carry on driving. I like it. It makes me happy.

Clare   Jimmy, you can't do that.

Jimmy   Yes I can. I can and I will.

Clare   What? And sleep in your car? And eat nothing but pork pies?

Jimmy   I like pork pies.

Clare   Jimmy. I'm being serious.

Jimmy   So am I.

Clare   You know those questions?

Jimmy   What questions?

Clare   The ones about the intransience of love and the communicability of the human spirit?

Jimmy   Oh yeah?

Clare   They were good questions.

Jimmy   Thank you.

Clare   I'll think about those ones for a while.

Jimmy   Do you want to stop, watch the morning break?

Clare   I should be getting back.

Jimmy   I love the break of morning. You know how you can tell when morning has broken in London?

Clare   How?

Jimmy   It's nothing to do with sunlight. Or birds singing or anything like that. It's when the cars come out.

Clare   Jimmy, what will I do if I decide I want to see you again? How will I get in touch with you?

Jimmy   Here. Take my card. This is the number of the company I work for. If you ever need a taxi ask for driver 42.

Clare   Can't I ask for you by name?

Jimmy   I don't think they know my name.

Clare (*almost surprised, as though suddenly realising*)   I'm glad I came, Jimmy.

Jimmy   Good. It's been good to see you, y'know.

Clare   It's been quite a night.

Jimmy   Yeah. It has.

Lights fade. **Clare** *leaves the stage.*

'My Girl' starts once more. Lights rises on **Jimmy** *sitting alone in his cab. Sound of the taxi radio blends in with the music. He lights a cigarette. Lights on cab fade, leaving only headlights. Montage of taxi radio instructions with the Otis Redding and the jungle music rises, then, with the headlights, fades.*

Christmas

This play is dedicated to G. N. Stephens

11/10/41–28/01/01

Christmas was first performed at the Pavilion Theatre, Brighton, on 6 December 2003 The cast was as follows:

Michael Macgraw	Alan Williams
Billy Lee Russell	Lee Ross
Giuseppe Rosso	Bernard Gallagher
Charlie Anderson	Bernard Gallagher
Fat Man	Ralph Brown
Man	James Lance
Young Man	Mark Enticknap
Small Man	Antony Ingram

Directed by Jo McInnes
Produced by Daisy Robertson
Designed by James Humphrey & Geoff Rose
Lighing by Matt Eaglan
Music by Will Matthews

Characters

Michael Macgraw, *thirty-eight*
Billy Lee Russell, *twenty-nine*
Giuseppe Rossi, *sixty-eight*
Charlie Anderson, *thirty-five*
Fat Man/Man/Young Man/Small Man

The play is set over the course of one night in a pub in east London.

Scene One

Very dim light on the interior of a pub. Loud music playing and the sound of a live band, a three-piece of drums, double bass and piano, leading a rousing, full-pub chorus of Frank Sinatra's 'That's Life'. Sound of laughter, shouting, singing, sparring. Yet the pub is empty. The intended effect is ghostly.

Lights rise. It is the early afternoon. The pub is sparse and dirty, the furniture wooden and broken. A few chairs stand around a few tables. Three bar stools stand by the bar. The bar looms, huge, out towards the audience, arched like a bullet. No brewery advertisement. Even the beer fonts look somehow dated. A photographic portrait of Frank Sinatra hangs above the bar. A huge, yellowing map of the world. There are Christmas decorations. An advent calendar with sixteen windows open.

Michael Macgraw, *the bartender, enters. A tired-looking, fractured man in his late thirties. He is hung-over, inches away from being still drunk. He is unshaven in a tieless shirt. He is a Londoner but having spent huge chunks of his childhood in Wicklow, Ireland, and having been surrounded by an Irish family all his life, he can speak with an occasional lilt to his voice. This is accentuated when he is drunk.*

He clocks his mail and collects it. Grimaces. Swears. Opens a small cupboard at the back of the bar and places two unopened letters inside it. Pours himself a cup of tea from the kettle behind the bar. Sups from it and opens and reads the third letter with great care. He moves round in front of the bar where he falls to the floor and starts on a series of ten press-ups. He counts every one. Returns to behind the bar. Takes a bottle of unopened poteen whiskey from beneath the counter. Holds it. Looks at it. Puts it back. Turns to the regular spirits behind him and adds a shot of whiskey to his tea. Toasts himself. Places the third letter into the cupboard and starts the process of opening the pub. He moves almost automatically. Connecting taps. Flicking switches. Attaching spirit bottles to optics. Opening fridges. Curtains. Letting in light. When the pub is ready he stops. Lights a cigarette.

The lights fade slowly.

Scene Two

Lights rise again, same pub, later that afternoon. The band is playing again – this time it's 'Luck Be A Lady'. **Macgraw** *is joined by* **Billy Lee Russell**, *an ugly, exasperated twenty-nine-year-old in a yellow raincoat over a grey sweatshirt and battered jeans. He is in a constant state of agitation. He taps, fiddles, twists, shakes, rocks constantly, especially when anxious. His throat is racked by years of smoking too much. He sups a pint of lager.* **Macgraw** *is reading the racing pages of a newspaper. Smoking a cigarette. Catching his breath as he reads. Trying to ignore* **Russell**.

Russell   I couldn't help noticing, Michael. The striking economy of your Christmas decorations. When did they go up?

Macgraw   Yesterday.

Russell   I quite admire that. As it goes. Christmas. Eh? What a . . . (*searching for the right adjective*) cunt. Innit?

Macgraw   Uh-huh.

Russell   Fucking, though, innit? Eh? Cunt.

Macgraw (*making notes on his paper*)   I don't know, Billy, I've always found something vaguely hopeful about it.

Russell   Hopeful? Have you? Well, fuck me on a horse. There you go. (*Pause.*) So. (*Another.*) How've you been, Michael?

Macgraw   Alive. Hanging on in there.

Russell *chuckles, taking the piss. He continues to do this for some time.*

Russell   Fucking dead in here.

Macgraw (*adding on a calculator*)   I can see that, Billy. Thanks.

Russell   Where the fuck is everybody?

Macgraw   A question so good you could frame it.

Russell   I should have brought my fucking mum.

Macgraw (*looks up*)   Thank you, no.

Russell   See the Hammers, this afternoon?

Macgraw (*back down*)   No.

Russell   What a shower of shite!

Macgraw   I read.

Russell   They've got an African fella, right midfield. Big tall gangly fuckwit. He's got a fucking broken leg.

Macgraw   Oh yeah?

Russell   They paid a million quid for a clueless sod with a broken leg.

Macgraw   . . .

Russell   Still playing, mind you. Still on the fucking first team. Best fucking player on the park this afternoon. (*No response.*) Cup starting after Christmas. (*No response.*) Is that a new shirt?

Macgraw   What?

Russell   That shirt, Michael. Is it new?

Macgraw   Are you taking the piss?

Russell   I've just not seen it before.

Macgraw   It's my Ralph Lauren.

Russell   Sweet. Seen Seppo?

Macgraw   Not tonight.

Russell   What's the matter wiv 'im?

Macgraw   Fucked if I know.

Russell   Gone down Bow Wharf, 'as he? Down the fucking wine bar? Developing a penchant for a bit of fucking Chardonnay?

Macgraw   Wouldn't fucking surprise me.

Russell   Pucker!

Macgraw   Every other cunt must be.

Russell   How's the horses?

Macgraw   Tragic.

Russell   Why's that?

Macgraw (*folds paper, puts calculator away*)   Don't ask.

Russell   See, you know what your problem is, don't ya?

Macgraw   I've got a fucking hatful.

Russell   You're a very closed person.

Macgraw   I'm what?

Russell   You don't fucking look it and you'd never fucking admit it but you're very closed. You want to open yourself up to a bit of advice.

Macgraw   Is that right?

Russell   Go fishing.

Macgraw   You what?

Russell   Friend of my mum's used to go fishing just up the Grand Union. Up in Dalston. Used to fucking love it. Catch these fucking big fucking pike. Catch 'em with his rod. Get 'em and he'd just throw 'em back in. Beautiful creatures. Very round eyes. Dead now.

Macgraw   Dead?

Russell   A terrible industrial injury.

Macgraw   I see.

Russell   That's the kind of thing you need, though. Bit of fucking fresh air, you wiv me?

Macgraw   How is your mother, Billy?

Russell   She's doing my nut in.

Macgraw   Oh yeah?

Russell   Tuesday. For no reason. My mum turns. Says to me. Billy Lee, you are one clumsy sodding bastard.

Macgraw (*rolls a smoke*)   Did she say that?

Russell   Very words. I hadn't fucking done anything! Fucksake! After a while, and this is what is so fucking maddening, I realised that she was most probably right.

Macgraw   ?

Russell   Sometimes you just get thinking about something about yourself that you'd never really thought about before. And then you realise it's true. You wiv me? I am a clumsy bastard. I'm always dropping stuff. She's started smoking cannabis.

Macgraw *moves to one end of the bar, where there is a hatch-way, to smoke his cigarette.*

Macgraw   Cannabis?

Russell   She's fifty-two.

Macgraw   That's quite unusual, Billy.

Russell   Never smoked in her life before. Not even a fucking fag.

Macgraw   To take up a drug habit at that age.

Russell   She has taken on the mannerisms of the traditional stoner. She hardly does anything else. Just sits in her room and smokes big bloody joints. She says it's for her arthritis.

Macgraw   Does she suffer from arthritis, Billy?

Russell   First I ever fucking heard about it.

Macgraw   How's your work, Bill?

Russell   It's fucking mental at the moment, Michael.

Macgraw   What are you doing just now?

Russell   I'm carrying hods, Michael. Bit fucking . . . does your fucking back in.

Macgraw   I bet it does.

Russell   It's been fucking freezing this week and all.

Macgraw   I'm sure.

Russell   I've been working in Shoreditch this week. Everybody's clearing away all the properties in Shoreditch. There's a lot of work out there.

Macgraw   There's always somewhere.

Russell   I've never seen so many cunting sandwich shops in one place in my fucking life before. How many fucking sandwiches do those people need?

Macgraw *smiles, rests his cigarette, opens a window on his advent calendar, returns to and relights his cigarette.* **Russell** *drinks.*

Russell   That photograph, Michael. I've seen that fucking picture hundreds of times now. I've always wanted to ask you. Who is that, Michael?

Macgraw   It's Frank Sinatra, Billy.

Russell   Now, you see, I thought it was Frank Sinatra. I was actually going to ask if it was Frank Sinatra. I was actually going to fucking ask that and all and I don't know why I didn't. People never do, do they? Frankie! You like him, do you? Frank Sinatra?

Macgraw   Yeah. I do.

Russell   My mum likes him an' all. Fucking mad for him she is. Always singing his fucking songs. Why do you like him, Michael?

Macgraw   Good songs, Billy, y'know? Good drinking music.

Russell   Is that right? I think he's fucking shite, myself. Dead now, isn't he?

Macgraw   That's right. Died couple of years back.

Russell (*laughing*)   Probably serves him right, I expect, eh?

Macgraw *ignores the laughter which falters and becomes embarrassed. He puts his cigarette out and cleans his ashtray. He starts distributing a rack of freshly cleaned glasses, washed from the previous night.* **Russell** *watches. After a while:*

Russell   I've got some cards.

Macgraw   Cards?

Russell   Would you like to play cards with me, Michael?

Macgraw   No. Thank you, Billy.

Beat.

Russell *drinks.* **Macgraw** *distributes glasses.*

Russell   Can I ask you a question, Michael?

Macgraw   Yep.

Russell   You ever fucking felt just like just throwing the towel in?

Macgraw (*stopping work*)   I'm sorry?

Russell   Just jacking it in. Giving it the fucking elbow. The whole kit and caboodle.

Macgraw   I'm not sure I know what you're talking about, Billy.

Russell   Have you ever had the fucking rug pulled from out of the bottom of your fucking feet? (*Demonstrates the metaphor with a physical gesture.*) Bouff! Like that?

Macgraw (*putting his work down, turning to him*)   I don't know what you mean, Bill.

Russell   I came home from here last Saturday. Got home at about one o'clock. I like to make myself a glass of milk before I go to bed after I've had a bit of a drink of a Saturday. For the alkaline, you understand? To soak up the acidity of the alcohol. I went into our kitchen. And I was surprised to find my mum still up. At that time of night. Sitting by the side of the kitchen. Crying her fucking eyes out.

Macgraw   Jesus.

Russell   Crying like a baby. I said to her, 'Mum?' y'know? 'Mum, what's the fucking matter? What the fuck's the matter wiv ya?' I was trying to be, y'know, gentle and that. I asked her what was going on. And she told me, Michael.

Macgraw   Told you what?

Russell   She told me about the old man.

Macgraw   Fucking hell. She never.

Russell   Straight up.

Macgraw   I don't believe it.

Russell   You don't believe it? *You* don't fucking believe it? Fucking *I* didn't believe it, mate. I'm the fucker who didn't believe it. How long has it fucking been now?

Macgraw   I don't know, Billy.

Russell   All my fucking life, mate. All my life is all.

Macgraw   What did she tell you?

Russell   So this is why I'm asking you about the rug being pulled out from under your arse.

Macgraw   I see, yeah.

Russell   It seems that Christmas has proven traditionally quite a harrowing time in the life of my mother. It was like a fucking novel.

Macgraw   What?

Russell   It would appear that it was twenty-nine years ago, on Christmas bloody Eve, that this fuckwit who was apparently my old man popped his fucking clogs. I never knew that.

Beat.

She never told me that.

Macgraw   No.

Russell   What a cunt that is, eh?

Macgraw   I don't know what to say, Billy.

Russell   There's no reason for you to say anything, Michael.

Macgraw   Christmas Eve?

Russell   It's fucking unbelievable, though, Michael, innit? Eh?

Macgraw   Who was he, Billy?

Russell   A geezer by the name of William White. Seems he was a bit of a tosser. Which is a strange thing to realise about your father. He used to run a newsagent's. Just off Mile End Road, behind Stepney Green tube station. A shite newsagent's. A really fucking bad one. Inadequate merchandise. Local papers. Out-of-date milk. Bad fags. You know what I mean?

Macgraw   I do.

Macgraw *rolls another cigarette. Maybe one or two for later which he keeps in his tobacco pouch. Moves to his 'smokers' end' and lights his smoke while he listens.*

Russell   It seems he had debts up to his eyeballs. 'Cause his newsagent's was so shit. 'Swhat my mum told me. He borrowed money off some fucker. Some gangster type. (*Beat.*) And he couldn't pay it back. At all. So it looks like they started to get heavy. He doesn't tell Mum nothing but she can tell that he's starting to sweat for a while. Acting oddly.

Eating too much. She's worried. So she wants to calm him down. Get him back as he was. And she has this great idea. She decides she's going to have a baby.

Macgraw   Good thinking.

Russell   For a bit of bonding. Hold 'em together. And it doesn't take her very long. Before she succeeds. And gets to letting him know. And by that time it's Christmas. And the stupid fucker goes mental. Loses it. Goes ballistic. Smacks her about a bit. Tells her to get herself sorted. Runs out on her. Two days later. He comes back. Starts going on about everything being all right. She shouldn't worry. He'd sort it. She didn't know what he was talking about. And then it gets to Christmas Eve. And she's expecting to spend the weekend with her new beau, the new fella. Taking him round to her folks and that. They arrange that he's got to be round at her place at one o'clock. Gets to one o'clock. He doesn't show up. Gets to two thirty and he's still fucking nowhere to be seen. And it seems that he's fucked off. Disappeared. She can't find him. Doesn't know where he's gone. She starts to get a bit anxious, you know. Goes round to his house. He's not there. Rings his mum. No fucking sign. So she decides to go to the shop. The place is on fire. Michael. He's still in there.

Macgraw   Fuck me.

Russell   No shit. Reckon it was an insurance grift that got fucked up. They could never work it out. Cunts never paid up.

He rolls himself a smoke out of **Macgraw***'s tobacco, just picking up the pouch left on the bar, doesn't look at* **Macgraw***.*

And my mum keeps all this to herself. I've been asking her for as long as I can fucking remember. Who's my dad? Where's my dad? Why the fuck don't I have a dad when every other cunt that I know does? Doesn't even fucking tell me. Nobody fucking tells me. And then one night. It's mental, Michael. It does my head in. I think I'm going to get fucking really quite drunk tonight. Ruined my cunting week.

Macgraw   It would do.

Russell   It has.

Macgraw   How's your mum now?

Russell   I don't know. I haven't seen her much. Went straight to bed. Left her awake. Got up. Went to work. Working all week. I've no idea how she is. It kind of threw me a bit.

Macgraw   I see.

Stares at **Russell** *for a while as he finishes his smoke.*

It must have been hard for her, Billy. Keeping something like that in. You know?

He rubs his smoke out. Cleans his ashtray.

Russell   She spends too much money.

Macgraw   Course she spends too much money, she's a fucking bird.

Russell   She buys the most expensive of everything. The most expensive toilet paper. The most expensive cereal.

Macgraw   She might be your fucking mother, Billy, but she's still a bleeding bird.

Russell   The most expensive light bulbs.

Macgraw   It's easy to forget that about your own mother.

Russell   One time she tipped a bus conductor.

Macgraw   Fucking hell. That's actually quite good.

Russell (*laughing*)   We haven't got any money left. Seriously.

Macgraw   I know that feeling.

Russell   We can't afford to pay the rent this month. They keep knocking it up. All these fucking City boys moving in down our street. Are you able to afford the upkeep on this place?

Macgraw   With what?

Russell   Bills due?

Macgraw   After Christmas.

Russell   What are you going to do?

Macgraw   I've taken to exercising. I do press-ups to compensate for the anxiety.

Macgraw turns away. Starts wiping down last night's stale beer from the bottom of the drip trays on the bar.

Russell   Do they work?

Macgraw   Do they arse.

Russell   I see.

Macgraw (*turns back*)   Billy, can I tell you summink – ?

A thirty-eight-year-old man enters. He is slightly fat and wicked-looking. He approaches the bar grinning. **Russell** *and* **Macgraw** *are surprised, stopped mid-track.*

Fat Man   Do you want to see a magic trick?

Macgraw   What?

Fat Man   Can I have a pint of lager, please?

Macgraw   Pint of lager.

He pours it. Serves it. Takes the money.

Fat Man   Watch this.

He drinks it, in one go so that it is empty.

Can I borrow a bar towel, please?

Macgraw   What for?

Fat Man   For my magic trick.

Macgraw   OK.

The **Fat Man** *takes the bar towel and drapes it over the pint glass, thus obscuring it from* **Macgraw**'s *and our view.*

Fat Man   Abracadabra! You bastard.

Removes the bar towel. The glass is still empty. Nothing has happened. There is a pause of a few seconds as **Russell** *and* **Macgraw** *stare in disbelief.*

Fat Man   Shit. Never works.

The **Fat Man** *leaves. They watch him go. Stunned.*

Russell   You know something, Michael?

Macgraw   What's that, Billy?

Russell (*putting down his drink*)   I'm twenty-nine. What do you think, Michael, what do you fucking think most fucking twenty-nine-year-olds are doing right now? Saturday night? Nearly fucking Christmas?

Macgraw   I wouldn't know.

Russell   I bet they're not, the vast majority of them, stuck in shit-holes like this, no offence intended. Drinking lame Guinness, moaning about their fucking mothers and watching fat weirdos doing fucking random magic tricks. I bet they're not doing that, are they? Last year, I was invited to spend Christmas Eve with a geezer I knew at school. Michael Wood. We used to call him wanker. That was his nickname. Based on his hobby. Rather than his character. He rang me up. Asked me if I wanted to come out with some of the old boys and get pissed.

Macgraw   Did you not go?

Russell   I was going to.

Macgraw   What happened?

Russell (*goes to light a cigarette, but doesn't yet*)   I got dressed up and fucking everything. Had a couple of whiskeys to get myself sorted. I was meant to meet him at eight thirty down by Bethnal Green Tube. (*Beat. He puts cigarette down.*) Couldn't do it.

Macgraw   What?

Russell   I don't know. I just couldn't fucking do it. Stayed in.

Macgraw   Oh yeah?

Russell   Finished the whiskey.

Macgraw   Aye.

Russell   And then came out here.

Macgraw   I see.

Russell   I don't know what is fucking wrong with me sometimes. Y'know what I mean? I mean, I . . . I like this place.

Macgraw   Good man.

Russell (*flicks lighter, talks into cupped flame, lights his smoke*)   I don't like too many places, y'know. Most places give me the fear something terrible but I don't get that here. I like it here. It's all right.

Lights fade.

Scene Three

Macgraw *and* **Russell** *remain on stage,* **Russell** *drinking and* **Macgraw** *working. The band is heard again. Again it's a Sinatra cover. This time it's 'You Make Me Feel So Young'. It is one hour later. In the semi-light* **Giuseppe Rossi** *enters. A smartly dressed, clean-shaven, sixty-eight-year-old Italian hairdresser. When the light rises again he has joined* **Russell** *at the bar and stands admiring the map of the world.*

Macgraw *is pulling cleaning fluid through one of the taps on his bar, one of the lager or bitter taps. This is a lengthy job. It takes some time. At the moment the process involves pouring half a wine bucket of fluid through the tap which is connected to a huge bottle of the stuff in the cellar. And then waiting. Then pouring more. And waiting. Until the whole bottle has gone through. Then the tap must be flushed with a huge amount of fresh water. This will come later. He is pouring cleaning fluid through while* **Rossi** *talks.*

Rossi (*considered*)   I think I have crossed the road outside to come into this pub on several hundred occasions now. I realised that, just now. That thought. And yet I've never crossed in front of the same collection of cars.

Russell   What?

Rossi   Never, in all of the times that I have crossed the road to come towards this pub, has the same collection of cars waited for me to cross in front of it. Maybe the same car has been there more than once. But not necessarily the same driver. And if the same driver then with different passengers. Or sitting in different seats. And certainly never with the same few cars collected together waiting in the same order. Yet this is a small street. Before this last month I came to this pub at almost exactly the same time every night. I always take the same route. And yet it struck me that this would never happen to me. No matter how many times I came to this pub this phenomenon would never occur.

Pause. They stare at him.

Russell   Christ on a fucking rubber bike.

Rossi   Life is a sad and beautiful thing, Billy. A sad and beautiful thing. (*Without turning from the map.*) Would any of you gentlemen like a drink?

Russell   I think I fucking need one now.

Macgraw *starts pouring their drinks.*

Rossi   Michael. Billy. If you could go anywhere in the world, any one place, where would you go?

Russell   There're a lot of places.

Rossi   I went to Vienna once. Just after I left Italy, just after the war.

Russell   What was Vienna like?

Rossi   Beautiful. It rained a lot. I went up in an air balloon. I swore I'd move back there to live. Work. Open up my own shop there, one day. All my life I swore this. Maybe it's not too late, Michael, who knows?

Macgraw   Not seen you for a few weeks, Seppo. What have you been up to?

Rossi *goes to join them now, collects his drink from the bar, pays for them.*

Rossi   I've not been too well, Michael. My doctor said to me, I need to stop drinking.

Russell   Cunt, eh?

Rossi   He said that I was an old man and that I could die very quickly if I didn't stop drinking. This is what he says to me! What does he know? Fucking doctors, eh? Very strange people. But with the shop being so quiet, I decided that I would try to take his advice. See if I could do it. Ended up chewing my fucking fingers off.

Macgraw   It's nearly Christmas. You've gotta have a drink at Christmas, Seppo.

Russell   If you can't get fucking whacked off your head at Christmas, doctor, you bastard, when can you fucking do it? That's what I'd say.

Macgraw   Right!

Rossi   You go back home at Christmas, Michael?

Macgraw   Home? I live in London, Seppo, this is my home.

Rossi   This isn't a home. London is nobody's home, Michael. Not really.

Macgraw   It's the Queen's home, Seppo.

Russell (*smiling, with a mouthful of beer*)   And it's my fucking home as well, you cunt!

Rossi   You never want to go back to Wicklow?

Macgraw   I don't really know too many people in Wicklow any more, Seppo.

Rossi   And do you not miss it?

Macgraw   Not normally, Sepp, no.

He goes back to pouring more cleaning fluid through. His concentration is meticulous at this point. Perhaps dips in and out of the cellar at the back. Only half conscious of the conversation in the bar.

Russell   If he missed it, he'd go back there, wouldn't he?

Rossi   Life is not always as easy as that, Billy.

Russell   Here we fucking go.

Rossi   Sometimes I think it is possible to miss a place but somehow never quite go back. Am I right, Michael?

Russell   Fucking hell.

Rossi (*turns to him*)   Do you have a phone book, Billy?

Russell   A what?

Rossi   Your own phone book with the names and addresses and the phone numbers of your acquaintances and your colleagues and your friends. Do you not have one of these?

Russell   Of course I do.

Rossi   You never catch yourself staring at those names. All those people you never talk to or hear from or telephone any more?

Russell   Yes, but what – ?

Rossi   And you will not telephone them. Ever again. (*Raises his glass to his lips, doesn't drink.*) Sometimes places can be like that. Sometimes you just can't go back. No matter how much you want to.

Russell   I've never left. London.

Rossi   So maybe you should listen to people who have, eh, Billy?

Russell   Fuck off.

Rossi   Before you go shooting your big fucking mouth off. Young people today, Michael!

Russell   Oh, give it a fucking rest, will ya?

Rossi   Fucking bunch of little wankers. You know what happened to me today?

Macgraw   Tell me.

Rossi   This is two weeks before Christmas. I'm working up to the Christmas holidays. Very busy. Everybody wants to look smart at Christmas. It's natural. So I'm working and there are two or three people waiting and reading their newspapers and smoking their cigarettes. Bit of music on the radio. It's all right. Everything is fine. You understand?

Macgraw   I do.

Rossi   One fuck. One dumb fuck. He is maybe seventeen years old. He wants a number two. He comes and sits down. You know what he says to me?

Macgraw   What?

Rossi   He tells me that he has been waiting for forty-five minutes. He says that he has been waiting for forty-five minutes and he wants to understand what I think I've been doing. This is what he says: 'What have you been doing, man? You're so fucking slow, man. What have you been doing, playing with your dick while you cut people's hair?'

Macgraw   Dickhead.

Rossi   This is what he actually says to me. Those are actually the fucking words he used. He thinks he can fuck with me! I told him to get his skinny fucking arsehole out of my chair and out of my shop. Nobody speaks to Giuseppe Rossi like that. Nobody. You understand me? It makes me sick.

Russell (*giggling*)   What did he look like? I probably know him.

Rossi   Physically sick. You know. Retching. (*He demonstrates.*)

Macgraw   Steady on, Seppo.

Rossi   I sometimes think, Michael, seriously, that people don't care any more. Sometimes I worry about that, y'know? They want everything fast and covered in plastic. (*Gesticulates with his glass.*) Nobody knows how to cut hair any more. Nobody knows how to barber any more. You ever notice that? Everybody runs salons and hair care centres, and hair design specialists. I was walking down the Roman Road last week. This is the truth. There's a new place open there. All fucking neon and flashing chrome lights. Calls itself, listen to this, calls itself a hair surgery. I mean, my God! I am not a surgeon! You understand me? I'm not a fucking surgeon. I'm not a specialist or a designer. I'm a barber. I've been a barber all my life. People still come to me. I have charged the same price for five years.

Macgraw   Fucking good man.

Rossi (*looking at* **Macgraw** *still*)   I had a letter from my brother yesterday morning. He's given me a problem. My little brother Pauli. He's made me very angry, you know? I ever tell you about Pauli? Very thin man. Red face. Beautiful hair. He writes to me every month. He's a good man. You understand? He's a little bit younger than me but he has a good heart. He has a great amount of generosity. He wants me to move back. He wrote to me, he said, 'Giuseppe, I will pay for your return. I will pay for your flight. I will buy your ticket. I will do all these things for you. You can live in my house. I will pay for your food. Just come home now, eh?'

Macgraw *pauses in the cleaning to look up, grins.*

Macgraw   Well, if that's the kind of problems he's causing you, I mean, fucking hell. Just give us his fucking address. We'll send the boys around, eh, Billy?

Rossi   You don't understand.

Macgraw   If that's the aggro that fucking Pauli is giving our Giuseppe then we'll sort the fucker out. I mean, fucking hell, Seppo.

Rossi   'It's been three years now since Barbara died.' This is what he says to me. Three years. You know what he wrote to me? He wrote to me, he said, 'You have no reason to stay in England any more.'

Rossi *sniffs his Drambuie. Doesn't drink it.*

Macgraw   I see.

Rossi (*replaces his glass on the bar*)   He writes to me. He says to me, 'Barbara has been dead for three years, Seppo . . .' As if I didn't know this.

Macgraw   People don't think –

Rossi (*interrupting*)   As if I don't count the days. I know how long she's . . . (*He stops, looks away and then back.*) I know that.

Russell   He sounds like a tosser, your brother.

Rossi   No. He's not a tosser, Billy. He's just a baby. Yes? Like you. He doesn't think very hard about things. It made me very angry. I have everything to stay for here, Michael. I have everything to live for here. People need their hair cutting.

Macgraw   That's true.

Rossi   People still need their hair cutting.

Macgraw *resumes cleaning the pipes.*

Macgraw   Billy for a start.

Rossi   And if I leave here, this is my point. If I leave here, how do I stay in touch and stay in control of what Barbara meant to me? Heh? How am I meant to do this?

Macgraw   You'd never lose that, Seppo.

Rossi   Don't you believe that. You know what the women in the village near my home do when their husbands die?

Macgraw   I have no idea.

Rossi   They cover their faces. They wear black. They stay in the house, in the marital home, for the rest of their lives. They don't leave. Not ever. Because they know that there is a relationship between a person and a place that is absolute.

Russell (*moved*)   Fucking hell.

Rossi   People live in times. They live in places. And as soon as the place goes then the person goes too. If you move on then you change. That is what they believe. Maybe that is no bad thing but the women of my village believe that if they leave their marital homes then they desert the ghosts of their husbands and that is no different from leaving them, from divorcing them. They would never do that. I believe that too.

Macgraw   That's very romantic.

Russell   It's beautiful is what that is, Sepp.

Brief pause. Cigarettes are crashed (shared). **Macgraw**'s *crash. Which means the men each roll their own cigarettes.*

Rossi   Yes.

Another pause.

Would you get married again, Michael? Do you ever think about it?

Macgraw   I think about it all the time, Seppo. I think I would look to wed an Irish girl next time. Maybe that'd take me back home, eh? Get me back to Wicklow.

Rossi   There's nothing bad about that idea.

Macgraw   Never make that mistake again. Fucking English women.

Russell   There's nothing wrong with English women.

Macgraw   There fucking is. They're fucking mad. Every last one of them.

Russell   Fuck off.

Macgraw   Every one of them. Total fucking dur-brains.

Rossi   I love all women. English women. Irish women. Italian women. American women. I love their hair. And the way that they walk. I love their round soft arses and their clothes and the way they shop for food and the way they hold their knives and forks and the way they smell. I love their teeth.

Macgraw   I never realised old men looked at women's teeth.

Rossi   Barbara had fabulous teeth. They were always very clean. She used to spend a great deal of time brushing her teeth.

Appreciative pause.

Macgraw *picks a box of matches from a rack behind the bar. Takes ten pence out of his pocket and opens the till to pay for the matches. He stares at the till for a few seconds. Rests his hand on the cupboard above his head.*

Macgraw   Funny.

Rossi   What is?

Macgraw *looks at him for a short time.*

Macgraw   I was just thinking.

Rossi   What about?

Macgraw   Nothing. It doesn't matter.

Pause.

I'll tell you fucking what, though.

Russell   What?

Macgraw   Got something a little bit special for yous two later on.

Russell   What is it?

Macgraw   You'll find out.

Russell   Is it a porno?

Macgraw   Is it a what? A porno? No it's not a fucking porno. It's a Christmas present. A little treat. Just wait and see. (*Beat.*) 'Is it a porno'!

Rossi (*starts to sing*)   'I'm dreaming of a white Christmas. Just like the ones I used to know. May your days be merry and bright.' EVERYBODY!

Macgraw *smiles.* **Russell** *joins in. He is absolutely tuneless.*

Rossi/Russell   'And may all your Christmases be white.'

Rossi *becomes resolutely, defiantly cheerful.*

Rossi   Let me buy you two gentlemen a drink!

Russell   Good man.

Rossi   We'll get drunk together.

Macgraw   Good idea.

Rossi   There is nobody else here, Michael. On Saturday night.

Macgraw   No.

Rossi   They don't know what they're missing, eh?

Macgraw   You're fucking right.

Rossi   Still. Tonight we won't care. Not about the wine bars in Bow Wharf. Not about the women of County Wicklow! Not about Pauli Rossi and his stupid bloody letters. Tonight we drink. One more week, boys, and it's Christmas Day. Happy Christmas, Billy!

Russell   Happy Christmas, Sepp.

Rossi   Happy Christmas, Michael.

Macgraw   Happy Christmas.

Rossi   Won't see another one.

Macgraw   Fuck off.

Rossi   Eh? You never know, Billy. You can never tell. Gentlemen! To Christmas! To our wives!

Lights fade.

Scene Four

Again the band starts to play. This time it's 'Drinking Again'. When the lights rise it is one hour later. **Russell** *and* **Rossi** *have settled down nicely.* **Rossi** *still has untouched drink in front of him.* **Macgraw** *is pouring water through the pipes now. It is a louder job. More physical. Involving the more rapid emptying of more wine buckets of water.* **Charlie Anderson** *has entered. Thirty-five-year-old, ill-shaven, Manchester-born postman, in uniform. He has propped a cello up against the bar. He is drinking Guinness, quietly. There is no communication between him and the others yet.*

Some time.

A **Man** *enters. Wet, harassed.*

Man   Have you seen a dog around here?

Macgraw   A what?

Man   A dog. I've lost my dog.

Macgraw   No. I've not. Have you seen a dog, boys?

Russell   A dog?

Macgraw   This fella's lost his fucking dog.

Russell   No.

Anderson *stares straight ahead.*

Macgraw   Not any apparently unaccompanied dog, y'know. Not as far as I could tell.

Man   It's a ratty little shit of a dog. But I kind of liked it.

Macgraw   Well. People make these attachments.

Man   It had very small eyes.

Macgraw   Were they very close together?

Man   They were, yeah.

Macgraw   An awful thing in any animal.

Man   Fucked off from the park trying to fuck a Pekinese. Little prissy Pekinese comes prancing into the park and my little bastard sees it. Springs its tiny purple cock out of its foreskin and legs it. Fucks off before I get the chance to catch up with it. I don't suppose I'll ever get it back now. If you see it, just hold it down until I come back, would you?

Macgraw   Yes, of course.

Man   I'll be back in about an hour. Unless I find the bastard.

He leaves. Bewildered laughter. **Anderson** *stares straight ahead.* **Macgraw** *goes back to his work.*

Russell   Who the hell was that?

Macgraw   I have no idea.

Russell (*still chuckling*)   What a terrible story.

Macgraw   . . .

Russell   A fucking fable is what that is. Fucking tragic.

Rossi   Still . . .

Russell   What?

Rossi (*goes to close the door that the* **Man** *has left open*)   We should be so lucky. Little Pekinese girl. Eh, boys?

Russell   Seppo.

Rossi   Billy.

Russell   For such an old cunt you've got a very sick mind, you know that?

Rossi   Still very cold outside, Michael, eh?

Russell   Nearly fucking Christmas, Seppo, it's the middle of winter. Of course it's fucking cold.

Rossi   Maybe this year we'll see a bit of snow.

Macgraw   Coldest night we've had all year.

Rossi   Coming through the park tonight, I thought my fucking toes would freeze off my feet. I'm still not used to this weather. I've been living in England now for over forty years, Michael. Forty years. It still feels fucking freezing to me.

Russell   Oh-oh. He's fucking off now!

Rossi   You go to the match today, Billy?

He flashes a quick smile at **Macgraw**, *who leaves to go to the cellar.* **Anderson** *still stares straight ahead.*

Russell   Don't even fucking even think about reminding me of that bunch of fucking tosspots. I couldn't believe it. The boys around me were laughing by the end of it.

Rossi   I had a man in the shop. We had the radio on. Listening to the match. He's getting his hair cut. He starts jumping up and down in his seat. Yelling at the radio. I'm trying to cut his hair. He makes my hands nervous. I say, 'Mr! Fucking sit down your big arsehole or my hands will slip and cut your fucking big head off!' He says he's sorry. Sits

down. Listens to the game some more. Starts crying. He was
very, very sad. You shouldn't let it get to you, Billy.

Russell Well, you say that, Seppo. You miss the fucking
point. There's no fucking choice in this. It's not a question of
me letting it get to me. I was born with it fucking getting to
me. You don't choose who you get to support, do you?
Football is not a fucking lifestyle choice, Michael, is it? It's a
pain in the cunt inflicted on you from birth. (*To* **Anderson**,
who lights a cigarette. **Macgraw** *returns from the cellar.*) I love it. I
love all sports, me. Cheers.

Rossi Cheers.

Macgraw Cheers.

Anderson *stares straight ahead. Pause.* **Russell** *looks at him.
Looks away again.*

Rossi You have any preparations for next week? Michael?
You having a party?

Macgraw (*looks up slowly*)   I think we might have a little
one.

Russell Good man.

Macgraw Get the fucking mulled wine out. Few fucking
mince pies. Bit of fucking tinsel. Something of a tradition in
this place, boys, is it not?

Rossi And a rich one.

A pause for drinking and smoking. **Macgraw** *checks his watch.*
Anderson *looks around the pub without moving any part of the
lower half of his body.*

Rossi Michael. Have you heard whether you will you get
to see Danny over the holiday?

Macgraw I don't think so, Sepp. (*Tries to busy himself with
the tap.*) I got a letter from the solicitor this morning. They
knocked me back.

Rossi I see. I'm sorry, Michael.

Macgraw (*looking right up*)   One fucking time, Seppo. I clipped him. That's all. I grazed his – it was a fucking – I wouldn't mind if I'd been a mad old cunt or nothing but – Ah. Bollocks to it, eh?

Macgraw *resumes his work. Pulls lager through the cleaned tap. Pours a pint. Tastes it. Gives it to* **Russell**.

Rossi   How long has it been now?

Macgraw   Seven years.

Rossi   I see. He must be bigger now.

Macgraw   Well, he's not exactly big, Seppo. He's tall but he's scrawny, you know?

Macgraw *goes to his 'smoking point' to relight and finish a rested cigarette.*

Rossi   I do. How old is he?

Macgraw   Fourteen next month.

Russell   Lanky, I think the word is.

Macgraw   Yeah. Lanky. That's right. He's a lanky, stringy boy.

Russell   The rightful heir to this place, eh, Michael?

Macgraw   By rights he should be.

Russell   The Macgraw legacy. Lucky bastard!

Rossi   Have you spoken to his mother?

Macgraw   No.

The nozzles for the tap are being cleaned in soda water. **Macgraw** *removes them. Scrubs them with a small brush. Attaches them again.*

Rossi   You would have thought, at Christmas, that she could have . . .

Macgraw   No.

Rossi   Do you speak to him on the telephone?

Macgraw (*up at* **Rossi**)   As from this morning, Seppo, that is actually against the law. Can you fucking believe that?

Beat. Starts cleaning the nozzle again. Polishing the fonts.

I send him cards.

Russell   Cards?

Macgraw   I sent him a Christmas card. Postcards from time to time. When I go on holiday. I don't know if he gets 'em or nothing.

Russell   Holiday? When do you go on holiday, Michael?

Macgraw   I've been on holiday. I went to Southend in 1999.

Russell   Southend isn't a holiday, Michael. Benidorm is a holiday. Florida is a holiday. Marrakesh is a fucking holiday, mate. Southend is a day trip.

Macgraw   I was there for a fortnight.

Russell   Holy Mary, Mother of Jesus!

Macgraw   I sent our Danny a postcard.

Russell   Well. I'm sure he fucking appreciated that.

Macgraw   He did and all.

Russell   A happy postcard from the arse-end of the A13. I bet he took it to school and showed it to all his mates like it was the best thing in the whole of fucking history.

Macgraw   Fuck off.

Russell   You know, I remember him, your Danny.

Macgraw   Who could forget him, eh?

Russell   Sweet fucking kid, you know that, Michael?

Macgraw   I do.

Russell   No, but honestly.

He starts to direct his memories towards **Anderson** *who stares at him but barely shows any sign of understanding.*

His kid. Fucking total sweetheart. He used to come in here, you remember, when he was a little boy. Come in here, run up to me, of all fucking people. Run up to me and throw his fucking arms around me and he'd say to me, 'I love you, Uncle Billy.' Right in the middle of the pub. Mad bastard!

Macgraw   I do remember that.

Russell   I used to teach him how to play pool. Didn't I? When he was what? Seven years old.

Macgraw *is polishing the rest of the fonts now, with an old torn shirt and a glass-spray.*

Macgraw   Seven, yeah. About that.

Russell   He was shit at pool. Fucking hell. He was terrible.

Macgraw   He was.

Russell   He couldn't even hold the fucking cue properly. I used to play him seriously and all. Eh? I didn't fuck about. I told him. 'Danny,' I said, 'Danny, you're a loser. That's your problem, son. You're a born loser. Loooseeer. Loooooseeer.' I used to sing it to him. To try to make him determined not to lose again. It never fucking worked. Did it, Michael?

Macgraw   Never.

Russell   And Christmas. He'd do your fucking nut in. Wouldn't he? All this running around and, 'Uncle Billy, what have you got me, you cunt?'

Rossi   He never used language like that, Billy . . .

Russell   Fuck off.

Rossi   . . . he was seven years old.

Russell   I miss him, Michael. I miss your son. I thought I saw him once. Danny. Down Roman Road market. Woman and her kid walking up ahead of me.

Macgraw *turns to him. Stops his work.*

Macgraw   Really?

Russell (*to* **Anderson**)   I started walking faster. Trying to catch up with them. Wasn't working so I actually started running. I'm running. Running even. After a few minutes I catch up. They turn round. Boy was about nineteen. Didn't look anything like Danny at all. Don't know what came over me.

Beat.

Anderson   What did she take him away for?

Macgraw   I'm sorry?

Anderson   Your wife. What did she take your son away from you for?

Macgraw   I actually don't think that's any of your business.

A slight beat. **Anderson** *moves in his seat. His eyes aren't focused.* **Macgraw** *glares. Moves to him.*

Macgraw   I'm sorry?

Rossi   Michael.

Face-off. A slight beat. Then **Macgraw** *searches for a cigarette. Struggles to light it. Lights it.*

Macgraw (*to* **Seppo**)   He was always really sick at Christmas. There was always some kind of illness.

Rossi   The excitement.

Macgraw   Yeah. Maybe.

Pause.

Macgraw *glares at* **Anderson**, *then begins to rack glasses.*

Russell   Does anybody know any good jokes? (*Beat.*) Just an idea.

Anderson   These two rabbits escape from the laboratory.

Russell   Here we fucking go.

Anderson   Where they have been the subject of a series of immoral experiments.

Russell   I see.

Anderson   Scampering through the fields that surround the labs. Flopsy and Mopsy. Running, running, running. Come across a big field full of carrots. The biggest, juiciest carrots you've ever seen. And the two of them turn to each other, high fives, and get to work with the eating. After a couple of minutes Flopsy looks up and notices that Mopsy has left the field of carrots and is slumped down at the side of the field. Moping.

He chuckles, drunk.

Flopsy asks him what's the matter and he goes, 'Oh! I'm just not really into it.' Flopsy looks bewildered for a second and then decides. Fuck it. Finishes the carrot and away they go. Running through more fields, they come across a field of lady rabbits. Delighted, they turn to each other, high fives and get working. If you know what I mean. And Flopsy's having the time of his life. Been through five of these lady rabbits before he notices that Mopsy has moved again and sat by the side of the field. This time he's pissed off. Goes over to Mopsy and says, 'Look, Mopsy, we were in a beautiful big field of carrots and you just turned and left it. Said you weren't into it. Fine! Did I say anything? Did I fuck! We find a field full of beautiful lady rabbits well up for it, and after a few minutes what do you do? Same thing. What the fuck is going on?' Mopsy looks up. 'You wouldn't understand.' 'Yeah, I would.' 'You reckon?' 'Aye.' 'You really want to know what it is?' 'Aye.' 'I want to go back to the lab.' 'You what?!' 'I want to go back to the lab!' 'What? And leave these bunnies? These lady rabbits? And the fields? And the carrots?' 'Aye.' 'Why? Why on earth would you

want to do that?' 'You really want to know?' 'Aye.' Mopsy
looks up. 'I want a fag!'

Macgraw (*stopping, putting the rack away*)   Fucking hell!
That's actually excellent!

Rossi   The rabbit wants a cigarette!

Macgraw   Very good.

Russell   I don't get it.

Macgraw   Billy, for God's sake.

Anderson (*placing down his Guinness for the first time*)   People
say, gentlemen, that poverty concentrates a community.

Russell   Fuck!

Anderson   They claim that in times of financial hardship
people are bound together. They find a spiritual solidarity in
the face of economic collapse. In my experience this is a
crock of shit. In my experience poverty, economic collapse,
financial hardship, being and becoming stony fucking broke
destroys people.

Russell   Hear, hear!

Anderson   Today I won three hundred and sixty pounds
on a horse. One week before Christmas I put twenty quid on
a horse at eighteen-to-one running at Portsmouth and the
fucker won.

Macgraw   Frigging fuck.

Anderson   This was a horse called Blind Willy. I only put
twenty quid on the bugger because I was drunk and I
thought the name was quite funny.

Russell   Fucking hell.

Anderson   This was a horse that had, during the course of
this season, run only three times. The first two times it failed
to finish. The last time it finished sixth in a field of six. It was
a horse of singularly poor parentage. It was running in

conditions that its trainer, a Welsh alcoholic by the name of Jones, described as 'unfortunate'. It was a shit horse. It won.

Russell   Bastard.

Anderson   Subsequently I have become momentarily wealthy. I have spent the past four hours drinking in different pubs around the East End. Some pubs that I have never been into before. Some pubs that I have been into many, many times. And others that I am returning to after a period of enforced absence. My wander has encompassed a two-square-mile area. Going as far east as Bromley-by-Bow and as far south as Wapping Wall. It has been remarkable day. I am very, very happy.

Beat. Finishes his Guinness. Offers **Macgraw** *his hand.*

Anderson   What's your name?

Macgraw   Michael.

Macgraw *shakes, though doesn't hold eye contact.*

Anderson   Good to meet you, Michael. How are you? Charlie. Happy Christmas.

They remain slightly guarded still. **Macgraw** *goes back to work. He pours* **Anderson** *another Guinness. Takes his dirty glass off him.*

Macgraw   Thank you.

Anderson   And I apologise if I offended you with my stupid fucking questions about your family. (*To* **Rossi**, *with a handshake.*) Charlie Anderson.

Rossi   Giuseppe Rossi. Seppo.

Anderson   Charmed, I'm sure.

Russell   Billy Lee Russell.

Anderson   What a remarkable moniker! Happy Christmas!

Russell   And to you!

Rossi   Happy Christmas.

Russell (*drinking*)   You jammy bastard!

Macgraw (*without looking*)   You a postman, Charlie?

Anderson   Too right I am.

Macgraw   Tredegar Road?

Anderson   That's right.

Macgraw   How's it been?

Anderson   You have no idea. Last week I worked six fourteen-hour days.

Rossi   You deserve a day off.

Anderson   I do. I bloody well do, as well. I cannot believe it sometimes, gentlemen. The amount of cards people actually send to each other. It's astonishing.

Macgraw *brings over the settled Guinness.*

Macgraw   Do you not find it quite touching? Human contact. A little residue of hope. Do you not find it warms your heart?

Anderson (*stares first*)   To the fucking core. (*Drinks.*) Cheers.

Shares his salutation with **Rossi** *and* **Russell** *who return it.*

I like this pub. I like the wallpaper.

Rossi (*concerned*)   How many pubs have you been in this afternoon?

Anderson   Seven.

Macgraw *sucks in his breath.*

Anderson   This is my favourite.

Rossi   Good.

Russell   Poor bastard.

Anderson   Best wallpaper.

Rossi   It was Michael's father's idea. He was always very fond of red and gold. As a colour combination.

Anderson   And he was right to be, Michael, he was right to be.

Macgraw *throws a glare at him.*

Russell   Three hundred and sixty quid. Fucking cunt.

Drinkers' beat. **Seppo** *raises his drink to his mouth, sniffs it, lowers it without drinking.* **Russell** *stares at* **Anderson** *while sucking the froth from his pint.* **Macgraw** *rolls and lights his own cigarette without crashing, staring too at* **Anderson**. **Anderson** *contemplates the colour of his Guinness, holding it in mid-air, theatrically extravagant.*

Macgraw   I see you have a cello. With you. There. Charlie.

Anderson *(still staring at his lifted Guinness)*   That's right.

Macgraw   Now. Why might that be?

Anderson   I'm selling it.

Macgraw   Good reason. And whose cello might you be selling there?

Anderson   Mine. It's my cello.

Macgraw   I see. *(Beat.)* Now. What have you got a cello for, Charlie? If you don't mind me asking.

Anderson   I used to be a cellist.

Macgraw   Fair enough, boys, eh?

Russell *(fascinated)*   Did you?

Anderson   Aye.

Russell   Liar.

Anderson   It's true.

Russell   A cellist?

Anderson (*only now lowering his arm*)   Before I were a postman.

Russell (*laughing*)   Fuck off.

Anderson *laughs*.

Russell   You don't exactly look like a cellist.

Anderson   Before I became a professional postman I was a professional musician. Honestly.

Russell   Bugger me.

Macgraw   We don't get many classically trained musicians in this place, Charlie, you know?

Rossi   I wish I could play a musical instrument.

Macgraw   Used to be a guy who played the fiddle, in here. But he was a tosser.

Anderson   I went out after work this afternoon. Took it all the way to a gentleman in Becontree. The fucker changed his mind.

Macgraw   And how much would your cello be costing, Charlie?

Anderson   Two and a half thousand quid.

Exhalations of awe and appreciation. **Anderson** *shakes his head vigorously, clearing it of alcohol.* **Macgraw** *begins to restock a bottle fridge from a crate on the floor.*

Rossi   How long were you a professional musician for, Charlie?

Anderson   Fifteen years.

Russell   Fucking musician, heh? Fucking hell. That's fucking rich, innit? Clientele in this fucking place, Michael. Things must be looking up.

Rossi   You get to travel?

Anderson   I did, Seppo, yes. I played all around the world.

Rossi   Did you?

Russell   I don't know that one.

Anderson   Twenty-nine different countries.

Russell (*the old joke*)   If you hum it, I'll probably remember it.

Anderson   It was a remarkable time.

Russell (*to himself, enjoying the joke*)   If you hum it . . .

Rossi   Did you ever play in Vienna?

Anderson   One, two, three times.

Rossi   I'm going to move to Vienna one day. Buy my own shop.

Anderson   Your own shop?

Rossi   A barber shop. I'm a barber.

Russell   'Ere! Stradivarius. I've got a question for you. If you're so fucking clever –

Anderson (*talking beneath him*)   I never said I was clever, Billy.

Russell (*who does not stop*)   – you tell me – what's the best piece of music, of classical music, that has ever been composed, for the cello?

Anderson   The best?

Russell   That you've ever played.

Anderson (*without hesitation*)   The second movement of Beethoven's cello sonata in D major.

Russell   Is that right?

Anderson   It's very refined. I used to play it with Katherine. My wife.

Russell   That's pretty fucking impressive, isn't it?

Rossi   It is.

Russell   The second movement of Beethoven's fucking cello sonata in D fucking major!

Rossi   With your wife? That's very romantic!

Russell   Innit, though? Eh? Fucking marvellous is what it is.

Anderson (*talking over him*)   I came here once before, Michael. Some time ago. I had a particularly memorable night.

Russell   People often fucking do, mate!

Macgraw (*still stocking fridge*)   How long ago was that?

Anderson   Fifteen years. More. I always swore to myself that I would come back here one day. I'm very glad that I made it. Were you here fifteen years ago?

Macgraw (*stops briefly to answer*)   Yes, I was. I've been here twenty years. I come over to work with my father before he got ill.

Anderson   You own this place, Michael?

Macgraw   I do.

Anderson   It's magnificent.

Macgraw (*turning away*)   Last fucking Saturday before Christmas.

Anderson   I've got an idea.

Russell   Luck like yours, I'd fucking bet you had an idea. I bet you fucking piss ideas. I bet you shit 'em for fucking breakfast.

Anderson   How about a few shorts to warm these beers up with?

Russell   Now that is an idea.

Anderson   Whiskey?

Russell   Yes, please.

Anderson   Michael.

Macgraw   Thank you, Charlie.

Anderson   Seppo.

Rossi   I think I'll have a Drambuie, Charlie. If that's all right with you?

Anderson   Pleasure. Michael. Three whiskeys. One Drambuie. And a box of matches.

Macgraw *pours and serves their drinks, takes money from* **Anderson***. A* **Young Man** *comes in. Slightly cautious.*

Young Man   Excuse me, mate, I'm looking for a pub called the Crown.

Macgraw   Oh, aye. Out the door. Left. Three hundred yards. Fourth turning on the right. Twenty yards down. Big stained-glass windows. Big cross on the top. Fucking marvellous place.

Rossi *and* **Russell** *grin at one another without the* **Young Man** *seeing.*

Young Man   Thanks, mate.

Macgraw   No problem, son. You have a good night.

Young Man *leaves.*

Macgraw   People are fucking always doing that. Always coming in here to ask me directions to get to a pub. This is a fucking cunting pub! What's wrong with these bastards? Jesus, I ask you!

Russell *and* **Anderson** *drink their drinks.* **Rossi** *sniffs his. Cigarettes. Each crashes their own.* **Macgraw** *begins to roll.*

Anderson (*without looking at them at first*)   What are you boys all doing for Christmas?

Russell   I'm spending Christmas with my fucking mother.

Anderson   And is this something that you are looking forward to?

Russell   I love my mother. I still live with her as it goes. (*Beat.*) It'll be all right, you know? We normally have a fucking great time. Go fucking mad with the tree. She cooks the turkey and I cook the veg. We'll watch a bit of telly and go to sleep. I'm normally quite drunk.

Macgraw (*not looking up from his cigarette*)   I'm going to be on my own.

Anderson (*who has stayed looking at* **Russell**)   Is that right?

Macgraw (*lights it*)   Watch *Only Fools and Horses*. Maybe do a bit of dancing! Get into the spirit of the occassion, you know?

Anderson   And are you going home, Seppo? To . . . ?

Rossi   To Rome.

Anderson   What a magnificent city!

Macgraw *looks back to the sporting pages of his paper, only occasionally looking up.*

Rossi   Not for Christmas. I go to my wife's brother's family house for Christmas dinner. My wife died three years ago. He looks after me. I play with his grandchildren. Try to corrupt them a little bit. He has a very good collection of wine. He's very tall. Very English.

Macgraw   What about yourself, Charlie? You got any plans?

Anderson   I think I'm going to have a bath.

Macgraw   Good idea.

Anderson   Drink some whiskey. Maybe listen to some of the early recordings of Frank Sinatra.

Macgraw   Good man.

Russell   That fucker.

Anderson   This will be the first Christmas that I've spent on my own.

Russell   What is it about him?

Macgraw   Ever?

Anderson   Ever.

Russell   He can't even fucking keep a fucking tune.

Macgraw (*looking back to the sporting pages again, only occasionally glancing up*)   It's strange. No matter how hard you try to convince yourself that it's no big fucking deal, that it's just a normal day. Even if you don't believe in God and all that. Even if you fucking hate it, I bet. You can't ignore it either.

Anderson   I'm sure I'll find out.

Macgraw   You will.

Beat. He looks up. **Rossi** *exits for a piss.*

Ah! Fuck it. I went for a walk the other morning. Through the graveyard down at the bottom of Bow Road. There was a beautiful, gorgeous girl there. Long red hair. Great arse.

Russell   I like a good arse.

Anderson *and* **Macgraw** *glance at* **Russell**. **Anderson***'s glance lingers.*

Macgraw   So I said to her. I sidled up. Said to her, 'Morning!' She said, 'No. I'm walking the dog.' My round, I think.

Russell *laughs, loudly.* **Anderson** *smiles. Drinks are poured. Cigarettes crashed.* **Anderson***'s crash.*

Russell   I was travelling on the tube the other day.

Macgraw (*back to the paper again*)   Fucking hell. Here we go.

Russell   I noticed, on the tube. In the journey between Bank and Mile End. On the Central Line. That there were three different greyhounds. On one tube. Three of them.

Anderson   Is that right?

Russell   With strangely fat bellies.

Macgraw   You're a fucking wonder, Billy, you know that?

Russell   They have these bellies. These big overweight greyhounds. Makes you think, doesn't it? What the fuck do people want overweight greyhounds for? The greyhound should be a lithe beast.

Macgraw   One day I would very much like to live in your head.

Russell   These greyhounds with big bellies and surprisingly big balls. I have a feeling that they might be intended for eating. Taste very much like pork. Apparently.

Silence. **Macgraw** *and* **Anderson** *both look at* **Russell**. *Then* **Anderson** *turns back to his drink.*

Anderson   What do you do, Billy?

Macgraw *resumes stocking his fridge.*

Russell   You what?

Anderson   Your job. What is it?

Russell   I'm a builder.

Anderson   You work for yourself?

Russell   No. Yeah. I mean, I do casual stuff. Mainly. You know. Go along to the sites. There's a little fucking network, you wiv me?

Anderson   I am.

Russell   It's all right. Y'know? It's pretty fucking knackering and that sometimes.

Anderson   I'm sure.

Russell   And it's as cold as a cunt at the moment.

Anderson   Right.

Macgraw *dips into the cellar to refill his crate in order to continue restocking the fridge.*

Russell   I'm just lugging the fucking hods at the moment and all. Which is diabolical. I quite like the creativity of the actual laying of bricks. You know what I mean?

Anderson   How long have you been doing that, Billy?

Russell   Fucking. Ten year. Off and on.

Anderson   You must have made a fair whack of money, though, eh? I mean, there's a bit of fucking cash hanging around in that line of work. Especially if you do it casual and all. Dotting on and that.

Russell   It's not bad. It's not brilliant but it's not fucking terrible either.

Anderson (*doesn't let him finish*)   Never fancied getting your own place?

Russell   What?

Anderson   You never fancied getting a place on your own. Leaving home. With the money you make and that.

Russell   Nah.

Anderson   Why not?

Russell   Just, never really did is all.

Macgraw *comes back in. Beat.* **Anderson** *stares at* **Russell** *while he drinks.* **Macgraw** *continues to refill the fridge.*

Russell (*changing the subject*)   I wish you still had your fucking pool table.

Macgraw   Yes. We could all have a little tournament.

Russell   We could play charades.

Macgraw   What?

Russell   Actually, that is a fucking great idea. A game of charades. Right now.

Anderson   I'm starting to like you, Billy, you know that?

Russell   Are you?

Anderson   I think you might prove to be a little fucking interesting, you with me?

Russell *mimes 'a film'.*

Macgraw   Billy!

He stops.

Anderson   No, go on, Billy. This'll be fun. (**Russell** *continues*.) Film.

Russell *mimes 'a single word'.*

Anderson   One word.

Macgraw   Would you fuck off with your fucking charades. For fucksake.

Anderson   I'm good at charades. Shut up.

Russell *mimes something inexplicable. Then he takes to pointing desperately at* **Rossi** *who returns from the lavatory. He repositions the cello as he sits.*

Anderson   Billy . . . Er . . . Italian . . . *The Italian Job* . . . *The Godfather* . . . Fuck. You're not really doing it right.

Rossi   Why are you pointing at me?

Anderson   *The Hairdresser's Husband* . . . Fucking hell! I give up, Billy, honestly.

Russell   *Shampoo.*

Anderson   What?

Russell   I was doing *Shampoo*. With Warren Beatty. Seppo's a hairdresser.

Macgraw   He's a hairdresser, Billy. Not a bottle of shampoo.

Anderson   Billy.

Russell   Yes.

Anderson   I think you might be a genius.

Russell *sits down between* **Anderson** *and the cello. Gently props the cello so that it doesn't fall.*

Russell   Thank you.

Anderson   But you're very, very bad at charades.

Russell   Fuck off. It was fucking obvious.

Anderson   Please don't ask me to play charades with you again. (*Beat. With a laugh.*) You mad bastard.

Beat. **Macgraw** *wipes the bar, throws* **Anderson** *the occasional glance.*

Russell   So this money, Charlie? This three hundred quid? What are you going to do with it?

Anderson   I'm going to invest it.

Russell   Invest it?

Anderson   In property.

Russell   Three hundred quid?

Anderson   I'm going to buy West Ham. (*He laughs.*)

Russell   Fuck off, you northern cunt.

Anderson   I'm going to drink a bloody toast! To West Ham United! To the East End. A remarkable fucking place. Salt of the fucking earth, the lot of you, with your rollmop herring and your fucking funny accents.

Rossi   This used to be quite a place.

Anderson   And your shit fucking football teams.

Russell   Oy! Twat! (*Beat.*) I still fucking like it round here, actually.

Anderson   So do I, mate. Some great fucking pubs around here. Great fucking wallpaper.

Russell   I like to walk around here. I like looking at the buldings in Tredegar Square. I like the Roman Road. You can have conversations with people on the Roman Road. You can just go up to people. Talk to them. About all kinds of stuff. They don't really seem to care too much.

Anderson   Is that right?

Russell   It is.

Anderson   How often do you do that, Billy?

Russell   Quite often.

Anderson   Do you?

Russell   Yeah. If I feel like it. You should try it.

Anderson   Does your mother know you do this, Billy?

Macgraw *stops wiping, looks up at* **Anderson**.

Russell   What the fuck has my mother got to do with anything?

Anderson   I just think she'd be a bit surprised is all.

Russell   I think my mother gave up being surprised quite a while ago. She's too fucking stoned all the time.

Anderson (*laughing*)   Stoned?

Russell   Don't ask.

Russell *leaves for a piss.* **Macgraw** *works.* **Anderson** *watches him.*

Anderson   I was always transfixed by this place, you know, Michael?

Macgraw   Oh yeah?

Anderson   By the way it just sits here.

Macgraw   Is that right?

They stare at each other. **Anderson** *looks to* **Rossi**.

Anderson   How long have you been working here for, Seppo?

Rossi   Forty-three years. Same shop. Bottom of Grove Road.

Anderson   I imagine that you've encountered rather a lot of changes in that time.

Rossi   Changes?

Anderson   Sociologically. As it were. Politically. Architecturally. Culturally. You with me?

Anderson*'s leg, ever so gently, shakes for a while. His shaking knocks against the side of his cello case. Beat.* **Rossi** *weighs him up. And then softens towards him.*

Rossi   There are more buildings.

Anderson   Buildings?

Rossi   When I moved here the place was blown apart.

Anderson   Blown apart?

Rossi   It was amazing. Some parts around the park you can still see the traces of the bombs from where the buildings just stop. And the estates were built.

Anderson *raises a gentle toast to the estates. Is ignored.*

Rossi   We thought they were so beautiful. I used to stand underneath them and stare right up. I couldn't believe how magnificent they were. Reaching to the heavens.

Anderson *laughs once. Drinks from his pint.* **Russell** *returns from the toilet.*

Russell   Fucking Christ, Seppo, what have you been fucking eating, mate? It smells like a fucking horse in there.

Anderson   You know what I've always enjoyed?

Macgraw   What's that?

Anderson   I have always enjoyed watching the recorded highlights of football matches that have already been played. On the television. I like the sense of power.

Russell (*bewildered*)   Fucking hell. What's been going off in here now?

Anderson (*talks right over* **Russell** *as though he is not there*)   I always remember, few years ago. I came home at night after work and they were showing the highlights of a match between Oxford United and Chelsea. In the FA Cup. It's a fourth-round match. Big game. Oxford are beating Chelsea. One-nil. In the fucking cup! Ten minutes to go. The Oxford manager brings on this lad, huge bastard, six seven, Kevin Francis.

Russell   That's the cunt that went to –

Anderson (*continues, ignoring* **Russell** *now*)   And what this Francis boy doesn't know is that he's going to come on and concede a penalty with a big clumsy tackle on fucking Luca Vialli in the last fucking minute of the game. And Chelsea are going to equalise with the penalty and go on to win the cunting replay. And Oxford get knocked out of the Cup. Now when he comes on he doesn't realise that.

Russell   Of course he doesn't realise it. It hasn't fucking happened yet. You've fucking lost me, mate.

Anderson (*talking over him*)   But I realise it. And I love, I just fucking love looking at the big bastard and thinking, 'You poor fucker. You have no idea. Do you? Eh?' Right at that time in his life he has no idea what is about to happen to him. Do you ever think about that?

Russell   Think about what, exactly? I don't fucking get you at all!

Anderson   Just – (*Looks away from* **Russell**.) Don't worry about it.

Russell   No, Charlie, what you fucking cracking on about?

Anderson   Billy, honestly.

Russell   You're fucking breaking up, mate.

Anderson (*stares back at him*)   Yer reckon?

Russell   Fucking too right.

Anderson   If somebody told you, Billy, the exact date on which you were definitely going to die, what would you tell them?

Russell   You what?

Anderson   What would you tell 'em, Billy, you heard me. Exact fucking date and everything.

Russell   I don't fucking, what – ?

Anderson   It's just a question, Billy. Just a bit of fun, eh?

Russell   I think . . .

Anderson   What if it's today?

Russell   Today?

Anderson   When you leave this pub? What if somebody told you that you were going to get run over? Or stabbed? Or shot? That this was definitely going to happen? How would you react?

Russell   You're doing my head in now. This geezer's doing my fucking nut.

Anderson   I'm not, am I, Billy?

Russell   You know what your problem is, don't yer? Yer fucking nuts is your problem.

Anderson   Nuts?

Russell   Fucking nuts.

Anderson   Well, you should fucking know, Billy, eh?

Russell   You what?

Anderson   You heard me. (*Beat.*) Don't worry about it.

Pause. **Anderson** *grins into the top of his pint. Some time.*

Rossi (*to* **Macgraw**)   When I was a boy, before the war, I watched all of the adults, all of the grown-ups in my village, change. I saw posters of Mussolini on the walls of my village. It was a very small place. I knew that something horrible was happening. I didn't really think about politics at all. But I saw the changes in the eyes of all the people. And a man from our street was taken and shot for a reason I never learned. There were soldiers all over the place. I remember, though, one old man, from our village. He was a very well-known man. He used to live in a very small house. But he came into town quite often. Fell asleep in the benches in the centre of the village. One day I passed him. He was crying. I asked him, 'Hey! Dino! Why are you crying?' You know what he said? He said, 'I didn't realise.' That's all. 'I didn't realise.'

Suddenly **Anderson** *slams his empty glass down on the bar. His gesture unnerves the others. There is a slight ring from the cello.* **Russell** *settles it, stops it from falling.*

Anderson   Who wants a drink?

Russell   Me.

Rossi   Me too.

Anderson   We'll keep this place afloat yet, Michael. I'm fucking telling you.

Macgraw   You think so?

Anderson   Absolutely no fucking doubt about it.

Rossi   Charlie, let me get them.

Anderson   You know what, Seppo. I've been drinking in boozers around here all day. Not one fucker has talked to me before I came in here. Not one single fucking sorry dried-up flaky fucking cunt. I have three hundred quid to spend on drinks, boys, and I am happy to fucking spend it on you fuckers. Billy?

Russell   I'll have a Guinness, please, Charlie.

Anderson   And a whiskey to wash the fucker down. Michael?

Macgraw   Just a shot'll do fine for me, Charlie.

Anderson   Me also. Both doubles, Sepp?

Rossi *hasn't been drinking his Drambuie. Glasses are gathering in front of him.*

Rossi   I'd like a Drambuie, please, Charlie.

Anderson   Coming fucking right up, mate. Coming right up.

Macgraw *and* **Russell** *and* **Anderson** *finish their drinks simultaneously and more are poured, lined up and paid for. Cigarettes are lit. Each their own.*

Rossi   Charlie, are you all right?

Anderson   Am I what?

Rossi   You seem very . . .

Anderson   Very what, Sepp?

Rossi   It doesn't matter. It . . . You're a northerner, Charlie?

Anderson   Manchester, Seppo.

Rossi   And a musician.

Anderson   Not any more.

Rossi   A postman.

Anderson   That's right.

Rossi   I admire the postal service.

Anderson   Oh yeah?

Rossi   People writing letters to one another. Sitting down and making an effort to communicate. It's a rare thing nowadays.

Anderson   It's mostly bills, Seppo, you with me?

Rossi   And you've just come in here. From nowhere. To drink with us! To spend your money! To sell your cello! This is a magnificent gesture! (*Beat.*) Let me ask you a question, Charlie. I'll tell you my story, eh?

Rossi *raises a Drambuie glass to his lips, doesn't drink it though.*

Macgraw *begins polishing three whiskey tumblers, one by one. They are unusually old, ornate. They are rarely used. He polishes them with great care.*

Rossi   My wife died three years ago, Charlie. Barbara, a beautiful English girl. I was married to her for forty years. More. Forty-two years. She died three years ago. It wasn't a painful death. It was gentle. She was old. She was sleeping. I have lived three years now since she died. I follow the traditions of the town in which I was raised. As her widower I respect her ghost by staying in her house and tending her house and her grave and her memory. Where I am from, this is what people do. This is how respect is maintained. Two weeks ago my brother wrote to me. He wants me to move home with him. He wants me to leave my wife and her home and her grave. To break the tradition. I don't want to go. But I have very little money left in the shop any more. And the shop. The shop is so quiet nowadays that it doesn't bear thinking about. I am becoming an old man. I don't know what to do. What would you do?

Anderson   What would *I* do?

Rossi   Yes. An educated man. A classically trained musician. Share with us some of your wisdom, Charlie. What would you do?

Brief silence. The others wait for his answer.

Anderson   I don't believe in ghosts, Seppo, yer with me?

Russell *is starting to fidget.*

Rossi   It's not about ghosts, Charlie, it's about tradition.

Anderson   I certainly don't believe in fucking tradition.

Rossi   It's important to believe in tradition.

Anderson   But not to the point that it fucking kills you. Yeah? That's just fucking sad.

Macgraw (*stops cleaning*)   You can't do that.

Anderson   Do what?

Macgraw   You wanna watch your fucking tongue, mate, is what you wanna do.

Anderson   Watch my tongue? Watch my fucking tongue! What are you fucking going on about, 'watch my tongue'?

Macgraw   You can't just walk in here, talk to people like that.

Anderson   Like what? Like what, Michael? What are you talking about?

Macgraw   You know exactly what I'm talking about.

Russell   Fucking weird.

Anderson   You what?

Russell   You, yer fucking weird.

Anderson (*points at* **Russell**)   How old are you, Billy? Remind me.

Russell   What's that got to do with anything? How fucking old I am?

Anderson   Billy, answer my question.

Russell   I think you're a fucking strange cunt.

Anderson   Billy.

Russell   I'm twenty-nine. (*About the cello*.) What does this look like?

Anderson (*stares at him, for a second*)   Twenty-nine! And you live where?

Russell   At home. Charlie . . .

Anderson   With?

Russell   My mum.

Anderson   And your dad?

Russell   No.

Anderson   Why not?

Russell   He's dead.

Anderson   Oh yeah?

Russell   Yeah. Can I see your cello?

Anderson   When did your dad die, Billy? Billy?

Russell   Before I was born. Can I?

Anderson   Really?

Russell   Yes.

Anderson   That's a diabolical fucking tragedy.

Russell (*tries to unclasp the case*)   Fuck off.

Anderson   Don't you fucking touch that, Billy. I'm warning you.

A moment.

Macgraw   Maybe you should go.

Anderson   Maybe I should what?

Macgraw   You heard me.

Anderson (*claps his hands together*)   Nice one!

Macgraw   Maybe you should go now.

Anderson (*carefully, punching every word*)   You don't mourn Barbara because you loved her, do you, Seppo?

Rossi   What?

Anderson   People don't mourn out of love. They mourn out of fear and the fear makes them stop.

Russell   You don't know what you're going on about!

Anderson (*turns on him*)   Of course I do. I know exactly what I'm going on about. I was just thinking. Did you have a very hard time at school, Billy? Did you, though? I bet you fucking did! I bet you had a cunt of a time, eh, Billy? What did they used to say to you? What did they used to do? (*Singing.*) 'Where's your daddy gone?' That was before it was fucking fashionable and all, wasn't it? No fucking daddy. Poor bastard, eh?

Russell (*standing, turning to him*)   What did you say?

Macgraw   Charlie, stop it, now.

Anderson (*standing*)   Or what? Or fucking what, Michael? Come on! Flash of the old fucking Macgraw temper, is it? One more fucking time, is it? Bring it all back! Come on, then!

Macgraw *goes to move from behind the bar.* **Rossi** *stops him.*

Rossi (*calmly*)   Charlie, you're shaking.

Russell *is boiling with rage.* **Anderson** *props himself up on the bar, tries to shake the alcohol from his head.*

Russell   What kind of a fucking cunt are you?

Anderson (*squeezes his eyes closed tight, then looks straight at him*)   I'm not a cunt, Billy. I'm not a cunt! I'm your fucking guardian angel, mate.

Rossi (*standing*)   Charlie, you're shaking.

Anderson   You're so fucking young.

Russell   I'm what?

Anderson   You're so young, you haven't fucking done anything.

Russell   What are you fucking cracking on about, you?

Anderson   You've got to start taking control over your life, Billy, because it is just going to piss away –

Russell   You what?

Anderson (*talking over him*)   – in this place. And that would be too horrible to even think about.

Russell   Fuck this. Fucking, just –

Anderson   Billy, it would be just –

Anderson *goes to touch* **Russell***'s face.*

Russell   Get your fucking hands –

Russell *brings his arm down on the bar and smashes his pint glass. There is a long silence. For a while they are utterly still. The force of the blow causes the strings of the cello to resonate; in the silence we hear its hum subside.*

Anderson*'s shaking is more pronounced. His breathing rapid, recovering.* **Rossi** *is absolutely still. He stares at* **Anderson***, placing his hand on his shoulder to try to stop him shaking.* **Anderson** *doesn't notice it is there.* **Macgraw** *begins to collect pieces of glass from the bar.* **Russell** *is bleeding slightly.*

Russell (*about his hand*)   I'm . . .

Macgraw (*handing him a clean, damp cloth*)   Here. (*To* **Anderson**.) See what you've fucking done now. On yer way, son, away yer fucking go.

Russell *stares at* **Anderson** *for some time. Wounded. Confused. Not at all with him.* **Anderson** *stands to collect his cello, starts putting his coat on. Stops himself.*

Anderson   Sometimes I just, sometimes I wish I could just burn this fucking cunt. (*To* **Russell**.) You want it? I'll leave it for you, Billy, if you fucking want it, son, you can fucking have it.

Rossi   Why did you stop playing?

Anderson (*caught*)   What?

Rossi   Why did you stop playing your music?

Anderson   That's not an easy question to answer, Seppo.

Rossi   No, but it's the question that I've chosen to ask you. So maybe you could fucking answer it, eh? Running away, is that living?

Anderson   I'm not running away.

Rossi   Of course you are. Closing your account. Selling your instrument. How can you do that? That is a terrible thing to do! (*Beat.* **Anderson** *stares at him.*) You don't play your music with your wife any more.

Anderson (*continuing his drunken preparations to leave*)   No, mate. Not any more. No. No. No. No. I'm sorry. I've been a cunt. Too much fucking, yer know. (*Pauses. Looks around himself.*) With my wife? Seppo. The wife's . . . (*Looks to* **Macgraw**.) Where's the toilet? (*Beat.*) I just wanted . . . (*He screws his eyes up. Straightens his coat. Long pause. To* **Rossi**.) So we're burgled. She comes home too early. Finds them in the bedroom. They get scared. Smash her face up with the crowbar that they've used to break the key on the door. Stamp four times on to her ribcage. Leave the house without anybody noticing. Somebody notices, eventually, that the front door of the house has been left wide open for three hours and phones the police to investigate.

Short silence.

Rossi   Charlie?

Anderson   Where's your toilet?

Macgraw *doesn't answer. Brief silence.*

Rossi   When was this?

Anderson   Eight months ago. April.

Rossi   How old are you?

Anderson   I'm thirty-five. (*Beat. About the cello.*) I sit in my room staring at this fucking bastard thing.

A **Small Man** *enters. He is tired. Wrapped in an overcoat and scarf. Head down. Quiet.*

Macgraw   Evening, sir, what can I get you?

Small Man   Half of bitter, please.

Macgraw   Cold night.

Small Man   Yes. It's started to snow.

Macgraw   Is that right? That's ninety-eight pence, please.

The **Small Man** *hands over the money. Sits to drink his beer. Doesn't remove his scarf or coat. Drinks in silence. His presence stops all conversation. He drinks his beer fairly quickly, says goodnight and leaves. Everybody watches him go.* **Macgraw** *looks for a cleaning job to do. He can't find one.*

Macgraw (*to* **Anderson**)   Toilet's just through on the right.

Anderson   I think I'll be all right.

Russell (*a gesture of generosity*)   This geezer arrives at a desert island. He's on holiday. Bit of tourism. Arrives at the island and he gets in a taxi. Explains to the driver how he's new to the island and asks him if he'll drive him around for a bit. Taxi driver, a handsome fella by the name of Johnny, agrees. Gives him a guided tour. As they're driving he starts pointing things out. Goes down to the docks to look at the boats. 'Mister,' he says, 'you see those boats? Those three boats there. I built those boats. Me. Johnny. I built them. Do they call me Johnny the Boat Builder? No they don't.' They drive past a beautiful, elegant church. Taxi driver gives it, 'You see this church? This beautiful church. You know who built this church? I built this church. Me. Johnny. Do they call me Johnny the Church Builder? No they don't.' And they drive on. Past a row of lovely, stylish cottages. 'Mister! You see these cottages? The beautiful, lovely, stylish cottages. I built those cottages. Me! Johnny! Do they call me Johnny the House Builder? No they don't! One lousy fucking sheep!'

Crash cigarettes. **Russell**'s *crash.*

Anderson   This is where I first met her, Michael. Come in here with a mate of mine. She's sitting by the bar. The way she smiled at me when I saw her for the first time. We must have drunk until three in the morning. I thought I'd come back. See whether the place had changed or not. (*The others watch him.*) Whereabouts in Ireland are you from?

Macgraw   Arklow, County Wicklow.

Anderson   Beautiful place.

Macgraw   It is. It's magical. I spent a lot of time there when I was a kid.

Anderson   You've lost your accent, you know that?

Macgraw   There are traces.

Russell   Can I get you another drink, Charlie?

Anderson   I should be going.

Russell   Pint of Guinness, wasn't it?

Anderson   No, Billy, thank you.

Russell   Pint of Guinness, please, Michael.

Macgraw   Charlie, if I'd known, yer know. You're welcome to stay for another.

Anderson   No. Michael. Really. I want to go home.

Macgraw   Right.

Anderson   It's getting late. I should be on my way.

Macgraw   Right. (*Pause. After* **Anderson** *has done up every button on his coat:*)   Charlie.

Anderson   Michael.

Macgraw   Do me a favour.

Anderson   What's that?

Macgraw   See your fiddle?

Anderson   Aye. What about it?

Macgraw   Give us a tune.

Anderson   What?

Macgraw   Go on. Just give us a tune. Play something for us.

Anderson   Michael.

Macgraw   Come on, your fucking man, what's his face?

Anderson   Beethoven.

Macgraw   That's the fucker. Your fucking thing. That one you two were going on about. I've never heard that. I think it would be a wonderful thing to listen to. A wonderful way to see in Christmas.

Anderson   Michael.

Macgraw   I'd very much like to hear it and I'd very much like you to play it for us three. Here. In my pub. Just this once. Just tonight.

Anderson   I can't.

Macgraw   What?

Anderson   I can't, Michael.

Macgraw   I see.

Anderson   I'm sorry.

Macgraw Fuck off with your sorry. You're sorry? What the fuck have you got to be sorry for? Heh? I'm sorry. I'm the sorry one. Shooting my mouth off like a bloody idiot. I'm . . . y'know.

Anderson It's all right.

Macgraw It was just an impulse.

Anderson It's all right, Michael. Honestly.

He stands, again, to start finally to leave.

It's been good to meet you, Billy.

Russell *can't think what is the right thing to say so says nothing.*

Anderson Seppo.

Rossi Charlie, please, will you take one drink with us?

Anderson Thank you, Seppo. No. That's kind of you to ask. I need to be, yer know.

Rossi I hope you come back, Charlie.

Anderson Yeah. I hope so too. I'm such a fuckin', Christ. I'm fucked. (*He looks at them for some time.*) Goodnight, Seppo. Merry Christmas.

Rossi Goodnight, Charlie. Merry Christmas.

Anderson Goodnight, Billy. Merry Christmas, mate.

Russell Goodnight, Charlie. Yeah. Merry Christmas.

Anderson Merry Christmas, Michael.

Macgraw Yeah. Goodnight.

Anderson Have a good one, boys, eh?

He pulls his hat down over his ears and ties his cello on to his back. As he leaves, the others watch him go.

Rossi Very cold outside.

Macgraw   That's a bastard about his fucking cello, innit?
Becontree. That's a long fucking trip with one of those on
your back.

Russell   Fucking right it is.

Rossi   A strange man, eh?

Russell   Fucking right.

Macgraw   Very sad story.

Rossi   Very sad.

Russell   Sad? You reckon? I thought . . . Didn't you think
he went a bit fucking mad? I mean, a little bit too fucking
far?

Macgraw   I don't know, Billy.

Russell   I mean, you don't do that, do you? You can't just
come into a fucking pub and just start spouting shite like
that. I thought he was a fucking schizo! And a cunt. Taking
the piss out of West Ham. (**Macgraw** *and* **Rossi** *exchange
glances.*) And what was all that rabbit shit all about? With the
cigarettes? That was just fucking stupid. And I bet he was
lying about his fucking cello.

Macgraw   Billy.

Russell   I bet he fucking nicked it or something. I –
fucking – second movement of the fucking cello sonata.
Fucking second movement, my twat.

Pause.

Rossi   We'll say nothing more. It has been a long night.

Russell   It fucking has and all.

A long silence. The three men are almost completely still.

Rossi   Maybe I've been here too long. You never know,
gentlemen, do you?

Rossi *grins. Drinks a Drambuie in one. Stands.*

Macgraw   Are you gonna write to him, Seppo? Your brother?

Pause. **Rossi** *holds another to his nose. Sniffs it. Puts it back down again.*

Rossi   I think so. After Christmas. In the new year.

Russell   You wanna go, Sepp. Maybe he'll take you to fucking Vienna. Stop you fucking going fucking on about it.

Rossi   You taking the piss out of me now, Billy, yes?

Macgraw   You gentlemen like another drink? Before I close up? I got something a little bit special, my fucking Christmas present for yous.

Rossi   I need to go, Michael.

Macgraw   Are you sure?

Rossi   I think so, yes, I'm sure.

Macgraw   When you gonna be in again?

Rossi   I think I'll be in next Saturday.

Macgraw   Christmas Eve?

Rossi   I think so.

Macgraw   Seppo. I was gonna tell you summit.

Rossi   What's that? Michael?

Macgraw *looks at him for a short time. Smiles.*

Macgraw   It don't matter. Honestly.

Rossi   Christmas Eve, Billy.

Russell   You got me a fucking present yet?

Rossi   Of course I have.

Russell   Good man.

Rossi   I've got you a fucking joke book.

Russell   Cheeky bastard.

Rossi   I'll see you soon, Billy.

Russell   I'll see you next week, Seppo, eh? See you in here, next week?

Rossi, *too, pulls on his coat, gloves, scarf, hat. Readies himself.*

Rossi   Yes. Yes. Of course. Next week.

Macgraw   You look after yourself, Seppo. Get home safely.

Rossi   Of course I will, Michael. Goodnight.

Macgraw   Yes. You have a good night too.

Rossi *leaves. They watch him go.*

Russell   I should be going too, Michael. Mum. Y'know. It's getting late. I worry about her.

Macgraw   Do you?

Russell   She's just looking very old at the moment.

Macgraw   I see.

Pause.

Stay a bit, Billy.

Russell *looks at him.*

Macgraw   Here. That thing. Cap your night off.

He goes beneath the bar, searches for a bottle of poteen, opens it and pours into the whiskey tumblers he was polishing before.

Here, taste this.

Russell *does. It is strong, makes him cough.* **Macgraw** *pours him more.*

Macgraw   Happy fucking Christmas. Poteen whiskey. Made with potatoes! Wonderful, isn't it?

Russell   Fucking magic.

Macgraw   Are you all right, Billy?

Russell   Of course I'm all right, Michael.

Macgraw   I mean, you've had quite a fucking day, haven't you?

Russell   I fucking have.

Macgraw   With your mum and with West Ham and that.

Russell   Don't bleeding remind me of that.

Macgraw   He was a fucking funny fucker, wasn't he? That Charlie Anderson cunt.

Russell   He fucking was and all. Fucking northerners, you know?

Macgraw   I do.

Russell   Fucking wankers.

Pause. **Macgraw** *clears glasses.* **Russell** *smokes, drinks his beer.*

Macgraw   I tell you what's done my head in.

Russell   What's that?

Macgraw   That letter. Them solicitors. I thought I – Took me by surprise a bit. Stupid cunt. Would've been all right and all, wouldn't it?

Russell   Would've been fucking great.

Macgraw   Makes me want to . . .

Russell   What?

Macgraw   Just, yer know. Fucking . . .

Russell   What, Michael? What you going on about now?

Macgraw   Nothing, Billy. Honestly. Don't matter.

Pause. **Macgraw** *can't look at* **Russell**.

I have fucked so many things up, Billy. I don't know fucking anything any more.

Russell   Michael? You all right?

Macgraw   I'm fine, Billy, yeah. I'm fucking cracking.

Looks at him for a short while.

Russell   Funny.

Macgraw   What?

Russell   I was kind of thinking.

Macgraw   Fuck me, well done.

Russell   Fuck off.

Macgraw   What about?

Russell   I was thinking about my dad.

Macgraw   I see.

Russell   What do you think he must have thought about? Dad? Eh? Sitting there. With the shop just starting to burn up?

Macgraw   I have no idea, Billy.

Russell   He might have fucking thought about me, Michael, eh? About what I was going to be like when I came out? What was going to happen in my life? He might have wondered about that, mightn't he?

Macgraw   I would say he probably did, Billy, yes.

Some time.

Russell   So what do you think you're gonna do, Michael? About this place?

Macgraw   Billy. Here. Billy. Come here. Look at this, would you?

Russell   What?

Macgraw   In here. Have a look.

*He goes to the cupboard behind his bar and pulls out a black bin bag.
Plants it on the floor in front of* **Russell**.

Open it. Have a look.

Russell   It's full of envelopes.

Macgraw   That's right.

Russell   Are these what I think they are?

Macgraw   What do they look like?

Russell   Jesus fucking Christ.

Macgraw   They're bills, Billy.

Russell   I know they're fucking bills, Michael. I can see
they're fucking bills. There's rather a fucking lot of them, is
there not?

Macgraw   Phone bills. Electricity bills. Gas bills. Tax
charges. Brewery invoices.

Russell   Michael, they're not even open. Half of them are
not even bleeding open.

Macgraw   There's about seventeen thousand pounds
worth of debt in here.

Russell   Christ, Michael. How did you get all this?

Macgraw   I can't pay it.

Russell   What?

Macgraw   There's no way I can pay it all.

Russell   I see.

Macgraw   The brewery won't sell me any more beer. The
electricity company and the gas company and the telephone
are going to cut me off in the new year.

Russell   What are you going to do? (*Beat.*) Michael?

Long pause. **Macgraw** *starts smiling.*

Macgraw   I have no idea.

Russell   Michael. What are they going to do to you?

Macgraw   I don't have a fucking clue.

Russell *starts smiling too. The two of them begin to laugh, quietly. The laughter grows. And eventually settles.*

Russell   We do all right, don't we?

Macgraw   Yeah. Not so bad.

Russell   What would we fucking do without you? Me and, and, and Seppo.

Macgraw   You'd be all right.

Russell   You think so?

Macgraw   I know it, son.

Russell (*affectionately*)   I'm not your fucking son, you cunt.

Macgraw *looks at* **Russell** *for a while.*

Macgraw   Will you take another drink with me?

Russell   I don't think so.

Macgraw   Come on, you fucker. It's yer fucking Christmas gift.

Russell   I should be going.

Macgraw   We've got a whole bottle of this stuff to fucking finish.

Russell   Michael. No. I have to go.

Macgraw   Right. (*Clicks his tongue, once.*) I see. (*His face fallen, he puts the lid back on the bottle.*) We'll maybe save it for next week, eh? Next Saturday night, Billy, we'll fucking drink this shit.

Russell *stands. Collects his coat and puts it on. He fastens the buttons high up to his neck. Raises its collar. Speaks as he does so.*

Russell   He was right about one thing, mind you. This really is great wallpaper. I never even fucking noticed. Right. I'm going to piss off.

Macgraw *nods. He watches* **Russell** *go.*

Russell (*opening the door of the pub*)   So. Next Saturday, Michael, eh?

Macgraw   See you then, Billy.

Russell   Yes.

Macgraw   Look after yourself, eh?

Russell   Fuck off, would you? Swear everybody's going fucking mental on me.

Macgraw   Goodnight, Billy.

Russell   Goodnight.

Macgraw *turns away from the door. Returns to the bin bag and removes the third letter he placed in it earlier this evening. Rereads it. Screws it up and throws it in the bin behind the bar. He picks the bin bag up from the floor. Feels its weight in one hand. His face drops, only momentarily becoming gravely dark. He carefully returns the bag to the cupboard. Locks the cupboard.*

He pours himself a glass of water and begins to go through the process of locking up the pub. Turning machines off. Locking fridges. There is a buzzing light on the inside of one of his fridges. He adjusts its bulb and the buzzing stops. He pulls the curtains on the windows which he also locks. There is an unthinking rhythm to this.

A pause. Thinks. His face blackens.

He goes back through the door behind the bar from which he entered at the start of the play. Returns with a coat and a sports bag full of clothes. He places the sports bag on the bar and rifles through it. Pulls out a passport. He checks the date on the passport and returns it to the bag. He goes over to the till. Empties all of the money from the till. Puts the notes in his wallet and the change in his pocket. Opens up a locked cupboard again, pulls out an unopened bottle of whiskey and stuffs it in his sports bag.

He puts on the coat. Pulls up his zip. Before he leaves he opens a window on the advent calendar. He moves round to the front of the bar and, with his coat on, falls to the floor to start his ten press-ups. Counts all ten. Stops and stands again. Picks up the sports bag from the bar. Lights a cigarette with a match. Stands quite still.

Some time.

Lowers the bag back on to the bar. Unzips his coat again.

Lights dim and the version of 'That's Life' that we heard at the beginning plays again. This time we hear the end of the song and the singer thank his audience and wish them goodnight.

Lights fall.

Herons

I lie and stare at the blank ceiling, the neutral walls, the null air. God knows, adults find it hard enough to act on their knowledge of right and wrong. Can children, whose sense of right and wrong is newer but dimmer, fresher but fuzzier, act with the same clear moral sense? Do they grasp that badly hurting someone is much more wrong than stealing and truanting (which Thompson and Venables had got away with for months)? Do they have a sense of the awful irreversibility of battering a child to death with bricks? Can death have the same meaning for them as it has for an adult? I submit, your Honour, that the answer to these questions is no, no, no and no.

Blake Morrison, *As If*

But the nowness of everything is absolutely wondrous, and if people could see that, you know. There's no way of telling you, you have to experience it, but the glory of it, if you like, the comfort, the reassurance . . .The fact is, if you see the present tense, boy do you see it! And boy can you celebrate it.

Dennis Potter interview with Melvyn Bragg, *Without Walls Special*, Channel 4, 5 April 1994

This play is dedicated to Oscar and to Dad

Herons was first performed at the Royal Court Jerwood Theatre Upstairs, London, on 18 May 2001. The cast was as follows:

Billy Lee Russell	Billy Seymour
Scott Cooper	Robert Boulter
Aaron Riley	Stuart Morris
Darren Madden	Ryan Winsley
Adele Kent	Lia Saville
Charlie Russell	Nicolas Tennant
Michelle Russell	Jane Hazlegrove

Directed by Simon Usher
Designed by Antony Lamble
Lighting by Paul Russell
Sound by Ian Dickinson

Characters

Billy Lee Russell *Fourteen years old. A dirty, scruffed mop of hair. Wears a thin and old Adidas jacket and a Nike Air baseball cap. He speaks in the manner of somebody with a desperate eagerness to please, to satisfy, to explain, to charm others. This eagerness manifests itself also in the way that he moves.*

Charlie Russell *Thirty-four years old. Billy's father. A hulking damaged man. He wears a blue jacket over a white T-shirt and jeans and he smokes roll-up cigarettes with remarkable constancy. His skill at rolling these cigarettes betrays surprising subtlety and dexterity. Charlie trips over his words when he talks, as though he can't possibly explain everything that he needs to. This struggle results in inarticulacy. And occasional accidental poetry. He is a man who has watched bewildered as almost everything that he once loved has been taken away from him.*

Michelle Russell *Thirty-two years old. Billy's mother. Separated from Charlie. She has a confident energy that she struggles to contain when she speaks to Billy, almost out of fear of frightening him. She takes great care over her appearance but there is something about her clothes, particularly about the coat she wears, which is somehow awkward. It is as though she is trying too hard. She can look, at times, monumentally tired.*

Adele Kent *Thirteen years old. She is a year below Billy in school. She wears her school uniform still. She wears it unruly. She has a disarming directness. She has bleached blonde hair and dark eyes. She has something of a reputation around and outside of the school – not for being feared, but she is respected. She is a friend of Scott Cooper's. Scott does not know she has taken to visiting Billy. At first she makes Billy nervous.*

Scott Cooper *Fifteen years old. He is big for his age and handsome. He is deeply damaged. He has a vulnerability which manifests itself in cruelty. He moves and speaks with a calmness that is disarming. Sometimes he appears slow-witted. He isn't.*

Aaron Riley   *Fifteen years old. The sharper of Scott's cohorts. He and Darren dress in a similar fashion. They are all tracksuits and jerky movements. Aaron grins a lot and hardly ever looks at the person he is speaking to. He absorbs information and language like a sponge.*

Darren Madden   *Fifteen years old. He is a simple, often bruised boy. He has the habit of spitting in thin, fine jets between his occasional comments. Blunter, more monosyllabic than either Aaron and Scott and less handsome than either of them. His clothes are cheaper.*

The play should be cast accurately to age.

The events take place in the present day around the lock of the Limehouse Cut and the Lee River in east London.

The seating should be arranged in such a way as to make it possible for actors to arrive on stage from all angles, even coming from behind the sides of the audience without the audience necessarily noticing their arrival.

A note on punctuation:
A dash (–) at the end of an incomplete sentence denotes interruption.
Ellipsis (. . .) at the end of an incomplete sentence denotes a trailing off.
Ellipsis in place of a spoken sentence denotes an inability to articulate a response.

Darkness.

*'Can I Pass? – instrumental' by the Rebel plays gently. After a while,
and as though from some distance, we hear the sound of water. As the
sound increases in volume it should become clear that it is the sound of
water running through the gate of a lock. The volume of the sound
increases with the volume of the water, drowning the music, and
growing in time to an almost deafening level.*

*As the water continues a pool of blue light on the centre of the stage
isolates* **Billy**.

The lighting should be gentle, not allowing us a clear view of him.

*He stares out to the audience for some time. In his right hand he is
holding a handgun. He examines it for a moment and then briefly
points it at the audience. Makes a gunshot noise with his voice and
moves to throw the gun away. The lights fall on him. The noise
crescendos with the fall of the lights and then quietens after a few
more moments.*

*Lights rise on the stage. It is late afternoon. Over the next five scenes the
lighting will fall into evening. There is a looming, damaged oak tree
hanging over the downstage area towards the right. A path of perfectly
still water runs across the front of the stage, narrowing as it runs. (See
Richard Wilson's* 20:50 *[1987].) There is a bench looking out over
the water. When characters look out over the water they can look
directly into the audience. For a short time there can still be heard the
sounds of a canal.*

After a few moments, we should become aware of the presence of
Scott, **Darren**, **Aaron** *and* **Adele** *on stage.* **Scott** *and* **Adele**
*are in the middle of an argument. She turns away from him. He presses
her.* **Darren** *is amused by* **Scott**'s *aggression and* **Adele**'s *anger.*
Aaron, *who smokes meticulously throughout the scene, should barely
pay them attention.*

Scott (*moving towards* **Adele**)   Everybody's always fucking
lying about the cunt.

Aaron   She was a fucking slag.

Scott   She comes over to us, comes over to our Ross and she's giving it all this fucking eye shit. Oh Ross, she says, your eyes are so dark. She said this.

Darren   Tart.

Scott   She actually even fucking touched the boy's face. And you tell me that it's sad.

Adele   It is.

Scott   And you tell me that you miss her.

Darren   Fuck off.

Scott   That you can't stop thinking about her and I'm telling –

Adele   I can't.

Scott   I'm telling you, Del. You don't even know what you're talking about. You haven't even got a clue.

Adele   I knew her.

Scott   You didn't, Del. Not really. You never did.

Adele   She was my friend.

Scott   She was white trash.

Adele   You're lying, Scott.

Scott   Del. Fucking just shut it.

Darren   Straight up.

Scott   Thick fucking twat.

Adele (*confronting him*)   Don't talk to me like that.

Scott (*grinning, closing up on her*)   See me. When it comes to Friday. See what I'm gonna fucking do. I'm gonna come out here. I'm gonna have me a fucking party. A fucking anniversary party for her. I'm gonna toast our Ross and our Bergsie.

Adele   It didn't need to happen.

Scott   And I'm gonna toast old fucking fuckwad Charlie Russell.

Adele   They didn't need to do what they did.

Scott   And I'm gonna toast his son.

Darren   His fucking retard son.

Scott   His fucking retard son.

Adele   They deserved what they got.

Scott   And I'm gonna dance around.

He demonstrates an elegant dance movement.

Darren   Sweet.

Scott   And and and celebrate the dearly beloved fat cunt and get stoned off me dick and be happy and (*stopping dancing*) if you ever say anything like that about my brother again, Adele, I swear to Christ I'll punch you in the face so fucking hard that it'll break my fucking fist.

Aaron   Sweet as.

Scott (*becoming very still*)   Do you hear me?

Adele (*standing her ground*)   You're wrong.

Scott   Do you hear me, Adele?

Adele   I hate it when you get like this.

Scott   Do you fucking hear what I'm saying about my brother?

Adele   Yes. I hear you.

Scott   Sweet. (*He kisses her. She ignores his kiss.*) I'm going for a walk, boys. You's coming?

Aaron   A fucking walk?

Scott   Yeah, man. A walk.

Darren   That'd be lovely, Scott.

Scott   Fucking get ourselves fucking sorted, eh?

*He moves to leave. The others follow him. And then he stops. He turns to **Adele**.*

You coming or what?

Beat.

I said. Are you coming with me or fucking what?

Adele   Yeah. Yeah, I'm coming.

*She follows **Aaron** and **Darren** out. As she passes **Scott** he strokes her back.*

Scott   Good girl.

They exit. The lights dim gently.

A moment. The sound of the water.

Billy *enters. There is an urgency about him. An eagerness. He has with him a battered school bag, and a thin bag for carrying a fishing rod. He checks that nobody is watching him and then he opens his school bag and takes out some fishing accessories. Bait, tackle, a small box of hooks, a net, etc. The final object that he removes from his bag is a black, small, well-kept book. A log or a diary of some sort. He opens it and presses down the correct page. He also opens up the case for his rod and fixes the two halves together. Attaches the tackle to the reel and a hook to the tackle and finally some bait. This whole process should be done quickly, with obsessive care and attention to detail. When he has finished **Billy** becomes completely calm. We stay with him for a short time. He makes a few notes in his book. He hums the melody from 'Can I Pass?' by the Rebel.*

Scott *enters and stands downstage to **Billy**'s right. Leaning under the oak tree grinning, and drinking from a bottle of Stella Artois with remarkable speed and thirst, **Scott** waits for some time before he speaks. He watches **Billy** who doesn't know that he's there.*

Scott   I thought you'd be here.

*There is a pause. **Billy** keeps calm, maybe smiles to greet **Scott**. **Scott** moves, slowly, upstage towards him.*

Billy   Scott.

Scott   What are you doing?

Billy   I'm fishing.

Scott   Fishing?

Billy   For tench.

Scott (*arriving close, examining* **Billy***'s equipment*)   What are tench, Billy?

Billy   They're really small fish.

Scott   What do you do with them, Billy? When you've caught 'em?

Billy   I normally throw them back in.

Scott   What's the point of that?

Billy   It's kind of like a sport.

Scott   What's the point of throwing them back in, Billy? Waste of time, eh?

Billy   It's all to do with –

Scott (*cuts him off, about his beer*)   You want some?

Billy   No thank you.

Scott *paces around the space behind* **Billy**. **Billy** *remains fishing, but is always aware of where* **Scott** *has moved to.*

Scott (*finishing his bottle, pointing offstage*)   Did you see them little kids just up Goresbrook just now?

Billy (*enthusiastically*)   Yeah.

Scott (*putting his empty bottle in his pocket*)   I was just coming down here. I'd just been with the boys all afternoon. And I was coming down here. I was looking for you. I had something that I needed to tell you. And I saw them. They were young, eh?

Billy   Their legs are shorter.

Scott   What?

Billy   I was thinking about what it was about kids, when they're young like that, that makes them look strange. It's their legs. In comparison to the size of their heads.

Scott   Did you see what they were doing?

Billy   No.

Scott   I think they were doing bad stuff.

Billy   Oh.

Scott (*pulls out a packet of B&H*)   Sex stuff.

Billy   What?

Scott (*offers a cigarette to* **Billy**, *half knowing that he doesn't smoke*) Seriously.

Billy   No thank you.

Scott   How old do you think they were?

Billy   Twelve. Thirteen.

Scott (*lights it*)   At the oldest.

Billy   They come round here most days.

Scott   That makes me sick. Seeing that.

Billy   Are you sure that's what they were doing?

Scott   I should fucking know, Billy, eh. What do you think I am? Don't tell me you think I'm a liar, mate.

Billy   I wouldn't. I'm not. It's just. That's horrible.

Scott   Horrible?

Billy   Yeah.

Scott (*with a smoke ring*)   Do you have any brothers or sisters, Billy?

Billy   No.

Billy *reels in his line.*

Scott   You wouldn't understand then, Billy, probably, eh?

Billy   I don't know.

Scott   You wouldn't though, would you? You know about my brother, eh, Billy?

Billy   Yeah.

Scott   But I've got a sister too. Now she's nine. If I ever heard that anybody was doing anything like that with my sister, Billy, if I ever saw my sister round here or round anywhere doing that kind of stuff I'd fucking go mental, me. I'd go apeshit. I wouldn't be able to stop myself. Sometimes I get a temper on me about things like that and I end up it's like I just want to kind of fucking just go round hitting stuff.

Billy   I see.

Scott   She's into all kids' stuff. You know like groups and that? Like Steps and shit?

Billy   Yeah.

Scott   She's into all that.

Billy   I see.

Scott   I came over 'cause I wanted to tell you something and I saw those kids and it just kind of did my head in a bit. (*Beat.*) Do you ever get a feeling like you're not allowed to be a child any more?

Billy   What?

Scott   It's just something my dad said. He said that the problem was that children aren't allowed to be children any more. I just wondered if you ever felt like that.

Billy   No.

Scott   No. Me neither. If I see them round here again I think that I'll tell them to fucking just go away.

Billy   They're here all the time.

Scott   Are they?

Billy (*starts preparing a second hook*)   Normally they just throw stones at each other. Swear. Call each other fucking cunts. They draw graffiti on the walls. Write their names. Draw dicks and tits and that.

Scott (*throws his cigarette into the water*)   Good idea.

Billy (*looks up at him*)   I think they look odd. I think they look out of place. I think they look like they're shaped all wrong.

Scott   Do you?

Billy   Yeah.

Scott (*picking up and examining **Billy**'s fish-bait*)   You think some pretty fucked-up stuff, you, eh? Don't you though, Billy? You do, eh?

*From here **Billy** starts to avoid eye contact with **Scott**. Concentrates more on his fishing.*

Billy   What was it that you wanted to tell me?

Scott   These fish, these tench. How often do you catch them? Say, every day?

Billy   I normally catch two or three a day. At least. Sometimes much more.

Scott   Nice feeling?

Billy   When they come out of the water. They flash. They're all silvery. They look just magnificent. That's the best feeling.

*The two boys take to staring out over the water. **Scott** moves closer to **Billy**.*

Scott   Two or three a day isn't many though, Billy, is it?

Billy   It's all right.

Scott   You end up waiting a long time though, don't you?

Billy   I don't mind that. What was it that you wanted?

Scott   I've been looking for you all day. I wanted to wait until I got you on your own. I wanted to tell you. I went to see our Ross yesterday.

Billy   Did you?

Scott   It was a bit mad. You know what I mean?

Billy   I'm not sure.

Scott (*sitting with* **Billy**, *who doesn't acknowledge him*)   He's changed. He seems quite quiet.

Billy   I see.

Scott   It was fucking horrible, Billy. I can't stop thinking about it. It actually made me want to throw up. Ross told me, and this is what I'm here for, Billy, Ross told me to say hello to your dad.

Billy   . . .

Scott   And I probably won't see him. I don't see your dad that much. And when I do he kind of avoids me.

Billy   I see.

Scott   Billy, tell him he's asking after him.

Billy   Right.

Scott   Checking that he's all right and that. Looking forward to seeing him soon. He'll be thinking about him Friday, Billy. It is very important that you pass this message on, Billy, you with me?

Billy   Yeah.

Scott   Are you sure?

Billy   Yes.

Scott   Because you fucking better be.

Billy   I am.

Scott (*ruffles* **Billy***'s hair,* **Billy** *doesn't move*)   How is your dad, Billy?

Billy   He's all right.

Scott   Good. I mean after everything that happened.

Billy   He sleeps a lot.

Scott   Right. Well, that probably helps I reckon, eh, Billy? (*No response.*) I would imagine that plenty of sleep is exactly what he needs even. To replenish himself. You know what I mean, Bill? (*No response. Pause. Grinning.*) I should be going, Billy. I'll probably come back later. See how you're doing and that. Maybe bring some of the boys with us if that's all right with you, yeah? (*Beat. He stands.*) Billy.

Billy   Yeah.

Scott   Were you lying about your brothers and sisters?

Billy (*turns to him*)   What?

Scott (*with a big smile*)   Good man. Laters, eh?

Scott *exits.* **Billy** *turns to look away into the opposite direction from where* **Scott** *leaves. He reels in his hook and sits back on his heels for a short time. The lights are dimming gently.* **Billy** *is trying to calm himself, rocking back and forth on his heels. He is unsure what action needs to be taken but he understands that something must be done. He stands after a short time and exits upstage right.*

Lights dim faintly and rise a little again.

Charlie *enters. He sits looking out over the water.*

Billy *enters from downstage left after a few minutes and watches him.* **Charlie** *talks to* **Billy** *without looking at him.*

Charlie   One time. I come down here. There was a heron. Perched. Just resting. You know up by Goresbrook House?

Billy   Where have you been, Dad? I've been looking for you for ages.

Charlie (*grins*)   Just resting. Just there, like. Sitting. Beautiful it was. It had these white feathers. And you look closely you can see these feathers just getting touched by the wind. Gorgeous black eyes it had. And still like nothing you'd ever see. I come down here. Watched it. And you wait two seconds and the cunt just swoops. Drops like a lead ball. The weight of it. Plunges down. Comes up in a second with a carp in its beak, Billy. Honestly. It was one of the most breathtaking sights that I ever saw.

Billy   How long have you been here?

Charlie   So I come back. Two days later. Bring a gun with me, don't I? Wait to shoot the bastard. I was going to shoot it. Blow its head off and stick it on the wall at home. Buy one of those little wooden plaques. One of those things. Just glue it up there. Waiting two days. Cunt's fucked off 'a'n' it? Never comes back.

Billy   How long have you been here, Dad?

Charlie   Not long, Billy, don't worry.

Billy *moves to sit with his father. He fidgets while his father speaks.*

Charlie   I remember when I bought the bastard. Lewis Matthews. Geezer who sold it to us. I told him that I wanted it to shoot the herons that were eating my fish and also for protection from robbers and that and he says to me, he said, 'Charlie,' he said. 'Don't ever leave it around unloaded.' Which surprised me. At the time. He said, ' 'Cause one day you're going to fucking want to shoot the cunt. You'll fucking wake up and some cunt'll be fucking robbing you. So always put a fucking bullet in it. Four chambers round the barrel and it's one two three four BANG!' (*Pause.*) Sometimes I just take it out. Think about all the people I could shoot. Y'know what I mean?

Billy   Dad, I've got to tell you something.

Charlie   I've been waiting for you, Billy.

Billy   Dad, something's happened.

Charlie   You get out late, did you?

Billy   Dad –

Charlie   Fucking detention again, was it? You been mouthing off again probably, have you?

Billy   Dad, just listen to us for a minute, will ya?

Charlie (*containing his violence*)   You're not fucking trying one over on me, are you, Billy? Because I'm fucking warning you . . .

Beat. **Billy** *decides to wait for a while.*

Billy   Course I'm not. I've been looking for you.

Charlie *starts fishing with the equipment that* **Billy** *left from the last scene.*

Charlie   Well, I've been here. What was it you needed to tell us?

Billy   It can wait.

He sits with his father. Some time.

Did you get out today?

Charlie   Yeah.

Billy   Did ya?

Charlie   I'm out now, ain't I?

Billy   Did you go down the dole?

Charlie   Yeah.

Billy   And did you tell 'em about the water bill?

Charlie   Yes.

Billy   'Cause we don't need to pay that. They shouldn't even be sending us that.

Charlie   I told 'em.

Billy   Was there anything going? Any jobs, was there?

Charlie   I didn't get a chance to have a look.

Billy   You what?

Charlie   I didn't have time.

Billy   What do you mean you didn't have time? What takes up your time, Dad? What have you been doing all day?

Charlie   Billy, son, just fucking, just give it a break, will you?

Billy   Honestly, Dad, you can't even sort it out to go and have a look at the noticeboards in the dole while you're actually in there even, you're actually in the actual office, Dad. You do my head in sometimes. You do. (*Beat. Collecting it from his pocket.*) Here. My report. You've got to sign this.

Charlie   What's this?

Billy   It's my punctuality report, Dad. I've told you about this.

Charlie   What do you need a punctuality report for, Billy? What the fuck's wrong with your punctuality?

Billy   Everybody gets them if they're a little late a couple of times. I wanted to be on it.

Charlie   You what?

Billy   I wanted to be on it because I was getting a bit worried.

Charlie   Well, if you were getting a bit worried, Billy, if you were getting a bit worried, mate, what were you being so late for, eh?

Billy   I don't know, Dad, honest. It's not that big a deal. I told you this. Here. You've got to read it. And sign it. They need it.

Charlie (*reading*)　'Excellent. Excellent. Very good
behaviour. Very good, if a little quiet.' Who's that? Biology.

Billy　Mr Warren.

Charlie (*putting out his cigarette*)　What's he fucking going on
about? 'If a little quiet.' He should be fucking glad is what
he should fucking be. Dickhead. (*Beat.*) 'Good. Very good.
Very good day, Billy.' Well, fuck me. Billy, this is a fucking
bleeding miracle is what this is. I need to sign this then,
do I?

Billy　At the bottom. They need it.

Charlie *pulls a pen from his pocket and signs the report. Hands it
back.* **Billy** *takes it, smiling, folds it neatly and goes to put it back in
his bag.*

Charlie　Who needs it?

Billy　The school. They need to keep a track on me. It's
important.

Charlie　Right.

Billy　For the records.

Charlie　Right.

Billy　'Cause, because if we, if we move and I go to
another school then they're going to need all this
information so they can send it on to my new school. Dad.

Charlie　Billy, just don't . . . best not lose it then, eh?

Billy　I won't. I'll give it back to him tomorrow.

Beat.

Dad.

Charlie　Billy.

Billy　Can I ask you a question?

Charlie　Go on.

Billy   Have you changed your shirt?

Charlie   You what?

Billy   Have you?

Charlie   . . .

Billy   You haven't, have you?

Charlie   I . . .

Billy   You've got to change your shirts, Dad.

Charlie   Jesus fucking Christ on a bike.

Billy   I even, didn't I, I even just washed 'em for you. I even just left one out for you.

Charlie   Will you give it a rest?

Billy   What's going to happen, Dad, say they have to have an interview, say somebody comes and they're trying to sort out a new flat for us or they're checking up on us or that –

Charlie   Billy.

Billy   Say they are though.

Charlie   I don't think that's going to happen, son.

Billy   It might do. Say they do. And you're there. And you're looking like a right tramp. I really worry about it. Sometimes. I really do.

Charlie   Well, fucking don't.

Billy   Well, I can't help it.

Charlie   Well, try.

Billy   Dad. I saw Scott Cooper.

Charlie   Did you?

Billy   Yeah. He told me to tell you something. He told me to tell you that he'd been to see his Ross.

Charlie   Right. (*Beat.*) I see. (*Another.*) Billy.

Billy   Yeah.

Charlie   Is that what this is all about?

Billy   All what's about?

Charlie   All fucking this palaver. Billy, do I look like a twat?

Billy   What?

Charlie   Do I look like a fucking twat, Billy? You heard me.

Billy   No.

Charlie   No. Of course I fucking don't. I'm a handsome bastard, me, and I'm not a fucking stupid twat. So why do you think, Billy, thinking about it and everything, why do you think I should even, even for the slightest moment even, why should I even care what that prick Scott Cooper has fucking been up to with his spare time? Eh, Billy? Answer me that one, pal.

Billy   Dad, he's been to see his Ross.

Charlie   I don't care.

Billy   And his Ross had told him that he was thinking about you.

Charlie   Billy, I couldn't give a monkey's fuck.

Billy   Dad, I think I'm scared.

Charlie   What?

Billy   I think I'm scared of what's going to happen when they get out.

Charlie   Oh fucking listen to it, will ya?

Billy   Dad.

Charlie   Listen to it fucking going on! Jesus fucking H. Billy, you're worse than your fucking mother!

Billy   Dad, don't.

Charlie   Billy, son. I don't give a shite. I don't give a shite what Scott Cooper has been doing. I don't give a shite about what his retard fucking brother's been saying. And you tell me that you're scared.

Billy   I am.

Charlie   Well, Billy, I promise you, son. You have fucking nothing to be scared of, mate. Fucking nothing. You hear me? Do you?

Billy   Yeah.

Charlie   Fucking . . . good. You better. So just fucking quit it, all right?

Pause.

Billy   Dad.

Charlie (*treads his cigarette out*)   Billy.

Billy   I saw Mum yesterday.

Charlie (*turning to look*)   Where?

Billy   Down the market.

Charlie   What were you doing down the market yesterday?

Billy   After school.

Charlie   Did she see you?

Billy   I don't know. I don't think so.

Charlie (*looks to* **Billy**, *concerned*)   Did she speak to you?

Billy   No.

Charlie *watches* **Billy**. **Billy**, *not sure how his dad will react, finds it difficult to hold his stare.* **Michelle** *enters. Stands below the oak tree. Neither* **Charlie** *nor* **Billy** *acknowledges her. It is* **Billy** *who breaks the tension between the two.*

Billy   Dad, I think if we're going to leave here, Dad. I think we should think about going soon.

Charlie *watches* **Billy** *for a short time. He never says what he is thinking. Instead he hands him some money.*

Charlie   Get yourself some chips. I want you home by ten o'clock.

Billy   Right.

Charlie   Ten o'clock, Billy. I want you back home.

Billy   Dad, do you know what day it is on Friday?

Pause. **Charlie** *glares at* **Billy** *and then breaks the tension with some reluctance.*

Charlie   Don't be late. I'll see you later.

He turns and leaves. Exchanges a long glance with **Michelle** *as he exits.* **Billy** *watches him go.*

Billy *turns to look at* **Michelle***. The lights should dim, almost imperceptibly.*

Michelle   Hello, Billy. How are you, darling?

Very long pause. She buttons her coat up.

Billy   There's something I've got to tell you, Mum, it's very important.

Michelle   I thought it was you. The other day and that. Up on Roman Road. I thought, I thought it was you.

Billy   Mum.

Michelle   You've grown, you know? Billy? You've really grown. And filled out, like. In your shoulders and that. Billy. Billy, you look lovely, you know.

Billy   Mum, do you know somebody called Scott Cooper?

Michelle   Scott who?

Billy   Scott Cooper, Mum, he's a boy from down Goresbrook?

Michelle   No, Billy, I've never heard of him.

Billy   Well –

Michelle (*cuts him off*)   How's school? Billy?

Nervously, half shaking, she lights a cigarette.

Billy   You've got to tell something to Danny and Leanne.

Michelle   And how's, how's, how's Charlie? Are you all right? Are you eating all right? The pair of you?

Billy   Yes, Mum, we're fine.

Michelle   And are you staying out of trouble? Out of bother with your teachers? And doing your homework?

Billy   You've got to tell Danny and Leanne that if they come across a boy called Scott Cooper that they mustn't, they, they mustn't talk to him or look at him or listen to him or anything. They've got to, it's very important that they've got to just leave him alone. Are you with me, Mum?

Michelle   Of course I am, Billy.

Billy   Will you tell them?

Michelle   Of course I will, Billy.

Billy (*making to leave*)   If Dad knew I was talking to you he'd do his nut, I swear.

Michelle (*stopping him*)   Billy. Don't go. Just not yet.

He turns. She moves towards him, slowly, cautiously. As soon as she makes the slightest movement to touch him he explodes at her.

Billy   Don't touch me.

She freezes, pulls back and leaves.

He turns away from her and begins to pack away his fishing equipment.
He packs furiously and chaotically. Interrupting his packing by writing
occasional phrases or sentences in his book.

Adele *enters. She stands some distance away from* **Billy** *and from*
where he is packing and writing. Upstage. She waits. She spends some
moments staring out over the water before she turns to watch **Billy**.
When she speaks he stops his packing for a short time. But only for a
short time.

Adele   You're Billy. Billy Russell. You go to our school.
(*No response.*) You're in Mr Webster's form. 4D. I hate him.
He's a fat cunt. (*No response.*) You live on the Cotall Street
Estate. Up Limehouse. Opposite Stainsby Road, your flat is.
I've seen you. Not only at school and that. I live just near
you. I'm not being a funny cow. Honestly. I've just noticed
you. I'm Adele.

Billy   I know.

Adele   What you doing?

Billy (*continuing to pack up*)   I was fishing.

Adele (*approaches him*)   You're always fishing, aren't you?
Heh? Every day I come here you're here fishing. With your
dad normally. Where's your dad today, Billy? (*No response. He*
continues to pack.) Don't you want to talk to us? It's all right.
I'm not going to bite you or nothing. It's a bit fucking weird
though. Don't you think, Billy?

Billy   No.

Billy, *packed up, carrying only his book separately, goes to leave.*

Adele   Where are you going?

Billy (*stops*)   Home.

Adele (*taking the piss*)   What are you running away from,
Billy? What are you trying to escape from?

Billy   Can I ask you something?

Adele   It speaks!

Billy   Can I?

Adele   Go on.

Billy   You come down this way, every day. At, at the same time every day. Exact same time. And you stop. Just for a second and that. But you do, you just, you stop. At the same point. Just looking up there. Out there across the other side. And then you carry on. Can I ask you?

Adele   What?

Billy   Why do you do that?

Adele   It's none of your business.

Billy   No. I know that. I just thought I'd ask you. I'm sorry. I'm just inquisitive. I'm a strange fucker sometimes. (*Pause.*) Is it . . . ?

Adele   What?

Billy   Is it because of Racheal?

There is a moment between the two. And then **Adele** *grins.*

Adele   You know something I noticed. (*No response.*) You're going to think this is well weird.

Billy   What?

Adele   You've got the same eyes as your dad.

Billy   That's not true.

Adele   Yeah, it is. Was it your dad who found her?

Billy   What?

Adele   Racheal. Was it your dad who found her?

Long pause.

Billy   Yes. It was.

Adele   That's what I heard. Did you see her too?

Billy   No.

Adele   What was it like?

Billy   What do you mean?

Adele   Did he never say, your dad, what it was like? What happened? How come he found her? Anything like that?

Billy   No.

Adele   Did you never ask him?

Billy   No.

Adele   'Cause I would have. I would never have shut up about it. It was Ross Cooper, wasn't it? And Berg Kempton. And his mates? Who did it?

Billy   Yeah.

Adele   Your dad saw 'em, didn't he?

Long silence.

Did you know her?

Billy   Not really.

Adele (**Billy** *turns to her as she speaks*)   I used to sit with her in English. She was very quiet. She was quite, you know, she was like quite fat and that. Never said anything but sometimes, if you were working in pairs and that, she used to know so much stuff. She used to talk about why people did things. She had all these ideas. Never told them to anybody. Except she'd tell them to me, though, and I'd tell the teacher and he'd think I was a right boffin. But it was all her.

Billy   I'm not in your year. I'm in Year Ten.

Adele   I know. (*New tactic. She moves towards him.*) I remember when you arrived at our school. You only came a couple of years back, didn't you?

Billy (*keeps his ground*)   Yeah.

Adele   Where did you go before?

Billy   Morpeth.

Adele   Did you? (*No response.*) How come you changed?

Billy (*looking away*)   We moved.

Adele   To Cotall Street?

Billy   That's right.

Adele   How come?

Billy (*turning back to her*)   Aren't you Scott Cooper's girlfriend?

Adele   No.

Billy   That's not what I heard.

Adele   I'm not.

Billy   Isn't he going to be a bit fucked off that you're coming round here talking to me?

Adele   I'm not his girlfriend. How come you moved?

Billy (*moving to collect his fishing bag*)   If I know Scott Cooper he'll be fucking angry and he'll probably most likely fucking want to batter the pair of us.

Adele   Scott Cooper's a needledick.

Billy   But he'll still fucking batter us.

Adele   How come you moved?

Billy   I came to live with me dad. I used to live with me mum.

Adele   How come you changed?

No response. **Billy** *looks away from her.*

You know what your problem is? Billy, don't you? You're just fucking plain rude sometimes. It's no wonder you've got no mates.

No response.

And I'm trying to be dead friendly. And you just ignore us.

Billy (*explaining*)   I was leaving school one time last week. There was a lad waiting outside the school. An older lad. About eighteen. I watch him waiting at the bus stop. And he's waiting for a kid in Year Ten.

He turns to confront her with his justification. She doesn't break eye contact with him.

As I'm coming out of the gates the kid in Year Ten is walking ahead of me and this lad gets him. This eighteen-year-old. Gets him. Gets him by his coat. And he pulls his head down and smacks it against a lamp-post. Four times. Back and down against the metal bit on the lamp-post.

Adele   So?

Billy   I've seen teachers talk to kids as though they are worthless scabby shit. Bully them. Humiliate them. Never think about stopping and asking if they need help but instead, they just, instead they just say stupid cruel things. And the reason they do it is because so many of the kids, not all of them, but so fucking many are so fucking stupid and dick around and act like tossers. They think it's funny. It's not. It's shitty. And it ruins things.

Adele   What the fuck has that got to do with anything?

Billy   I come down here, Adele Kent, and there is litter, pissy fucked litter everywhere. And it's kids that have left it.

Adele   Billy.

Billy   Even here. Even the surface of the water. The place looks like it's fucking ripped up. People don't care. Do they? Even about trees and that? People just, why do they, just fucking, the way people treat trees around here is despicable!

Adele   What has that got to do with anything?

Billy (*concluding*)   It's not just me.

Adele   That's not an excuse.

Billy   What do you want?

Adele   How did you know my surname?

Billy   I found it out. I asked somebody. What do you want?

Adele   Why did you do that?

Billy   Because I wanted to know. What do you want from me, Adele?

Adele   I found out about your dad. And I thought it was interesting. I wanted to meet you.

Billy   It isn't.

Adele   What?

Billy   Interesting.

Adele (*proving him wrong*)   When I was four my mum was put into mental hospital because she tried to kill herself. I only found that out just this year. My dad's psychic. He's got psychic powers. He can see people's souls. What they look like. I don't know if I like him or not. Parents are *always* interesting.

Billy   That's not true.

Adele   Parents are always interesting. Because they're always fucked but they're very close to how you are yourself. You do things and it's just the same as them.

Billy   I'm nothing like my dad.

Adele (*ignoring him*)   So when I heard about Charlie I thought that the easiest way to find out about what happened, about him, was to find out about you.

Billy   I'm nothing like my dad.

Adele   I bet you are. (*No response.*) I used to know Berg Kempton. My mum used to work in their pub up Ilford. She used to be a cleaner. They used to come down Cotall Street. I saw him once get a baseball bat and smack this kid's arm up. The kid was, what, fifteen. How long's he gone down for?

Billy   Ten years.

Adele   When he comes out do you think he's going to look for your dad?

Billy   I don't know.

Pause.

Adele   It was this time last year, wasn't it? (*No response.*) Billy. It was a year ago on Friday. You remember? (*No response.*) It was horrible, Billy, wasn't it?

Billy   Yeah.

Adele   There was six of them, I heard, wasn't there?

Billy   Yeah.

Adele   What do you think she thought? When she saw them?

Billy   I don't know.

Adele   You wanna know something?

Billy   What?

Adele   I'm on seven different types of medication.

Billy   You what?

Adele   I take two different types of pills for epilepsy. I've had fits. Two fits. Not for years.

Billy   So what do you want me to do about it?

Adele   And I have nightmares.

Billy   What?

Adele   I think it's almost funny sometimes. I've seen people, people I know, take speed, pills, draw, gas, booze, charlie, glue, smack. I've seen people smoking smack outside my flat, Billy, on our estate. Right in front of the Old Bill.

Billy   So what are you telling me this for?

Adele (*moving towards him*)   Sometimes at night I still get frightened. Of the streets near where I live. Of the gangs there. The junkies. The scumfuckers. The scuzzbags. The perverts.

Billy   What are you going on about, you?

Adele   I just wanted to meet somebody. To talk to somebody. Somebody who knew her. I wanted to meet you, Billy. To see if you were all right. Billy, I think about her all the time.

Long pause. They should be quite close by now.

Billy   You know who frightens me?

Adele   Who?

Scott *has entered with* **Aaron** *and* **Darren***. The three boys drink beer. Smoke cigarettes. They surround* **Billy** *and* **Adele***, but remain around the peripheries of the stage for now, allowing them to continue uninterrupted.*

Billy   All the winos and that. The boozers. When you walk past them, you never know if they're going to smack out or what.

Adele   No, you don't.

Billy   I have this theory about what happens to you when you're dead.

Adele   Oh yeah?

Billy   I think when you're dead you go up to heaven and you meet God and He asks you if you think that, after the things that you have done in your lifetime, you deserve to go to heaven or to hell. And you have to answer. And the answer decides where you go but you have to be completely absolutely honest about it. And there's nothing worse than lying in this test. Because God can, He can just fucking well tell, can't He. And if you lie, well, you're really fucked. And those winos, all those, those people. They're fucked too. I think.

Adele (*bewildered*)   That's about the stupidest idea I've ever heard.

Billy   Where do you think you'll go?

Adele (*still bewildered*)   Jesus.

Billy   Where do you think Racheal will be?

Adele (*serious*)   I don't believe in heaven. Or hell.

There is a slight moment. **Adele** *and the boys ignore each other when* **Scott** *starts to speak.*

Scott   We was just thinking about you.

Billy   What?

Scott *removes a cigarette from his packet. Leaves it unlit for now, occasionally dangling it between his teeth.*

Scott   We were having a conversation. About Bergsie. Ross. And that. And the conversation kind of came around to you.

Billy   Right.

Scott   Which might surprise you. But might not. I was gonna ask you a question.

Adele *touches* **Billy**'s *face. Leaves. Takes a swig from* **Scott**'s *bottle as she goes. Nobody, however, pays any attention as she leaves. The lights fall darker to night-time.*

Billy   Go on.

Scott   You moved schools, yeah?

Billy   Yeah.

Scott   We couldn't remember. We couldn't figure it out.

Aaron   Remember, I think, is fairer, Scott.

Scott   Yeah. Fair enough. We couldn't remember. Why did you move schools, Billy?

Billy   Moved house.

Darren   Makes sense.

Aaron   Although it is a little evasive.

Scott   Yes. You moved house. Why?

Billy   What?

Scott   Why did you move house?

Billy   I went to live with me dad.

Scott (*moves in*)   What was wrong with your mum?

Billy   Nothing.

Aaron (*moves in*)   Well, if there was nothing wrong with her, Billy, then how come you fucking fucked off and left her, boy?

Billy   Just did, that's all.

Scott   And your brother and your sister?

Billy   I haven't got a brother and a sister.

Scott (*strikes a match*)   Liar.

Billy   What?

Scott (*lights his cigarette*)   Isn't he, lads? He's a fucking liar.

Darren (*moves in, with a big swig from his bottle*)   He's a fucking dick.

Scott   I mean, it's not a big deal. But to deny your own brother, Billy, your own sister. I think that's a little out of order. Don't you, boys?

Aaron   I think it's fucking abject!

Scott   Mind you, boys, have you seen his mum?

Darren   What?

Scott   Billy's mum. Have you seen her?

Darren   Nah.

Scott   Straight up, man, she is fucking tight.

Darren   Right!

Scott   Ain't it, Billy? Don't you think, I mean, I know you're not meant to think stuff like this but your mum, Billy, even you can see that she is one straight up fucking sweet bit of pussy, yeah?

Billy   Why are you talking as though you're American?

Some time. Some tension. **Scott**'s *cigarette close up to* **Billy**'s *unflinching face.*

Scott   Billy.

Billy   What?

Scott   Billy.

Billy   What?

Scott   Billy.

Billy   What?

Scott   Shut your mouth or I'll cut your eyes out.

Darren (*finishes his beer in celebration*)   Damn straight, Scott.

Scott   Billy's mum's got a sweet little pussy though, Billy, ain't it?

Darren   What are her titties like, Scott?

Scott   Fucking I never saw her titties, man.

Darren   Nah?

Scott   Nah, I fucked her with my eyes closed.

Darren   Sweet.

Scott   Tight little cunt but, to tell you the truth, Billy, eh? Her face is a mushy pile of shit.

Darren   You know what I heard about his mum, Scott? I heard his mum works hard.

Scott   Damn hard.

Darren   Works all night sometimes.

Aaron   I seen her. But I spent my money elsewhere. Because I figured she's a fucking filthy cunt. With lice. Crabs. All manner of venereal disease.

Darren (*swigs from* **Aaron**'s *bottle*)   Aids.

Scott   Billy, has your mum got Aids?

Aaron (*wipes bottle neck*)   Did she get it from fucking monkeys, Billy, 'cause I heard she's hungry for monkey cock? Although that's an unsubstantiated rumour.

Darren   Billy's mum's got Aids big time.

Aaron (*lights a cigarette*)   Billy, do you ever think about what it would be like to fuck your mum? Do you ever think about that? 'Cause if you ever do, just ask Scott, and I'm sure he'll tell you. (*Hacking cough / laugh.*)

Darren   He's told us enough times.

Billy   Shut up.

Darren (*claps / rubs his hands*)   Ooooohhhhh!

Aaron (*in a fake scientist's voice*)   I do believe that this peculiar worm is turning, Scott.

Scott (*threatening, quiet*)   I can see. (*Beat.*) Boys. (*Another. Release.*) Lay off, eh? We're just joking, Billy. Just pissing you about. No offence, eh? Billy? No offence? Is it? Boys? Billy? You're not offended, are you, Billy? We're sorry, aren't we boys?

Aaron   Yeah. Right.

Scott (*perhaps ruffles his hair*)   Billy. You need to chill, man. I mean, I'm not saying anything but you're a bit of an uptight cunt, Billy, sometimes. You need to learn to take a bit of a joke, you with me? Billy? (*Beat.*) Billy. Have you got any money?

Billy   What?

Scott   Have you got any money for us?

Billy   I've got one quid fifty.

Scott   That's fine, Billy.

Billy   What?

Scott   Just give us your one quid fifty then, if that's all you've got.

Billy   I need it.

Scott   I'm sorry?

Billy   It's my bus fare.

Darren   You need it?

Billy   I . . .

Aaron   I'm a little surprised by that comment, frankly.

Billy   I need the money to get home.

Scott (*not menacing*)   Just give it to us, Billy, would ya? Stop confusing the issue with irrelevant fucking horseshit.

Billy *hands over the money. He starts to move away from them.*

Billy   I won't be able to get home now.

Scott   I'm sorry?

Aaron   Billy, you can fucking walk, man, can't you?

Scott   How's your dad, Billy?

Billy *stops.*

Darren   I was speaking to Bergsie's brother.

Aaron   Fucking hell. He is certainly not happy.

Scott   Year ago this week, innit?

Aaron   Friday.

Darren   Apparently Bergsie's had to tell his brother not to go near your dad or nothing because he wants to cut him himself when he comes out.

Scott   No shit?

Darren   That's what he said.

Scott   Won't be long now, will it? Good behaviour and that. Couple of years maybe.

Darren   If that.

Aaron   Billy, I heard something about your dad.

Darren   I heard lots of things about his dad.

Aaron   Is it true that your dad likes a nice pull.

Darren   A nice what?

Aaron   A nice pull. A nice wank. A nice little shuffle.

Scott   Don't we all, Riley, eh? That's not a crime.

Darren   Fucking hope not.

Aaron   Yeah. But a nice quiet pull when he's fishing.

Scott   What?

Aaron   Gets it out in public.

Scott   No?

Aaron   No shit. My sister saw him.

Darren   Fuck off!

Aaron   He grinned at her and everything.

Darren   Just where Racheal was and that.

Scott (*treads his cigarette out*)   You think he's thinking about it?

Darren   Damn right he is. Wanking himself off, thinking about Racheal.

Aaron   Thinking about pulling her body up again.

Scott   Thinking about what he saw!

Aaron   Sick fuck.

Darren   Sick fucking cunt, I think.

Scott (*closing in on* **Billy**, *pronounces every consonant*)   You know that, Billy? Your dad is a sick fucking cunt and when Bergsie cuts him, and when our Ross fucking stabs him, there are going to be many more people who are happy than there are who are sad. Because he's a cunt. And a grass. And a pervert.

Billy (*turning to confront them*)   That's not true.

Scott   You what?

Billy   That isn't true.

Scott   What isn't true, Billy?

Billy   Anything that you said. About my mum. Or about my dad. It's not true.

Scott   Are you questioning me?

Darren (*quietly*)   Fucksake!

Aaron (*concerned*)   Billy, man, don't!

Scott   Billy, are you questioning me?

Billy   It isn't true.

Scott   Don't be fucking questioning me, Billy. Really. Don't fucking do that. FUCK!

He explodes at him and knocks him back slightly. Clasps his face between his hands.

'Cause I'm not pissing you, Billy. I'm not fucking joking, son. If you ever fucking so much as ever fucking question me, talk to me. To me, like that. Touch fucking ME! Like that. Again. I swear to Christ, Billy, I will cut your tiny dick off. You understand me?

Billy   I didn't touch you.

Scott   Do you understand me?

Billy   Yes. I do.

Darren *and* **Aaron** *watch as* **Scott** *stares at* **Billy** *for some time, still holding his face.*

'Can I Pass? – instrumental' by the Rebel plays as the lights fall to darkness for a while.

Lights rise. It is early afternoon. **Billy** *and* **Charlie** *are together on stage, facing out towards the audience. They are fishing. There is a long pause as they fish. As they fish* **Billy** *occasionally looks to his dad, as though waiting for the right time to speak. When he answers his dad's questions he seems more detached than we have seen him before.*

Charlie   Keep calm. Don't move unless it is absolutely necessary. Keep still. Stay absolutely steady. Watch the details of the water. They'll come eventually. (*Pause.*) How was school?

Billy   It was all right.

Charlie   You done your homework?

Billy   Yeah.

Charlie   All of it?

Billy   Yeah.

Charlie   Already?

Billy   Yeah.

Charlie   Properly?

Billy   Yeah.

Charlie   I bet you fucking ain't. I bet you fucked it all up, knowing you, probably.

Billy   I never.

Charlie   Well, they don't fucking give you much, do they?

Billy   No.

Charlie   Probably don't like fucking marking it all, heh?

Billy   Probably.

Charlie   Lazy tarts. Probably just like want a fucking afternoon off. Probably. (*Beat.*) You staying out of bother?

Billy   Yeah.

Charlie   Are you?

Billy   Yeah.

Charlie   You better had be.

Billy   I am.

Charlie   'Cause I don't want to find out about you doing all kinds of mad stuff again, Billy.

Billy   You won't.

Charlie   I don't want you getting in with any bad old bastards.

Billy   I won't.

Charlie   You better not be.

Billy   I won't.

Charlie   I'm warning you.

Billy   I'm not. (*Beat.*) Dad, have I got your eyes?

Charlie   What do you mean?

Billy   It's just something somebody said to me.

Charlie   I hate it when people say all that shit. I can never figure it out. You've got your own eyes.

Billy   People have said it before though, eh? I remember even Mum used to say I had your eyes.

Pause. Tension for a short while.

Charlie   See, you know what your fucking problem is, don't ya? You're up with the fucking fairies half the fucking time. You're away with the fucking stars. Cloud fucking cuckoo land, Billy, isn't it? Got a head like a fucking Teletubby sometimes, Billy, honestly.

Billy   I got cut today.

Charlie   You what?

Billy   Today. At school. I got cut.

Charlie   On what?

Billy   On a fishing hook.

Charlie   On a what?

Billy   A fishing hook.

Charlie   How the fuck did you get cut on a fucking fishing hook?

Billy   I took a little box of fishing hooks up to the school to show our teacher and I was fiddling about with one of them in science and it went right through my thumb. I had to pull it out. Tore the skin right off my thumb and all. I thought I'd better tell ya.

Charlie   You fucking stupid bastard.

Billy   I thought I better tell you, Dad, because I didn't want you to get mad or anything.

Charlie   Billy, for crying out loud.

Billy   You should have seen Mr Thompson. He nearly puked up. And the woman in the office, the secretary who does all of the injuries and the sick notes and that. She was looking at it going, 'Oh, Billy! What are we going to do?' I said, 'I could just pull it out, Miss.' She wasn't sure what to do, so I did. I just pulled it out. Blood spitting all over the place. It was funny. Made me laugh.

Charlie   Billy, what the fuck is the matter with you?

Billy   Some people get a bit sick around the sight of blood but it never really bothers me too much.

Charlie   Billy, you can't take fucking fishing hooks into school with you, you daft twat.

Billy   I wanted to show Mr Thompson what they looked like.

Charlie   I don't care.

Billy   He'd been asking about them.

Charlie   Billy.

Billy   What?

Charlie   I'll tell you something for nothing, son.

Billy   What?

Charlie   If I hear you've been fucking about with fishing hooks or shit like that again, at school or fucking anywhere, I'll take 'em fucking off you, so help me God I will, and I will stick 'em up your fucking arse.

Billy *never even looks at him.*

Billy   Right.

Charlie   For fucksake. I've told you.

Billy   What?

Charlie   Haven't I? About why this is important. Billy. Haven't I told you?

Billy   Yeah.

Charlie   You have just got to be, just you've got to be just bang on, Billy.

Billy   I know.

Charlie   Just absolutely bang on, mate.

Billy   You've told me that, Dad.

Charlie   I don't want no cunt from anywhere coming round here and saying that you're not, that you are not allowed to stay here any more. Billy. That you're not allowed to stay with me. And if you fuck up. If you fuck up, Billy, they will. They told us that. They'll come, Billy, they'll come and they will take you. You know that, don't you?

Billy   Yeah.

Charlie   So, just, fucking be good.

Billy   I try.

Charlie   You what?

Billy   I said I try. To be good. I really do.

Charlie   Well, try fucking harder.

Billy   Dad.

Charlie   Billy.

Billy   Can I ask you a question?

Charlie   Fucking hell, Billy, what are you like? What is it with all these fucking questions? I feel like I'm on fucking *Wogan*.

Billy   Can I?

Charlie   Go on.

Billy   It's a bit strange.

Charlie   All right.

Billy   Dad. When you, when you found Racheal, Dad, what was it like?

Pause.

Charlie   Why?

Billy   What?

Charlie   Why do you want to know?

Billy   Because I think about it all the time.

Charlie   It was a long time ago, Billy.

Billy   Dad, it was a year ago. It's not that long.

Charlie   I don't remember much about it, Billy. I try not to think about it.

Charlie *reels in his line, removes the bait from the hook.*

Billy   Dad, did you see them get her? Ross and Bergsie? Did you see them?

No response.

Ross's brother reckons you saw them and that you phoned the police. Is that true?

No response.

Dad, are you scared about what's going to happen when Bergsie gets out? Because I am. I think we should think about going, Dad.

Charlie   Billy, I've told you. I'm waiting.

Billy   I don't think it makes any sense waiting, Dad.

Charlie   Billy.

Billy   Dad, Ross's brother reckons that when Bergsie gets out that he's going to try and stab you. And I believe him, Dad. I honestly do.

Charlie *removes his line and packs up his rod. Stands to leave.*
Adele *enters quietly and lies down staring at the sky.*

Charlie   He won't.

Billy   Dad, I really think that he's going to try.

Charlie   He won't. He won't be out for ten years, Billy. We won't be here then.

Adele   When it gets as hot as this I can't even think.

Charlie *leaves.* **Billy** *watches him go. He opens his book and writes. He continues to write while* **Adele** *talks to him. The lights should brighten and become warmer throughout this scene.*

Billy   I like it.

Adele   I feel like I'm trapped in a cupboard. They shouldn't make us go to school when it's as hot as this. They shouldn't make us do anything. Nothing.

Billy   I find that it clears my head.

Adele   And the teachers get pissed off. Treat you like wasps. (*Beat.*) Has Scott spoken to you?

Billy   I watch all of the people who come down here. On their way somewhere.

Adele   Has he, Billy?

Billy   No. Nobody ever stops.

Adele   'Cause he told me he was going to.

Billy   Well, he hasn't.

Adele   Good. I was worried that he would find you.

Billy   Do you remember when you were little how aeroplanes sounded?

Adele (*propping herself up*)   What?

Billy   Did you ever lie on your back and look up at the sky and watch the aeroplanes fly over your head and listen to the sound that they made?

Adele   All the time.

Billy   As they get older, people just don't notice things like that.

Adele   They don't get time.

Pause. **Billy** *gets up, starts to reel in his line and remove the bait and the hook.*

Adele (*considered*)   Sometimes I wish I could still be in primary school. I used to love it there.

Billy   There's no point wasting time thinking about things that have finished, Adele. You have to, I have to, I look forward to stuff all the time.

Adele   What do you look forward to?

Billy   Going away. We're going away. Me and our dad. We're going to leave here and go down and live by the sea.

Adele   When?

Billy   Soon.

Adele   I'd like to meet your dad.

Billy   You said.

Adele (*turning to him*)   Do you like him?

Billy (*stops packing, sitting*)   Sometimes. Mostly. He's been all right. My mum's a bit of a fuck-up and he's looked after me and that. Sometimes he gets angry. Sometimes he don't say nothing. For days. Just sits there staring at his toe or something. Sometimes I think he wants to fucking kill me. When he gets angry it gets quite bad. A lot of the time he just warns me about stuff and then never does anything about it. Mostly he's all right.

Adele   Did you ask him about Racheal?

Billy (*resumes packing*)   No.

Adele   My dad's a weird fucker. He says he can look into your soul.

Billy   Do you believe him?

Adele   Sometimes I do. Sometimes it's just weird. He gets really into it. He gets obsessed about things. Sometimes it seems quite believable. He told me once that I had the same powers. As he did.

Billy   Fucking hell.

Adele   I don't think it's true. But last summer I saw Racheal. Honest.

Billy   Fuck off.

Adele   I did. In our house. Running up the stairs in front of me. This was, what, two months after she died. (*Pause.*) Her mum gave me all her schoolbooks. To help me with my coursework and that. I still read them. Look at her handwriting. (*Pause.*) Billy, do you ever get the feeling that you're not allowed to be a child any more?

Billy   Why do you ask that?

Adele   It's just something my dad said to me.

Billy   No. I never feel like that.

Billy, *packed up, sits looking out over the water, away from* **Adele**.

Adele   No. Me neither. (*Beat.*) Do you know Aaron Riley?

Billy   Yeah.

Adele (*standing, straightening her skirt*)   Last Saturday, yeah, he was down the Anglers. He took four pills. Four Es. In half an hour. Passed out. He had to go to hospital and have his stomach pumped. He's fifteen. I saw him at school yesterday. Asked him how he was. He said he was fine. He didn't know what all the fuss was about. Somebody asked him if he would do the same thing again. He said he didn't know. But he might do. I think he's a fucking thick cunt and he's probably going to fucking die.

Billy   Right.

Adele (*coming to join him*)   Do you know what worries me?

Billy   What?

Adele   It worries me that I've not got anything to look forward to.

Billy   That's not true.

Adele   Sometimes I think it is.

Billy   Isn't there something you've always wanted to have? Or always wanted to be.

Adele   See, that's the thing. I don't think there is any more.

Billy   That's bad.

Adele   Sometimes I get so angry about stuff.

Billy   You shouldn't.

Adele   I get frustrated.

Billy   What about?

Adele   About all kinds of things. About how stupid boys our age are. I prefer twenty-year-olds, me. They know what you want. And about how petty and stupid and bitchy the girls are. I end up clenching my fists up, sometimes, when I'm angry. Pull at my hair. Hit my face with my hand, hard. But that's not the same, is it? As having ambition, Billy?

Billy   Bergsie was twenty, Adele.

Adele (*walking away*)   I know.

Billy   And Ross.

Adele   I know that.

Billy (*turns to her*)   They were twenty. Did you know them?

Adele (*facing his confrontation*)   Why do you think I come here so often?

Billy   I heard that she wouldn't drown.

Adele   What?

Billy   That's what I heard. That's what the police said.
That there were signs of a struggle. That she fought and
kicked. So in order to keep her down under they threw
rocks at her. To knock her out. And to weigh her down.

Adele   She must have realised what was happening.

Billy   She must have done.

Adele   She must have known that she was going to die.

Billy   I know.

Adele   Can you imagine?

Billy   No.

Adele   She was thirteen, Billy.

Billy   They must have been very scared.

Adele   Who?

Billy   Bergsie. Ross. The rest of them. They must have
been frightened. (*Pause.*) I keep finding things. Here. Things
that people have left here. Pieces of paper with phone
numbers on. Photographs. Porno mags. And graffiti. And
everything that I find seems to lead back to what happened
to Racheal and how much she must have known –

Adele   That's bullshit.

Billy   – and what they were feeling when they realised that
she was going to die. There are so many things that I find.
That I come across. I don't know what to do with them all. I
don't know how to make them all make sense. I end up just
writing them down.

Adele   You what?

Billy   I write them down. I've got a book.

Adele (*quietly, angry*)   That's fucking weird.

Billy   No. It's not though.

Adele   Billy, it is. (*Beat.*) Do you know what I was asking about Scott for?

Billy   No.

Adele   Do you know what he did to me?

Billy   No.

Adele   He's found out about me coming here. To see you and that. So he's just been acting, like, like just a wank.

Billy   I see.

Adele   I've been off this week for three days because I've been ill. And while I've been off he's told everybody in my class that I was pregnant. Which was why I was off.

Billy   Dick.

Adele   I came into the form room this morning. And he was in there. He went into my bag when I wasn't looking and he got a tampax out of my bag and stuck it on the board. In front of everybody. He was just laughing and that. Teacher saw him and he didn't even do anything.

Billy   He's just a dick.

Adele   No. It's more than that. He keeps boasting about what happened. And joking about it being a year ago. He's a fuck. He makes people feel crippled. And people let him get away with it because they're scared of what he might do. It's just not, it's not fair, Billy. It's cruel, is what it is. And it's not enough, Billy, to just, just, just write it down, Billy. It's not enough.

Billy   What is it that you want me to do, Adele?

Adele   I don't know.

Billy   Tell me what it is that you want me to do and I'll do it. I'll honestly do anything that you ask me.

Adele   Billy.

Billy   'Cause I don't have any fucking clue for myself any more.

Adele *moves towards him but stops herself before she touches him.*

Adele   Billy, I think he's going to try to come and find you.

Long pause.

Billy   Do you know what my ambition is?

Adele   What?

Billy   I've got two.

Adele   Go on.

Billy   I want to go out to the sea. Into the ocean. With my dad. I want to see dolphins swimming, real dolphins swimming in the ocean. And I want to be able to ride on a roller coaster. A big fucking proper one. In like Disneyland and shit. I'd fucking love that.

Aaron, **Darren** *and* **Scott** *have emerged from the peripheries of the stage. They are drinking bottles of Stella Artois and smoking cigarettes and scrawny joints.* **Adele** *leaves, unable to touch* **Billy**. *The lights begin to fall into evening.*

The physical gestures of the boys, especially of **Aaron**, *should be exaggerated, demonstrative.*

Aaron (*giggling, stoned, drunk*)   See that tree?

Darren (*the same, but more so*)   What?

Aaron   The fucking tree, man! See that tree?

Darren   Yeah.

Aaron   I hate that tree.

Darren   Right.

Aaron   I piss on that tree.

Darren   Right.

Aaron   Tree! I piss on you! From great, great, unthinkable heights!

Darren   Right!

Aaron   And what does the tree do?

Darren   The tree?

Aaron   What does it do?

Darren   The tree does . . .

Aaron   What does it fucking do, Darren?

Darren   Nothing.

Aaron   Fuck all.

Darren   Diddley squat.

Aaron   Stupid green motherfucker.

Darren   Star!

Aaron   See this grass?

Darren   This grass?

Aaron   I hate this grass.

Darren   Yeah, man.

Aaron   I laugh at this grass.

Darren   Excellent.

Aaron   Grass. I laugh at you! From the very bottom of my bollocks. Ha ha ha!

Darren   And I laugh at you too, grass. Ha ha ha!

Aaron   'Cause it's thick!

Darren   The grass is dumb!

Aaron   Just plain stupid.

Darren   For real.

Aaron   See these fish!

Darren   I see them.

Aaron   In the fucking canal.

Darren   I know it.

Aaron   I hate these fish!

Darren   I hate them too.

Aaron   I rape these fish!

Darren   You rape them?

Aaron   Up the batty!

Darren   Fucking thick fish!

Aaron   Waggling fish on my dick, man!

Darren   Right!

Aaron   Big fucking fish waving in the air! Flapping in the breeze.

Darren   Raped!

Aaron   Right!

Darren   Nature!

Aaron   You're thick!

Darren   Nature is thick!

Aaron   I rape it. I piss on it. And I laugh at it. (*Beat.*) Billy.

Billy (*sober*)   What?

Aaron *and* **Darren** *begin to close on him slightly. They pass the joint between each other.*

Aaron   You know nature, Billy?

Billy   Do I know nature?

Aaron   I hate it.

Billy   I know that.

Aaron   I rape it.

Billy   You said.

Aaron   I laugh at it. I piss on it. I think it's fucking funny.

Darren   It makes him chuckle. Giggle.

Aaron   And I think you and your dad are fucked in the head.

Darren   But we like ya.

Aaron   We do.

Darren (*offers* **Billy** *a blast on the joint,* **Billy** *ignores him*) 'Cause you're a funny boy.

Aaron   Nature boy!

Darren   It's lovely.

Aaron   And we like your dad.

Darren   In our own little way.

Aaron   He's all right.

Darren (*treading the joint out*)   He is.

Aaron   For a pervert.

Billy   Aaron.

Aaron   Billy.

Billy   I hope you fucking choke on your ecstasy tablets the next time you take them. I hope they stick in your throat and tear up your insides and burn up the sides of your rectum when you shit.

Billy *goes to collect his bags, tries to leave.*

Aaron   Star!

Scott (*still in the peripheries*)   Did you tell your dad, Billy?

Billy (*freezes*)   What?

Scott   Did you tell him that Ross was asking after him.

Billy (*turns to face him*)   Yeah.

Scott   And that Bergsie is set on him.

Billy   Yes. I did.

Scott   What did he say?

Billy   He's not worried.

Scott   He fucking should be.

Aaron   Damn shitting straight he should be.

Billy   He's not. He said it doesn't matter.

Darren   Did he?

Scott   I would say it mattered a lot.

Darren (*throws his beer bottle away, it smashes*)   He's a prick, man.

Scott   I would say it mattered a hell of a lot, Billy.

Billy   He said it didn't matter because they're not going to be out for ten years.

Scott   They'll be out before then, Billy.

Billy   He said they'll not be out for ten years and that we're not going to be around when they get out.

Scott   You're not going to be around?

Billy   We're going away.

Scott   Where are you going? (*No response. He moves in on him.*) Billy?

Billy   Southend, maybe.

Scott   What?

Billy   Or Portsmouth. Or Brighton, or Cornwall or somewhere, anywhere, somewhere by the sea. Somewhere where there's water.

Scott (*up very close*)   Is that what he said?

Billy (*not turning away*)   That's where we're going.

Scott   He said this, did he?

Billy   It's true.

Scott   When are you going there, Billy?

Billy   Soon.

Scott   Soon? Soon? Soon? When is soon, Billy? For fucksake.

Scott *moves away from* **Billy** *to enjoy the whole space.*

Aaron   He tell this to you?

Billy   Yeah.

Aaron   You believed him, Billy, did you? Did you really?

Scott   When's soon, Billy?

Billy   In a few months. After I've finished school.

Scott (*picks up* **Billy**'s *bag, feels the weight*)   He told you this, Billy. And, Billy, tell me. How is he going to afford to move you somewhere close by to the sea, Billy? How is he going to actually afford to do that exactly?

Billy   He'll get a job.

Scott   Will he? Will he really? (*Lowers his bag down.*) Fucking hell, Billy, you're a fucking wonder!

Aaron (*finishing his beer*)   I like him, Scott!

Scott   I like him too.

Aaron   I think we should keep him!

Billy   Fuck off.

A beat. **Scott** *finishes his own beer bottle, belches and throws it violently away towards the canal.*

Scott (*quietly, controlled, moves close to* **Billy** *again*)   Billy, let me tell you something. Can I? Billy, your dad is a fucking monkey. No one's going to give him a job, Billy. He's never going to leave this place. He's never going to leave this estate, Billy. It won't happen.

Billy   That's not true.

Scott (*gently, he maybe strokes* **Billy**'s *hair*)   It is true, Billy, of course it's fucking true, mate! And he knows it's true. You know what, Billy? He's been fucking lying to you.

Billy   No.

Scott   He's been lying because he's too scared to admit to himself, or to you, what the truth is.

Billy   No.

Scott   That he is just fucked.

Billy   No.

Scott (*prodding at, examining* **Billy**'s *face*)   And you know what, Billy, I think that you know he's been lying to you. I think that you've known all along. It's pathetic, Billy. It's fucked up, mate. It is so fucking fucked up that it's not fucking true!

Aaron *and* **Darren** *have become very still, watchful.*

Billy (*calmly, plucking up courage*)   Scott.

Scott   What?

Billy   Scott.

Scott   What?

Billy   Scott.

Scott   What?

Billy   I heard what you did.

Scott   What?

Billy   I heard what you did to Adele, Scott. And I think you're an arsehole for it, Scott. I think you're a coward. And I hope that your brother gets raped up the arse when he's in prison. Until it bleeds and fucking everything. Because he's a nonce, Scott. And everybody knows that he's a nonce. And everybody hates him and you and your whole family because of it. I hope you realise that. And I hope that you are haunted until the day you die, by the, by the, the ghost of Racheal King. And that you never forget her or what your brother did to her. And that you never, not for one second, ever know what it is to hope. I hope that happens to you, Scott. Because that is what you fucking deserve.

Scott   Billy.

Billy   Because you're a wanker.

Scott   Billy.

Billy   You're a wanker, Scott, and your brother's a nonce and everybody knows it and everybody has always known it.

Scott   Dick.

Scott *puts his fingers into* **Billy**'s *mouth, grabs hold of his cheek and pulls his head towards him. He holds the neck of his T-shirt and headbutts him twice in the face.* **Billy** *crumples and* **Scott** *pushes him to the ground. He kicks him in his side.* **Billy** *is whimpering.*

Scott (*to* **Billy**)   Shut the fuck up. (*To* **Aaron** *and* **Darren**.) Fucking hold him down.

Darren   What?

Scott   You heard me, hold him fucking down.

The two boys do and **Scott** *starts to pull* **Billy**'s *trousers down.*

Aaron (*giggling*)   What you doing, Scott?

Scott   Give me your bottle.

Aaron   You joking?

Scott   Fucking give it to me.

Billy   NO!

Scott   Give me your fucking bottle, Aaron.

He does. **Scott** *takes it and goes to force it up* **Billy**'s *rectum.* **Billy** *screams.*

Aaron   Shit, Scott, man. Take it easy, boy.

Scott   Don't you fucking tell me what to do. Don't you fucking dare tell me what to do.

Darren (*scared*)   Scott, man, please don't.

Scott (*snarled at* **Darren**)   What did you say? What did you fucking say?

Darren *and* **Aaron** *pull back, frightened by* **Scott** *and appalled by what he has done.* **Billy** *has stopped screaming and is sobbing now, hysterically but quietly. As the attack continues* **Scott** *becomes increasingly scared.*

Scott   This boy is fucking dead. He's a fucking deadbeat. This boy is a fucking deadbeat. (*To* **Billy**.) This is from Ross, Billy. A little fucking anniversary thank you. (*Rams hard once with the bottle.*) And this is from Bergsie. For everything you and your fucking dad have fucking done to my family. (*And repeats each time.*) This is from Adele. This is from your dad. And this is from your mum. And this is from your Danny. And this is from your Leanne. (*Stopping, crying.*) Nobody tells me what to do. Nobody speaks to me like that. Nobody speaks about my brother like that. Nobody speaks about my brother. Nobody speaks about me. Nobody.

Lights fade. Music briefly.

Lights rise on **Billy** *sitting alone, reading from his book. The lights reveal that it is a new day, perhaps sometime in the afternoon. He flicks back a couple of pages, forward a couple. He starts to write something but doesn't. He closes his book. He stares out for a few moments. For a moment he seems to be watching something move on the far bank of the water.* **Adele** *joins him on stage. He doesn't acknowledge her* *approach. He sits staring out front.* **Adele** *stands behind him watching him with great caution. She speaks with great gentleness and concern. He is even, detached.*

Adele Are you all right?

Billy Yes.

Adele Are you sure?

Billy I'm fine.

Adele I heard what they did. Aaron told me. I think you should think about phoning the police.

Billy . . .

Adele Billy, did it hurt you?

Billy You know what happened when my dad phoned the police.

Adele Did they hurt you, Billy?

Billy Yes.

Adele Maybe you should go to the hospital.

Billy I'll be all right.

Adele Maybe it will be easier when you leave.

Pause.

Billy Maybe.

Adele *moves closer.*

Adele He's a cunt. One day he's going to suffer. He's so going to suffer, Billy.

Billy Yes. He will.

Adele (*edging closer*) I used to watch him with Steph, his little sister. She's nine years old now, Billy. She's a sweet little girl. He used to punch her in the face with the ball of his hand to get her to do what he wanted her to do. And the stupid thing is that Ross was just the same with him. And he used to hate it. And his dad. You know some people can turn rooms horrible? They can twist the atmosphere of a room without actually doing anything. Scott's dad's like that. (*She sits with him, still looking at him.*) Billy, I'm so sorry.

Billy   It wasn't your fault.

Pause.

Adele   Did he say anything about me?

Billy   No.

Adele   Sometimes he lies about me.

Billy   He didn't this time.

Adele   He tells people all kinds of shit.

Billy   He didn't even mention your name.

Adele   He tells people that we slept together. Which isn't true. We never did. I've never slept with anybody, Billy. I haven't. Honestly.

Billy   Why are you telling me this?

Adele   Billy, talk to me.

Billy   What do you want to talk about, Adele?

Adele   I want to make sure that you're all right. I feel guilty. I feel that it was in some way my fault what happened to you.

Billy   You want to feel better about it all?

Adele   Billy, don't. (*Beat.*) I just want to talk to you.

Pause.

Billy, what are you going to do?

Long pause.

Billy   You should have been here earlier. There was a heron. Just sat on the other side of the canal. Down by Goresbrook House. It was magical. Sat still as stone.

Dropped into the water. Like a lead ball. Came up with a carp in between its teeth.

Adele (*turning away from him*)   I hate it when you go like this.

Billy   Like what, Adele?

Adele   I hate it when this happens.

Billy   When what happens?

Adele   I feel sick. Nervous. I feel like I'm waiting for something terrible.

Billy   Nothing terrible's going to happen, Adele.

Adele   When I was a kid, when I was little, I was suspended from my primary school. Because I took a kitchen knife into my class. And I warned people not to go near me. Because I was feeling sick and I was worried and I didn't know what I was worried about so I panicked about everybody. It felt exactly like this. It makes me feel that I'm too fat. That I'm ugly. That my skin is horrible. That my clothes are shit. It's how I feel, Billy, when I'm going to have one of my fits.

Long pause. **Billy** *looks at her for a short time. Looks away again.* **Adele** *still stares out.*

Adele (*turning to him*) . Billy. Can I see your book?

Billy (*to her*)   Why?

Adele   I want to know what it is that you write.

Billy   Why?

Adele   I want to understand how it helps.

He passes it to her. Looks back out. She opens it at the beginning. Reads a page. Flicks forward a chunk. And back. Reading random pages with great care.

What are these numbers at the end of each day?

Billy   They're all the people who have passed by where I fish. I count them.

Adele   Why?

Billy   I have no idea.

She reads more.

Adele   You write down all the graffiti.

Billy   . . .

She reads more.

Adele   I like this. Can I read a bit to you? 'Some of the people look like sticks. They look like they could snap. They have nodules in odd places.' I think that's very true.

She finds a new passage and reads it with care.

'When the sky gets blue like this it makes the colours on the buildings seem more acute. The orange of the chemist. The blue colour of the bookies.' (*Beat.*) Who's Leanne? And Danny?

Billy   They're my brother and sister.

Adele   I didn't know you had a brother and a sister.

Billy   They live with my mum.

Adele   Do they? How come?

Billy   They're younger than I am.

Adele   So?

Billy   I decided that I wanted to leave and come and live with my dad. They were too young to decide for themselves. So they stayed. I don't see them very often.

Adele   Do you miss them?

Billy   Yeah. I do.

Adele   Why don't you go and see them?

Billy   Because then I'd have to see my mum and I really don't want to see her.

Adele   Why not?

Billy (*as though confused by the question, it's so obvious*)   Because I hate her, Adele.

Adele   Why?

Billy (*almost spat at her*)   Why do *you* want to know?

Adele (*not flinching*)   Don't be angry.

They establish and then maintain eye contact.

Billy   I've got every right to be angry. Why do you want to know about my mum?

Adele   I just want to talk to you.

Billy   I hate her because she's vicious. She's horrible. She's horrible to me. And she's horrible to Danny and Leanne and she was horrible to my dad.

Adele   Was she?

Billy   She's a wino. A pisshead. A cruel drunken bitch.

Adele *lets him continue.*

Billy   One time, when she'd been on the drink, she hit me. She beat me up. She did. She got my head by my hair, this is, what, when I was nine years old. She got my head by my hair and she smacked it against the radiator in our front room until I was sick and until my head started to bleed. So I rang my dad up and told him what happened and he came to get me. And now he looks after me. Danny and Leanne were too young to come with us.

Adele   Fucking hell, Billy.

Billy   What?

Adele   I never realised.

Billy   People say all this stuff about Dad and what he's like and what he does. And none of it is ever true, Adele. They don't have the slightest idea.

Adele   Have you told him what happened?

Billy   No.

Adele   Maybe you should tell him.

Billy (*turns away*)   No.

Adele   Billy.

Billy   Do you know what I want most of all in the world?

Adele   What?

Billy   I want him to be all right. I want him to get over everything that Mum did to him. And I want him to get over, to just get over finding Racheal.

Adele   It won't happen.

Billy   What?

Adele   He won't get over finding Racheal. People don't get over something like that.

He refuses to look back to her so she returns to the book. She finds something there.

What's this?

Billy   Do you know what worries me?

Adele   What's this, Billy?

Billy   It worries me that I'm going to end up like him. Broken up like that.

Adele   Billy, what's this about?

Billy   What?

Adele (*reading*)   'She stands for maybe thirty seconds and then carries on walking. Doesn't say anything. Sometimes she looks at me or at Dad. She has blonde hair. Huge eyes.

She looks very sad and she looks fragile sometimes, like an eggshell. And other times she looks hard and cruel.' Billy? 'She has a small scar underneath her right eye. I watch the way she moves. I watch the rise and fall of her breathing. And the way her legs move when she walks. I watch her all the time.'

Billy (*standing, going for the book*)   Don't read that bit.

Adele (*standing with him, guarding it*)   Billy, is this about me?

Billy   Can I have my book back please, Adele?

Adele   Have you been writing about me, Billy?

Billy   Give me my book back.

Adele   Billy.

Face to face. Close.

Billy   What?

Adele   What is it that you want from me?

Billy   I just want. I just don't want you to go.

Michelle *enters. She pulls out a cigarette. Some time.* **Adele** *keeps watching* **Billy** *closely.*

Michelle   Is that a new jacket, Billy? It suits you. You look really smart, darling.

Billy   Mum.

Adele *leaves. She straightens the collar of* **Billy**'s *jacket before she does.* **Billy** *turns to his mum.*

Michelle   You always did used to look after your clothes, didn't you? You always took such a lot of pride in your, in your appearance. What you wore. Your hair, all of that. I remember.

Billy (*moving to her*)   Mum, I want to see Danny and Leanne.

Michelle (*joining him, moves to touch him but he gives nothing*)
They want to see you too, Billy. They ask about you all the
time.

Billy (*standing firm*)   Because we're going away. Me and
Dad. We're going away and I want to see them to tell them
where we're going and how they can get in touch with me.

Michelle   I see.

Billy (*still*)   But I don't want to come round.

Michelle   Where are you going?

Billy   I'm not going to come round to the house so I need
you to give a message to them.

Michelle (*lights the cigarette*)   Where are you going, Billy,
the two of you?

Billy   I'm not going to tell you, Mum.

Michelle   What?

Billy   I don't have to. I shouldn't even be here. If Dad
knew I was talking to you he'd go, he'd . . . He'd kill you.

Michelle   Why won't you tell me where you're going,
Billy?

Billy   Because where we go, you're never going to find us.
I'm not going to let you.

Michelle (*replacing her lighter*)   Billy, doll, don't be silly.

Billy   I'm not being silly, Mum, I'm being serious. (*Beat.
Closer still.*) Will you tell them to come and meet me?

Michelle   You can't stop me coming to see you, Billy –

Billy   I can, Mum. And I will. Will you tell them?

Michelle (*doing up her coat*)   How can you?

Billy   Will you?

Michelle (*perplexed, not bitter, moving slightly away from him*) How can you do this?

Billy   What?

Michelle (*turns back*)   How can you have become so hard?

Billy   You what?

Michelle   You never even talk to me.

Billy   Mum.

Michelle   You look at me as though you hate me.

Billy   After everything you did.

Michelle   Billy, what – ?

Billy (*cutting her off*)   You hit me so hard that it made me sick.

Beat. They talk over each other.

You used to say such terrible, horrible fucked-up just fucking shit –

Michelle   And I'm sorry, Billy, please –

Billy   – And what you did to Dad.

Michelle   To Charlie?

Billy   When you were on the drink, Mum, you did so many things that were just disgusting. Despicable.

Face to face.

Michelle (*over his next speech*)   Billy. Billy. Billy. Billy.

Billy (*bursting with a need to tell her*)   I remember, do you remember, that time, after Dad moved out, when you brought those fellas round. Those two bastards from Kempton's Bar? And told Dad to come and see you. And they were waiting there. When he arrived. They were waiting for him. Do you remember that?

Michelle   Billy.

Billy   They had bicycle chains, Mum, didn't they, and they just fucking beat him up so badly and I was watching. I was watching all the time. You knew I was and you still let them do it.

Michelle (*moving closer*)   I didn't know.

Billy   Of course you knew!

Michelle   Billy.

Billy (*containing himself*)   Will you give Danny and Leanne a message?

Michelle (*treads her cigarette out*)   You're not going anywhere.

Billy   I want them to come and meet me. Here. At three thirty tomorrow.

Michelle (*smiling, moving towards him*)   Charlie won't take you anywhere.

Billy (*standing defiant*)   He will.

Michelle   Charlie won't leave.

Billy   He will.

Michelle   He couldn't.

Billy   He's going to.

Michelle   He couldn't. He couldn't, Billy, because he couldn't leave me.

Billy (*exasperated, perhaps looking around as though trying to find somewhere to run to*)   What? What are you talking about?

Michelle (*close up*)   He couldn't leave me, Billy. He needs me too much.

Billy   You're cracking up, Mum.

Michelle (*calm, gentle*)   I'm not, Billy. He needs me too much. He loves me too much. Billy, he rings me all the time, love.

Billy   No he doesn't.

Michelle (*standing the collar of his jacket up*)   Billy, love, I'm not going to lie to you.

Billy   He doesn't.

Michelle (*very gently, perhaps stroking his face*)   He does. He speaks to Danny and Leanne. He talks to me for hours. He told me that he wanted to see me again. He won't leave, Billy, he just won't.

Billy (*backing off but not turning away*)   Fuck off.

Michelle   Billy.

Billy   Just fuck off. You liar. You fucking lying cunt.

Michelle   Billy.

His movements become slightly hysterical. Perhaps he hits himself as he backs off.

Billy   He wouldn't do that to me, after everything you did to me? No way would he do that. No way would he do that. You fucking lying bitch cunt.

Michelle   Billy, don't go.

Billy *moves away, upstage.* **Michelle** *watches him as he grabs his diary, opens it, and grasping his pen in the fist of his hand writes down his furious last note. She leaves gently. He reads some of his writing out loud as he writes. Perhaps he becomes isolated by light. He is exhausted. Gathers his breath. He speaks hurriedly. Pausing to recover his breath at points. His voice occasionally breaking. Perhaps bent over as though suffering from a stitch.*

Billy   This is the final entry into this journal. It is Friday. Today the sky is more purely blue than I can remember seeing it before. It seems terrible and huge and magnificent. This is everything.

He begins to change from writing into scribbling. Vicious sharp lines that almost tear the pages. And, shaking, he starts to tear up the pages of his book.

Isolating light falls on **Billy**.

Darkness. Perhaps music.

The lights rise again with **Aaron**, **Darren** *and* **Scott** *sat around the stage. Still drinking. Still smoking.* **Darren** *rolls a scrawny joint.* **Billy**, *some distance behind them, holds his dad's gun to* **Scott**'s *head. Until he speaks the boys don't notice him. He speaks calmly. He chooses his words with great care and he reasons with very simple, straightforward logic.* **Scott** *doesn't pay any attention at first. Perhaps we don't see the gun for a few moments.*

Billy   You need to apologise to me.

Aaron (*seeing the gun, confused*)   Billy?

Billy   You need to apologise to me.

Darron (*seeing the gun, alarmed*)   Fucking hell.

Scott   What?

Billy   What you did to me was unforgivable.

Scott *turns round and sees the gun.* **Aaron** *and* **Darren** *are slightly paralysed by surprise.*

Scott   Billy, for fucksake –

Billy (*interrupting him, calmly reasoning, pointing the gun clearly now*)   What you did, the things which you did. You shouldn't treat people like that.

Scott   Christ, Billy, is that real?

Billy (*coming forward*)   It's my dad's. He uses it for shooting herons because they kill his fish. And he uses it for protection against robbers. And if you don't apologise to me, Scott, I'm going to shoot you in your head.

Scott (*scrambling backwards*)   For fucksake, Billy, what –

Billy   For all this time. For all the money I've given you. For all the things that have happened here. All the things which you have said to me. All the things which you have done and which Aaron and Darren have done to try to impress you.

Scott   Billy, please.

Billy   And the things which you've said about my dad. And the things which you've said about my mum. And my brother and my sister.

Scott (*becoming more frightened*)   Oh! Fucking fuck.

Billy   And the things which you did to Adele.

Scott   No. No. No. No.

Billy   And what you did to me. Scott. What you did to me. You need to apologise to me for these things. Because it's just not fair. It's just not right, Scott.

Scott   I wasn't –

Billy   You need to apologise, Scott.

Scott   I'm sorry. I'm sorry. I'm sorry. I'm sorry. It wasn't me.

Billy   How do you know about my brother and sister, Scott?

Scott   What?

Billy   You heard me.

Scott   My sister knows them. My sister knows your Leanne. They're in the same class together. At primary school.

Billy *takes this in for a while. Might be backing off and then . . .*

Billy (*closing in*)   What did you mean it wasn't you, Scott?

Scott (*terrified now*)   I mean, I, I don't know. I mean. Shit. Please don't kill me.

Billy (*tighter*)   What did you mean it wasn't you?

Scott (*folding in on himself*)   I try. I try. I try. I try. I lose my temper. I try really hard to, to just. I try so fucking hard, Billy, but it's so fucked.

Billy   What is?

Scott   It's so mad. Please. It's just difficult because it's so. Terrible.

Billy   What is, Scott?

Scott   With, with, with Ross and with what you said and what happened and all that shit. People don't. Please don't, don't, don't hurt me, Billy.

Billy   That's not enough.

Scott   Please don't hurt me, Billy.

Billy   It's not enough.

Aaron (*frightened, maybe crying*)   Billy.

Darren (*the same*)   Billy, don't, for fucksake.

They perhaps move towards him, very cautious.

Billy   Shut up, fucking shut up just, honestly, just shut up. Or I swear I'll, I'll, I will kill him.

They freeze.

Scott   Please. I'm so sorry.

Billy   Are you scared, Scott?

Scott   What?

Billy   Are you scared?

Scott   Yes.

Billy   How scared are you, Scott?

Scott   I'm not my brother. I'm not my dad. I'm not . . .

Billy   Answer my question.

Scott   I'm so very scared. I don't want to die, Billy.

Billy I've nothing left to lose, Scott.

Scott Please, Billy.

Billy (*standing almost over him, like an executioner*) I've nothing left to lose any more. You took it all away from me, Scott. You and your brother. And what you did to my dad. And my mum. And this place. And all of this.

Scott I'm only fifteen, Billy.

Billy I'm fucking fourteen, Scott, you idiot.

Billy *pulls the trigger. The first chamber on the barrel is empty.* **Scott** *is terrified. A sharp, loud intake of breath. He sobs hysterically, pleading.* **Aaron** *and* **Darren** *are petrified.*

Scott Please. Billy, Billy, Billy, please. I don't want to die, Billy. I want to live, Billy.

Billy What for, Scott?

He pulls the trigger for the second time. Again an empty chamber. Another gasp for breath from **Scott***.*

There's nothing left for us now, Scott, is there?

He pulls the trigger for the third time. The chamber is again empty.

A moment. **Scott** *sobbing.* **Aaron** *and* **Darren** *stunned.* **Billy** *in total control. He grins.*

The sound of the water in the lock.

The lights fade to darkness.

They rise fairly quickly.

Billy *sits alone on stage. It is the morning. He stares out to the audience for some moments. Exhausted. Frightened. Moved.*

Adele *joins him. She is extremely cautious. Moves towards him.*

Adele Billy?

Billy Yeah?

Adele Did you kill him?

Long pause.

Billy   I saw my mum last night.

Adele (*moving closer*)   Oh yeah?

Billy   I told her to tell Leanne and Danny to come here. At three thirty. I hope she told them.

Adele   Did you kill him, Billy?

Billy   She was funny. She made me laugh. With her fucking stupid coat on and that.

Adele   Billy.

Billy   I don't want to talk about it, Adele. (*Pause. Looking away.*) If you could be any animal in the world, Adele. Any animal at all, other than a human being, what would you be?

Adele (*looking away*)   I don't know. A cat.

Billy (*looking to* **Adele**)   Why?

Adele   Just so you can sleep and that.

Billy (*looking away*)   I'd be a fish, I reckon.

Adele   Why would you be a fish?

Billy   Because they have no memory. They just swim around. If you have no memory you're never frightened about stuff.

Adele (*looking to* **Billy**)   What are you frightened about, Billy?

Billy   Everything that I can remember.

Adele   Everything?

Billy   Cats eat fish.

Adele   Everything, Billy?

Billy   But then cats are scared of water so I'd be able to swim away. (*Looking to* **Adele**.) Are you all right?

Adele   Am I all right?

Billy   Last time I saw you you said you were feeling nervous. Anxious.

Adele   No . . .

Billy   You said you felt like you felt when you were going to have a fit.

Pause.

Adele   I think I'm fine now, Billy, thanks. I think it's passed.

Billy (*new thought*)   Aren't you?

Adele   What?

Billy   Frightened of the things you can remember?

Adele   Some things. But some things I'm not.

Billy   Which ones aren't you?

Adele   I remember when my niece was born. I was there. I saw her getting born. That wasn't frightening. That was amazing.

Billy   Was it?

Adele   It was beautiful.

Billy   How old is she now?

Adele   She's three years old. I love her, y'know? She's very enthusiastic about things. (*Beat.*) Have the police been round?

Billy   It's a good age, Adele, isn't it?

Adele   Have they?

Billy (*looking away*)   It is, though, isn't it? That age? Don't you think? It's very creative.

Adele   Billy?

Billy   Can I ask you a question?

Adele   You answer mine first.

Billy (*looking back to* **Adele**)   Mine's important.

Adele   Have the police been round, Billy?

Billy   I don't know. I've not been home. I've not seen my dad. If they'd been he'd come and find me.

Adele   Did you kill him, Billy?

Billy   You said I could ask my question.

Adele   Did you shoot him?

Billy   You promised.

Adele   Go on.

Billy   Where did you get your scar from? On your cheek?

Adele (*after a beat*)   When my dad found out that I knew Bergsie and Ross, after I told him about Racheal's ghost, he smacked me with his belt.

Billy   Across your face?

Adele (*looking away*)   He just gets angry with stuff.

Billy   I see.

Adele   It doesn't worry me.

Billy   What was he like?

Adele   Who?

Billy   Bergsie?

Adele   You have to answer my second question first. Before I answer yours.

Billy   No. You first this time, Adele. What was he like?

Adele   He was very quiet. He didn't say much. I think he was nervous a lot of the time. I never found out about where

he came from or anything but I always had the impression
that it was horrible.

Billy   How?

Adele   Just the way he moved and stuff. He always looked
frightened that anything could happen.

Billy (*also looking away*)   I used to think Scott was like that.

Adele   No. Not Scott. (*Looking at* **Billy**.) Scott was nowhere
near. You answer my question now. (*Pause.*) Billy. (*Pause.*)
Did you kill Scott?

Some time. **Billy** *looks away out to the audience.* **Adele** *watches
him.*

Billy   No. Of course I didn't.

Adele   Thank God, Billy.

Billy   Why?

Adele   Just thank God, is all.

Billy   It was funny.

Adele   What?

Billy   He wanted so badly to live, Adele.

Adele   What?

Billy   He was crying. Like a little baby and everything.

Adele   Billy . . .

Billy   I thought there must be a reason for him wanting to
stay alive so badly.

Adele   He was scared you were going to shoot him in the
head.

Billy   I was thinking about Ross, Adele, and Bergsie. I
think I know why they were so scared. I think that they
realised what I realised when I saw Scott like that. The way
that things are wonderful. The way that colours work. The

sound of things and the way they smell, Adele. But they couldn't handle it. So they got frightened. And I started to figure out how everything joins up, Adele.

Adele   What?

Billy   The blue sky. And the flowers in the towpath.

Adele   What?

Billy   Everything is just joined up. . .

Pause. He looks to her.

Adele, I'm so glad you stayed.

Adele   I wanted to check that you were all right. I wanted to find out if you'd hurt him or if you'd got hurt. Or if the police had found you.

Billy   I was thinking about my test. I was trying to figure out what I'd say if I got asked if I deserved to go to heaven or if I should really go to hell. I think I deserve to go to heaven, I do. I think I really fucking do and all.

She holds his eye contact. He looks away again.

If the police find me, if they come, what do you think they'll do?

Adele   I don't know.

Billy (*back to her*)   Do you think that this means that I won't be able to leave here now, Adele?

Charlie *arrives on stage and moves slowly to join* **Billy** *and* **Adele**. **Adele** *sees him first. For a long time very little is said. It should be clear that* **Charlie** *knows that something bad has happened. There is a difference, a caution in the way that he moves or the way that he looks at his son that we haven't seen before. We can infer from this that the police have been round. He sits down next to* **Billy**. *The three of them look out at the canal together.* **Charlie** *rolls a cigarette but doesn't light it.*

Charlie   Billy.

Billy   Dad.

Charlie (*to* **Billy**)   You all right?

Billy (*to his dad*)   I'm fine, yeah.

Charlie   Good man.

Charlie *goes to light his cigarette but is interrupted by* **Billy**.

Billy   This is Adele.

Charlie   Sorry?

Billy   This is my friend Adele, Dad.

Charlie   Oh. All right, Adele.

Adele   All right.

Long pause. They look out again. This time his memory stops
Charlie *from lighting up.*

Charlie   Funny.

Billy   What is?

Charlie   I was thinking. On the way here.

Billy   What?

Charlie   Used to come here when you was a baby.
Sometimes. If I, like, if I was looking after you for the day
and that. I'd bring you down here. Used to look at the birds
and that. See if we could see the ducks. And the herons and
everything. You used to love all that. When you was just like
a little baby and everything. (*Pause.*) Billy.

Billy   Yeah.

Charlie   Billy, the, er, the police come round.

Billy   I see.

Charlie (*looking to* **Billy**)   They told us what happened,
Billy.

Billy   Right.

Charlie   Billy, what have you done, mate?

Billy (*turns to his dad*)   Dad, I didn't touch him. Dad, I didn't do nothing. I just . . .

Charlie   Billy.

Billy   I fucked it up, Dad. I'm sorry.

Charlie   Yeah, I know you are, son. It's all right.

Billy   Is it?

Charlie   Where's the gun, Billy, where d'you put the gun?

Billy (*looks out*)   I threw it in the canal.

Charlie (*slight laugh*)   Did you?

Billy   Yeah.

Charlie (*looks out*)   Right.

Long pause.

Billy (*looks to his dad*)   I saw Mum again, Dad. Yesterday. Dad, do you still ring her?

Charlie (*faces him*)   What?

Billy   Do you ring her, on the telephone? Speak to her and Leanne and Danny?

Charlie   No.

Billy   It's just what she said.

Charlie   It's not true.

Billy   Good, I'm glad. (*Beat. They both look out again.*) What did you tell the police?

Charlie   I told them to fuck off. That I hadn't seen you for two years. That you lived with your mum and I asked them if they could leave me alone and stop causing me so much anxiety.

Billy   Right.

Charlie (*looking to him*)   Do you know what I like about you?

Billy   What?

Charlie   You're very straightforward. You're very honest. It makes you seem quite, like, quite simple.

Billy   Right. (*Pause. Half turns to him.*) Dad.

Charlie   Yeah.

Billy   Dad, I've decided. I'm going. When the summer comes. When school's finished. I'm leaving. I just, I just am.

Charlie   I see.

Billy   I can't stay here for ever, Dad. It's just too difficult.

Charlie   I know.

Billy   You can come with me if you want to but I'm definitely, I'm just definitely just going.

Charlie   Right.

Billy   I'm going to go to Southend, I think. Or Brighton. Or Portsmouth. Somewhere where there's sea.

Charlie   I think that's a good idea, Billy.

Long pause. All three looking out.

Billy   Should we go home now?

Charlie   Yeah, let's go home.

There is a long pause as the three of them stare out front. Occasionally **Adele** *glances at the two of them. Occasionally* **Billy** *catches her glance. Lights fade. 'Can I Pass?' by the Rebel plays to close.*

Port

Nicky. Betty. Hazel. Christine. Sharon. Jane. Ta.

This play, like everything, is for Poll.

'Suppose, just suppose, nothing had ever happened.
Suppose this was for the first time. It doesn't hurt to
suppose. Say none of the other had happened. You know
what I mean? Then what? I said.'

Raymond Carver, *Chef's House*

Port was first performed at the Royal Exchange Theatre, Manchester, on 12 November 2002. The cast was as follows:

Racheal Keats	Emma Lowndes
Billy Keats	Andrew Sheridan
Danny Miller	William Ash
Christine Keats/Anne Dickinson	Siobhan Finneran
Jonathan Keats/Kevin Brake	Nicholas Siddi
Ronald Abbey/Jake Moran	Fred Ridgeway
Chris Bennet	Colin Parry
Lucy Moore	Rachel Brogan

Directed by Marianne Elliott
Designed by Rae Smith
Lighting by John Buswell
Sound by Ian Dickinson

Characters

Racheal Keats, *eleven–twenty-four*
Billy Keats, *six–ten / nineteen*
Danny Miller, *fifteen / twenty-four*
Christine Keats, *twenty-nine* ⎫
Anne Dickinson, *seventy-four* ⎬
Jonathan Keats, *thirty-four* ⎫
Kevin Brake, *twenty-eight* ⎬
Lucy Moore, *fifteen*
Chris Bennett, *fifteen*
Ronald Abbey, *fifty* ⎫
Jake Moran, *forty-eight* ⎬
Man in Home, *seventy-three* ⎭

The characters that are bracketed together should be played by the same actor. Although distinct there are fundamental shared resonances in their relationships with Racheal Keats.

The play takes place in a variety of locations in and around Stockport, Greater Manchester, between 1988 and 2002.

The set should remain spare and non-naturalistic throughout. The locations should be evoked by space, detail and lighting rather than replicated.

The character of Racheal Keats must remain on stage throughout the play. In between scenes we should be able to observe the adoption of nuances of physicality, aspect and dress that the actor employs in order to dramatise her increasing maturity.

An interval may fall after Scene Five.

A note on punctuation:
 – denotes interruption or a sudden halt
 . . . denotes a trailing off

Scene One

1988. A parked Vauxhall Cavalier in the car park of the flats on Lancashire Hill in Stockport. We should see the exposed interior of the car towards one edge of the stage. A real Vauxhall Cavalier should be used. The top of the car should be sawn off.

Isolating light on the car.

Racheal Keats, *eleven years old, sits in the passenger seat eating a bar of Dairy Milk.* **Billy Keats**, *six years old, sits slumped on the back seat. She wears a blue Adidas tracksuit top over her school uniform. He wears a huge battered Kappa coat over his.* **Christine Keats**, *their mother, twenty-nine years old, sits in the driver's seat.*

It is midnight.

Christine Keats *stares fixedly up at the fifth-floor flat where she lives with her children. Her husband, their father,* **Jonathan**, *is in there.*

The children are lively, excited. Throughout the scene the children's activity should be uninhibited, exploratory.

Christine *is desperately trying to ignore her children. This is her only means of tolerating their excitement.*

Billy *kicks the back of* **Racheal**'s *seat repeatedly. We should see his kicking. Maybe he sits raised up on the back seat. Maybe he even stands.*

Racheal   Billy.

He continues.

Billy, stop it.

He doesn't.

Billy, stop kicking me. God!

Billy   What?

Racheal   Mum. Tell him.

Billy   I'm not doing anything.

Racheal   Mum, will you tell him? He keeps kicking the back of my chair.

Billy   I don't. It's her.

Christine (*without turning*)   Billy, stop it. Now.

Billy   God. I'm not doing anything. Always sticking up for her. She's always lying about me. Always saying I'm doing stuff when I'm never. 'S so not fair.

Christine (*with a glare*)   Billy, one more word. I'm warning yer.

Billy *slumps back in his chair. Gives her the finger behind her back.*

Pause.

He kneels up on the back seat and looks out of the side and back windows of the car.

Billy   Mum.

Christine   What?

Billy   Mum.

Christine   What?

Billy   Mum.

Christine   What, Billy, for fuck's sake?

Billy   When are we going to Disney World Florida?

Christine   Oh, Jesus fucking Christ, Billy, would you shut your gob for one second, would yer? For fuck's sake.

He slumps back on the car seat. Huffs. Glares daggers into her back. Brief time.

Racheal   Mum. You know what Billy told me? You know what he told me? He told me. He goes. You know that path up our school, Mum?

Billy (*sitting up, urgent*)   I never.

He pushes his head between the front two seats.

Racheal (*grinning*)   He goes, if you walk off that path. If you go off the side of it and hop up and down three times –

Billy (*trying to thump her*)   I never. Liar.

Racheal (*chuckling, ignoring the thumps*)   You did, Billy. Stop lying. He goes, if you do that, he goes, you go to a magic place.

Billy (*slumping back, pissed off*)   I never said that.

Racheal (*with a big bite of chocolate*)   He's a dickhead.

Billy   I hate you.

Racheal   Int he, Mum? Int he a dickhead?

Billy   Shut it.

Racheal   No.

Billy   I'm gonna kill you.

Racheal (*with delighted mock horror*)   Mum. You hear that? You hear what he says? Mum heard that! You're going to go to Borstal now.

Billy   Fuck off.

Christine   Billy, shut it.

Christine *turns in her seat and smacks* **Billy** *in the face.* **Billy** *sits back in his chair. Holds his head down. Tries not to sob.* **Christine** *glares back at the window.* **Racheal** *sits still.*

Racheal   He should be asleep. Shouldn't he? Mum? Shouldn't he be asleep? Tell him, Mum. Tell him to go to sleep. He'll be knackered tomorrow. Falling asleep on his desk and that. Dribbling on his books. Proper gypsy. Should see him. I've seen him in assembly. Snoring. He's a right tramp.

Billy (*through his teeth*)   Am not.

Racheal   I saw Mrs Greenside with him. She was dead mad. Should have seen her. She gets him. Right in front of everyone. In her class and that. In juniors. And she gets him to the front of the class and she pulls his pants down and smacks his bum. Bare and everything. He was crying. Weren't yer?

Billy (*after a pause*)   No.

Racheal (*finishing the chocolate*)   You were, Billy. I saw you.

Billy   I weren't, right?

Christine (*still staring up at window*)   Go to sleep, Billy.

Pause. **Billy** *lies down on back seat.*

Billy   Can't.

Christine   You're not trying. Close yer eyes.

Some time. **Billy** *is still.*

Racheal (*quietly*)   Mum.

Christine   What?

Racheal   Why's our Billy always getting run over?

Christine   I don't know.

Racheal   Three times now, int it? Normal people don't get run over three times. Do they, Mum?

Christine   I don't know.

Racheal   I hate Mrs Greenside. She's got really bony wrists.

Silence.

He's going to sleep now. (*Singing, gently.*) 'Rock-a-bye baby on the tree top. When the wind the wind blows the cradle will rock –'

Christine   Shut it, Rachel. Fucking going on.

Racheal   I were only singing.

Christine   Well, don't.

Racheal   I was trying to get him to sleep.

Christine   Well, leave him.

Pause.

Racheal (*with a big shrug*)   Mum.

Christine   What?

Racheal   You remember when I got my hand caught int'
mangle?

Christine   You what?

Racheal   Did that hurt?

Christine   What?

Racheal   Did it hurt when I got my hand caught int'
mangle and that?

Christine   I don't know, do I? It were your hand.

Racheal   I don't remember it. Probably blanked it out of
my memory, an't I? What's the first thing you can
remember?

Christine (*still watching window*)   I don't know.

Racheal   You know what first thing I can remember is?

Christine   No.

Racheal   I remember finding that dead sparrow. In our
yard. You remember that? When I did that. Picked it up.
Put it in a paper tissue. You remember? Bring it to you? All
the bones and that. Dead tiny. You went crackers.

No response. Some time.

*She thinks aloud, counting aloud, proving something that she learned at
school to her mum.*

Next it'll be next year. And then it'll be two years and that'll
be the new decade and that'll be the nineties and then it'll
be ten years and that'll be the new century. We did that at
school.

No response. **Christine** *watches the window. Some time.*

I'll be twenty-three. God!

No response. Some time.

You know summit?

Christine (*still at window, but conceding gently*)   What?

Racheal   Sometimes, when you fart, it smells quite nice. You ever notice that? Yer own farts and that.

Christine (*turns to her*)   Racheal!

Racheal   It's true.

Christine   You're disgusting.

Racheal   You know summit else I think?

Christine   What?

Racheal   I think this is nice.

Beat. **Christine** *looks at her. Then back at the window.*

Christine   It's not.

Racheal   I think it is. I think it's all right. I do. I like it. You know what it's like? You remember when I was little. In the morning sometimes. You used to get us. Put us in your bed. To keep you warm. Always said I was like your hot-water bottle. Didn't you? You remember that? Mum? Do you? It's like that, I reckon.

Christine *looks at her briefly. Lights a cigarette and then looks back up at the window.* **Racheal** *opens another bar of Dairy Milk.*

Racheal   Shouldn't smoke. Not with our Billy asleep and that. Wind window down.

Christine   It's freezing.

Beat.

Racheal   You know when I grow up?

Christine   Yeah.

Racheal   You know who I want to be like?

Christine   Who?

Racheal   Leanne's mum.

Christine (*turning to her*)   You what?!?

Racheal   I think she's beautiful, I do.

Christine   You do not.

Racheal   I do. I think she's dead glamorous and everything.

Christine   Racheal, she's a fucking whore.

Racheal   So! That's what I want to be then!

Christine   Racheal!

Racheal   I do! I think she's beautiful. You should dress like her, Mum. You should. All the make-up and that.

Christine (*away again*)   You don't know what you're talking about.

Pause. **Racheal** *scans the windows of the car. Kneels up in her passenger seat to look around her. Perhaps sits on the top of the passenger door.*

Racheal   I like it here.

Christine   Do you?

Racheal   I like the park. Me and Leanne go up park sometimes. Did you know that?

Christine   No.

Racheal   We do.

Christine   You should watch it.

Racheal   Come and look for men.

Christine   For what?

Racheal   Men come up park sometimes. Get their willies out. We look for 'em. Scream at 'em. Peg it. It's dead funny.

Christine *laughs despite herself.* **Racheal** *puffs up with pride.*

Christine   You wanna watch that. All the perverts and that. Racheal, honestly.

Racheal   Ronald Abbey. He's a pervert. (*Beat.*) Can see the river from here. It's good down there. Stinks. But there's good stuff.

Christine   What sort of stuff?

Racheal   Just stuff that people leave. I like the water.

Christine (*serious*)   Racheal, it's filthy.

Racheal   I still like it.

Christine (*firmly*)   You better not go swimming in it.

Racheal   You what?

Christine   That water's filthy. You better not go swimming in it.

Racheal   Course not. I'm not thick, am I? Look, Mum. Can see clock tower in Merseyway. It's massive. It's a skyscraper that is, int it? Mum?

Christine   Is it fuck a skyscraper.

Racheal   I think it is. (*Long silence. She yawns. Looks up to her mother.*) Smells of tarmac.

Christine   What does?

Racheal   Here. In summer.

Christine   I don't know what you're going on about half the time.

Pause. **Racheal** *kneels up to look over into the back seat.*

Racheal   Billy's asleep.

Christine   Good.

Racheal   He looks right peaceful. He looks dead little when he's asleep, doesn't he?

Christine   Who?

Racheal   Billy. I wish he'd stop getting, you know, stop getting run over. He keeps going on about Disney World Florida and that.

Christine   I know.

Racheal   You gonna take him?

Christine   I don't know.

Racheal   Mum.

Christine   Racheal.

Racheal   Why's he done this?

Christine   What?

Racheal   Dad. Why's he done this?

Christine   I don't know, love.

Racheal   It's mental. As if you do this! As if you do though!

Christine   Racheal.

Racheal *turns back, sits up on her heels.*

Racheal   It is though, int it? Mental and that. You reckon he's in there?

Christine   Course he is.

Racheal   Lights off. Door locked. Sitting in there?

Christine   I could hear him.

Racheal   I hate it when he goes like this.

Christine   So do I.

Racheal   Why does he go like this, Mum? Mum? Why does he? Why does he go like dead mental and that?

Christine   I don't know.

Racheal   You're his wife.

Christine   So?

Racheal   You must know.

Christine   Would you shut up?

Racheal   You must though, mustn't you? There must be a reason.

Christine   Rachel, I'll fucking thump yer.

Racheal   You wouldn't.

Christine   You wanna try me?

Beat.

Racheal   I'm frightened of him.

Christine   You are not.

Racheal   I am. He's weird, he is.

Christine   He's your dad. He's not weird.

Racheal   Way he looks at us sometimes.

Christine   He's never weird.

Racheal   I think he hates us.

Christine   Don't be daft.

Racheal   Must though. Mustn't he? Big fat fucking bastard.

Silence.

This doesn't happen to most people, you know. Most normal people.

Christine   How do you know?

Racheal   It doesn't.

Pause. **Racheal** *stares at her mother who has taken to staring out of her side window.*

Racheal   Mum.

Christine   Racheal.

Racheal   What you thinking? Mum? Mum, what are you thinking? Tell us.

Christine   Has he put a light on?

Racheal   You gonna tell us or what?

Christine   Has he, Rache? Is that our flat?

Racheal   I don't know. I can't tell.

They crane their necks to look. And then settle back. **Christine** *lights another cigarette.*

Christine   You shouldn't say that he's weird. All right?

Racheal   Why shouldn't I? He is. He shouldn't lock us out of the flat, should he? Dickhead.

Christine   Racheal. Don't.

Racheal (*a little upset*)   Do you like him?

Christine   Course I do.

Racheal   Do you really?

Christine   You should go to sleep.

Pause. **Racheal** *settles down. Nestles her head against her seat belt.*

Racheal (*looking into wing mirror*)   You know Sarah Briard?

Christine   Who?

Racheal (*back to* **Christine**)   Sarah Briard. Out of our class.

Christine   No.

Racheal   She's dead.

Christine   You what?

Racheal She got smacked by a car. She was ten. Imagine that. Imagine being ten and you're dead. That's dead sad that is, int it? All the stuff she wanted to do, all that stuff. She's never, ever going to do that now. Not none of it. Wanted to play for Man U and everything. Fucking thick cow. As if you play for Man U and you're a girl. I never liked her. She was fat.

Christine Racheal.

Racheal Are you going to tell me what you were thinking?

Christine What?

Racheal Are you?

Christine No.

Racheal You know what I think you were thinking.

Christine Racheal, for fuck's sake.

Racheal I think you were thinking all about Dad and all about this and about how mental it is and about us and about how you want to kill him and about how much you love him, and about whether you're going to leave him and about whether you're going to leave us and about how old Billy is and about how old I am and about whether you're going to go and I think that you think that you're going to. That's what I think. Am I right?

Christine No.

Racheal What were you thinking then?

Christine I'm not going to tell you.

Racheal Liar. I can always tell when you're lying.

Billy *cries out, half asleep. He remains lying down.*

Billy I want to go in that car. I want to go in that car. Mum. I want to go in that car.

Christine Billy? Billy? Billy, love? You're dreaming!

Billy What?

Christine You were having a dream.

Billy What?

Christine You were dreaming. Started crying out. Go
back to sleep.

Billy (*sitting up, his head between the two front seats*)   Where are
we?

Christine We're in the car, love. Outside. It's all right.
Go back to sleep, sweetheart.

He settles. They wait until he is.

Racheal (*quietly*)   Funny bugger. 'I want to go in that car!'
What car? Bloody beamer, is it? Kip in a Merc, is it?

Christine You should go to sleep and all.

Racheal It's mad this, int it?

Christine What?

Racheal This. It's a bit mad, I think. Don't you reckon?

Christine It is a little.

Racheal You should tell Grandad. Imagine this and you
told Grandad. He'd go barmy. He'd smash Dad's head in, I
reckon. Don't you reckon, Mum? Don't you think you
should tell him?

Christine I don't think so, love, no.

Racheal I like Grandad. He's a right mad bastard. (*Beat.*)
Nana's a bit weird but Grandad's all right. Funny pipe-
cleaners and that. Mad Joe 90 goggles. Mum. (*Beat.*) Are you
thinking of going? Mum?

Christine No.

Racheal I wouldn't blame you. Dad's a knobhead.

Christine Racheal.

Racheal   You could take us with you.

Christine   You what?

Racheal   You could. You could take us with you. We could go now. We could just leave. Wouldn't need no bags or nothing. Nothing like that. Just start driving. Go to Grandad's and not come back. Go to country. Go to Disney World Florida. Couldn't we though, Mum? I reckon that'd be a top idea.

Christine   Racheal.

Racheal   I reckon that'd be well smart. Me and you and Billy in Dad's car. Pissing off with no bags or nothing. Going to Disney World Florida. Don't you reckon that'd be sound? It would though, Mum, wouldn't it?

Christine   Racheal.

Racheal   What?

Christine (*quietly, menacing*)   Just, fucking shut it, would ya?

Racheal   What?

Christine (*still menacing*)   We're not going to Disney World Florida. We're not going to countryside. We're not going anywhere. Jesus. Do you think? Do you really think that if I wanted to bugger off from here then I'd take you wirr us? I'm not daft, am I? Am I daft? No. No I'm not. Bloody dead weight, you two. Int you? Pair of yous. I'd piss off on me tod. Leave you two to fuckhead.

Racheal   Mum, don't.

Christine   We're not going. All right? We're staying put. You hear me? Do you?

Racheal   Yeah.

Pause. **Racheal** *screws up her chocolate wrapper. Stares at it. Then looks to her mum.* **Christine** *stares up at the window.*

Lights dim. In the dimness **Christine** *exits.* **Racheal** *removes her tracksuit top.* **Billy** *pulls up the zip of his coat and lifts the hood above his head. Perhaps the car remains on stage throughout.*

Scene Two

1990. The café of Stepping Hill Hospital, Stockport.
    We see a white plastic wipe-clean table with yellow plastic trim. Four plastic moulded seats attached to the table. The whole stage is lit very brightly. An antiseptic white light. There is a large bottle fridge full of Fanta Orange.
    It is nine o'clock at night. **Billy Keats**, *aged eight, sits on one side of the table.* **Racheal Keats**, *aged thirteen, sits on the other.*
    They are both doing their homework. **Billy** *holds his pen in his fist. He is unsettled. He unzips and zips up his coat repeatedly. After a short while he pulls his hood down. Sits grinning at* **Racheal**. **Racheal** *sits up straighter. She throws occasional glances at her brother. As though these glances will rein in his attention to his homework. They won't.*
    They continue with their work for a few seconds. **Racheal** *looks up at him.*

Racheal   What is it?

Billy   What?

Racheal   Yer homework.

Billy (*looking at the Fanta fridge*)   Maths.

Racheal   Yer want any help?

Billy   No. It's easy. It's adding up. It's stupid.

Racheal   If you get stuck. Just ask us.

She looks down. Continues with her work.

Mine's geography. My homework. (*Beat. Looking to him.*) Continental drift. Did you know that you're moving?

Billy (*looking back to her*)   Yer what?

Racheal   Right now. You're moving. Stockport's moving. England's moving. Getting closer and closer to America. Gonna smash up into it. Big fucking pile-up. Did yer know that? I bet yer never, did ya?

Billy   When?

Racheal   Not for ages. Thousands and thousands and thousands and thousands of years. Yer'll be dead. Before it happens.

Billy   Won't.

Racheal   Yer will. Like Grandad.

Billy   I'm gonna live for ever me.

Racheal   Yer not.

Billy   Grandad's never dead.

Racheal   Will be soon. Probably is already. Probably in there. Dead. Hope he is.

Pause. **Billy** *rests his head on the table. On his book. Writes with his fist.*

Lift yer head off the table.

Billy   Am thinking.

Racheal   Can't think with yer head on the table. Yer'll fall asleep.

Billy   Shut up. Yer not me mum.

Pause.

Racheal   Don't write like that. Yer not an idiot. Don't hold yer pen like that. Hold it properly.

Billy *looks long and hard at* **Racheal**. *Then looks around the room. Back at the fridge again.*

Billy (*enthralled*)   Look. They got Fanta Orange. In the fridge. Get us some.

Racheal   I've not got any money. Dad never gave us any money.

Billy *stands. Takes his coat off and drops it on the floor by the table.*

Billy   Am gonna nick some. Yer want some? I'll nick it. They won't do owt.

Racheal   Billy, sit down.

Billy (*goes to leave the table*)   They won't do nothing. They're fucking lazy bastards. Watch 'em.

Racheal   Billy, I'm warning you. Sit down.

He slumps back down in his chair.

Thieving little gypsy.

Billy (*head in hands now*)   He should have given us some money. I'm really thirsty.

Racheal   Well, he never. He'll be back soon. Just wait.

Billy   Mum'd have give us some money. She'd have let us nick a bottle anyways. (*Pause, looks at her. Brightly, inquisitively.*) Rache. What yer reckon it's like? Being dead?

Racheal   Better than what's happening to him.

Billy *stands. Leaves the table. Begins to explore the whole space. She tries to persuade him to come back to the table with the words that she says.*

Billy   Why?

Racheal   Yer see him?

Billy   No.

Racheal   Should have seen him. Flapping around and that. Screaming.

Billy   Was he?

Racheal   I saw him last week. He were like a fish. It was mental. You know what I'm going to do?

Billy What?

Racheal I'm going to go in there. And kill him. Put him out of his misery. Stop him flapping around and that.

Billy Yer what?

Racheal I'm going to. I've decided.

Billy Yer fucking not.

Racheal I am. There must be summit in here, eh? Be good, wouldn't it? Imagine it, Billy. Gagging for breath he'd be. Like a mongoloid.

Billy Yer wouldn't.

Racheal I fucking would.

Billy You're nuts, you are.

Racheal It'd be mental.

Billy You're crackers. I think you're on drugs.

Racheal Yer what?

Billy I think you are. I'm gonna tell our dad. You take drugs. You smoke drugs. You smoke blow.

Racheal I don't.

Billy I bet yer do. I bet yer on it right now. Stoned off yer fucking head.

Racheal Billy. Shut up or I'll fucking thump yer.

Billy So? I'd thump yer back. Where's our mum?

Racheal I don't know.

Billy Yer must do. It's her dad. She should be here by now. And Nana. Where's she?

She stares at him for a while. And then looks away.

Racheal Yer know summit?

Billy What?

Racheal   When Grandad gets better. When he comes out. Am gonna go and live wiv 'em.

Billy (*returning to the table*)   Yer never.

Racheal   I am. Dad said. You're not coming with us. Just me and Nana and Grandad. It'll be fucking great.

Billy   Fuck off.

Racheal *chuckles briefly.*

Racheal   Did you see that kid in the lift?

Billy   What?

Racheal   When we got in the lift to come down? Did yer see the kid getting out of the lift?

Billy   No. What about him?

Racheal   It were horrible. He was all crippled up. All bandaged up. Every part of him. Looked like a mummy. He was tiny and all.

Billy *giggles. Sits sideways on to the table, facing the fridge.*

Racheal   It's not funny, Billy.

Billy   Yeah, it is.

Racheal   It's not, Billy. It's horrible. This place is all fucking horrible.

Billy   I like it. I think it's all right. They've got Fanta Orange. Chocolate. It's good.

Ronald Abbey *enters. A man of indistinguishable weight. Fifty years old. Milk-bottle spectacles. Thinning hair. He speaks with a certain amount of saliva rattling around his teeth, smiles inappropriately nearly all the time and blinks a lot. He never, ever looks at the people he addresses. His evasion becoming more pronounced as the conversation becomes more personal. The children think he is, by turns, disgusting and hilarious. For a short time he hugs the side of the stage.*

Ronald   Hello, Billy. Racheal. Your dad said you were down here.

Billy   Arright, Ronald?

Racheal   Ronald.

Ronald   How are the two of you?

Billy   Arright, thank you.

Racheal   You been to see Grandad?

Billy *starts giggling again.*

Ronald   Yes. Yes I have.

Racheal   How is he?

Ronald   He was sleeping.

Billy *does fake snoring. And then continues to giggle.*

Racheal   Billy. Shut it.

Ronald   I wanted to say. I'm very sorry. About your grandad. And everything. I like him very much. He's a good person.

Racheal   It's all right, Ronald. He's going to get better soon.

Ronald   I do hope so.

Racheal   He will.

Ronald (*moving closer to their table, almost circling it*)   Are you bearing up? The two of you? Is everything OK?

Racheal   Yes. We're fine thank you very much. Billy, shut it.

Ronald   And your dad, is he all right?

Racheal   I think he's fine, yes.

Ronald   And have you heard anything from your mum?

Racheal   No we've not.

Ronald   I see. How long has that been now?

Racheal   Fourteen months.

Ronald   I see.

Racheal   On Tuesday.

Ronald   Good. Right. Well. If there's anything I can do for you. Anything at all. You know where I am.

Billy *bursts out laughing.* **Racheal** *stands, pissed off with* **Billy,** *backs away from* **Ronald.** **Billy** *remains seated between the two of them.*

Racheal   Billy. For fuck's sake.

Ronald   No, no. Racheal. That's all right. Is there something the matter, Billy?

Billy   No.

Ronald   Is there something very funny happening?

Billy   I know where you are.

Ronald   I'm sorry?

Billy   You said, 'You know where I am.' And I do. I know where you are. All the time. Up Lancy Hill.

Ronald (*closer*)   I'm sorry?

Billy (*rocking on his chair, drumming on his legs*)   Int he? She's seen yer. She tells us. Yer up there all the time. Get yer knob out and everything, don't yer?

Ronald   Maybe I should go.

Billy   Don't he? You said.

Ronald   Did she?

Racheal   Billy. You're dead.

Billy   Why? It's true.

Ronald (*closer still*)   Did she say that, did she?

Billy   Yeah. Get yer dick out for the little girls and that.

Racheal   I swear.

Billy   Can I see it, Ronald? Will yer gerrit out for us now? Will yer?

Ronald (*standing quite still, grinning*)   Well. Racheal.

Racheal   Ronald. I never.

Ronald (*still grinning, looking away from her, quietly*)   You little whore.

Racheal   Ronald!

Ronald   You little tart.

Racheal   Yer what?

Ronald   With your brother, Racheal. Surely not even you could go that far.

Racheal   What did you say?

Ronald   You heard me.

Racheal   I don't believe that.

Ronald   You heard me.

Moves to leave. **Jonathan Keats** *enters. Thirty-four years old. A sinewy man. Tattooed. Shaven-headed. He almost never registers any outward sign of emotional engagement. He is drinking coffee from a paper cup. He has a presence which registers immediately, not only with the children but also with* **Ronald**, *regardless of where they are looking. There is a stillness about him that is impressive.*

Jonathan   Arright, Ronald.

Racheal   Dad. You should have heard what he just said. I swear.

Ronald   Hello, Jonathan. Everything all right?

Jonathan   Everything's fine, mate. Yeah. Not bad.

Racheal   Honestly, Dad. Billy. Shouldn't he?

Jonathan (*without really registering*)   What?

Racheal   Hear what Ronald just said.

Jonathan   Why?

Racheal   It was barmy.

Ronald   I should be going.

Jonathan   Right. OK. Thank you for coming.

Ronald   No. Not at all. I was saying to Racheal and Billy. I like Gordon. He's a good man.

Racheal   I'm going to tell him. Ronald. After you've gone.

Jonathan   Tell him what? Tell who? What's going on?

Ronald   I must go. There's a bus. I'll see you soon I hope, Jonathan.

Jonathan   Yes. Right. I hope so too, Ronald. I'll see you later.

Ronald   G'bye, Racheal. Billy.

Billy   Tarrah.

Racheal (*laughing*)   Yeah. See yer, Ronald.

He exits opposite **Racheal**. **Billy** *and* **Racheal** *laughing bewildered as he leaves.*

I swear.

Jonathan   What's going on?

Racheal   You should have heard what he was saying. He's a psycho that one, Dad. I'm telling yer.

Jonathan   What did he say?

Racheal (*going to collect up her homework*)   Nothing. It don't matter.

Jonathan   Why? What was it?

Racheal It was nothing. I'll tell yer later.

Jonathan Right.

He moves towards the table. Sits down. Looks straight ahead for a few seconds before he speaks. Drinks from his cup.

Racheal. Billy. Yer grandad's died.

Billy *bursts out laughing again.*

Jonathan Just now. In his sleep and that.

Racheal (*crushed*) He never.

Jonathan He has, love. I'm sorry.

Billy's *laughing settles.* **Racheal** *backs off from the table.*

Jonathan I don't think it were painful or nothing. Didn't even notice at first. He just stopped breathing. Pulse stopped. You all right?

Racheal Yeah.

Jonathan You done yer homework?

Racheal Yeah.

Jonathan What about you, Billy?

Billy Didn't get none.

Jonathan Didn't yer?

Billy No.

Jonathan Right.

Pause.

Maybe you should go and see him. Yer can if yer want to. I think he'd have liked yer to.

Racheal No thank you.

Silence.

Jonathan What did Ronald say to yer?

Racheal   Nothing.

Jonathan   He's a funny cunt, int 'e? Mind you. Good of him to come and that. He liked your grandad. Remember that time he brought him round?

Racheal   What?

Jonathan   Maybe you weren't there. One time. Fucking freezing cold outside. Middle of winter. Knock on the door. It were Ronald. Holding your grandad up. Under his arm and that. Grandad's got his pants round his ankles. Reckon he was having a piss. Fell over and that. In the ice. Apparently loads of people walked past him. Ronald stopped to help him back.

Racheal (*defiant*)   He never.

Jonathan (*matter-of-fact*)   He did, love. Used to do it quite a lot. Could barely fucking walk half the time. He was never that big a man. Everybody said that he was but it weren't true. You with me? He was as much of a fuck as anything else. (*Drinks.*) You been behaving yerselves?

Billy   Yeah.

Jonathan   Yer better. You done yer homework properly, Racheal? Have yer, love?

Racheal   Yes.

Jonathan   Don't want fucking aggro, do we? Got to do your homework as well as yer can. Don't want to have to go up and see no teachers. Not unless it's Miss Ayling, eh? I'd go up and see her any time. Day or night. You wiv me? (*Finishes his coffee.*) So. What are you gonna do now, Rache? Eh?

Racheal   What do you mean?

Jonathan   Got nowhere to go to now, have you, love? Monday nights and that. Tuesdays. Wednesdays. Weekends. (*Screws up his coffee cup and throws it away.*) All the time she was round there, weren't she, Bill?

Billy   Yeah.

Jonathan   Can't do that any more. Can yer?

Racheal   It's your fault.

Jonathan   You what?

Racheal   This. Grandad dying. It's your fault.

Jonathan (*with a chuckle*)   What yer going on about, you, eh?

Racheal   Fucking bastard.

Jonathan (*shouting, suddenly*)   Eh!

Racheal   If you hadn't been such a fucking bastard he would have been all right.

Jonathan   What you nattering on about, you, eh? What she nattering on about, Billy?

Billy   Don't know.

Racheal   He told us. He used to tell us. What you did. To Mum.

Jonathan   Racheal. Enough. Now. Shut it.

Racheal (*starting to cry*)   Told us it used to break his heart. Yer fucking bastard.

Jonathan   You don't shut it now I'll fucking leather yer.

Racheal *stands, offers herself to her dad for a battering.*

Racheal (*becoming hysterical*)   Yeah? Would yer? Go on then! Fucking go on! Hit us! Hit us! Go on! I'd love it. I'd love it. Yer fucking bastard!

Her hysteria collapses into sobbing for a short time and eventually calms down. **Jonathan** *watches her simply and quietly, allowing her to calm.* **Billy** *stares down at his homework.*

Jonathan (*simply, quietly*)   Should go and see him.

Racheal   No.

Jonathan   Should do.

Racheal   I don't want to.

Jonathan   How come not?

Racheal   Scares me.

Jonathan   What does?

Racheal   People being dead. All that.

Jonathan (*with a gentle smile*)   Don't be daft.

Racheal   I'm not being daft. I'm being serious.

Jonathan (*moving to her*)   Racheal. It's all right. You know? He won't bite yer. You should. You'd feel better for it. It'd make it a bit, y'know. Go on. I'll look after Billy. You go.

She stares at him for a short time and then leaves. He watches her go. There is a silence between **Jonathan** *and* **Billy** *for a while. The two don't look at each other.*

Billy   Dad.

Jonathan   Yeah.

Billy   Can I nick a can of Fanta Orange. Out of the fridge. They won't do owt.

Jonathan (*sitting*)   Aye. All right.

He does. Comes back to the table and drinks with relish. His dad watches him for a while before speaking to him. This time, when the two address one another, they start to hold eye contact.

How are you, Bill?

Billy   Yer what?

Jonathan   Are you all right and everything? About Grandad and that?

Billy   Yeah.

Jonathan (*looking away for a bit*)   Your mum should have been here. Weren't even my dad. I held his hand. It were weird.

Billy   Dad.

Jonathan   Billy.

Billy   I don't think it were you. Who killed Grandad or nothing. I think it was all the fags he smoked. He was always smoking, him. Like a big old chimney.

Jonathan   I think so too.

Billy   Stupid. Smoking.

Jonathan   Yes it is.

Billy   Racheal smokes.

Jonathan   Does she?

Billy   All the time.

Jonathan   I see. Is she all right?

Billy   Yer what?

Jonathan   Racheal. Is she all right? Do you think?

Billy   Yeah. I think so.

Pause.

Jonathan   Billy.

Billy   Yeah.

Jonathan   I'm sorry, mate.

Billy   What about? (*Beat.*) Dad?

Jonathan   Just. Yer know.

Barely perceptibly, he starts to cry.

Look at me. Big stupid git. Crying and that.

Long silence. The two look away from each other. **Jonathan** *still only just crying.*

Racheal *comes back before* **Jonathan** *notices. Stands by the table. She catches him crying. He realises she has caught him. A vulnerable moment and then he inhales a big lungful of air.*

Racheal   You all right? Dad?

Jonathan   I'm fine, love, yeah. You OK?

Racheal   Yeah.

Jonathan (*smiling at her*)   Good girl. It weren't too bad. Was it?

Racheal   No. It was all right.

Jonathan (*standing*)   He was a funny fucker. Said to us. This morning. Tell Racheal and Billy that when I get better, we'll go out. Go to KFC. Go cinema.

Racheal   His skin was very loose.

Jonathan   Yer what?

Racheal   On his bones. It was warm. Yer press the skin down though and the muscles and the bone are all cold. It was weird.

Jonathan   Yeah.

He picks up **Billy**'s *coat. Neatens the collar. Passes it to him.*

You wanna go home, you two?

Racheal   Yeah.

Jonathan   See y'up at car.

Jonathan *exits.* **Billy** *follows.*

Billy (*leaving*)   Starving.

Racheal *goes to leave. Stops herself. Looks back.*

Lights dim.

Racheal *pushes down her school socks. Removes her tie and reties it in a fat knot. Pulls her skirt up, tightens it slightly. Applies some make-up. Ties her jumper round her waist.*

Scene Three

1992. The L section of the bus station in Stockport town centre. It is approaching night-time and darkening. The station is deserted except for the children. It feels huge, almost completely hollow. The children's movement is freed by the absence of others.

An aluminium queue divider centres the stage.

Racheal Keats, *fifteen years old, leans against the divider's pole. Breathless. Waiting.*

Chris Bennett, *also fifteen years old, follows her. Not breathless. In a tracksuit. Cocky, confident, very handsome and knows it. He joins her, leaning against the pole. Looks at her for some time without speaking. She grows increasingly self-conscious of this.*

They are waiting for their friends. He watches her while she talks. She can't look back.

Racheal   Gonna rain. Bet ya.

Chris   –

Racheal   Gonna slash it down.

Chris   –

Racheal *moves away from the pole – looks outwards and all around her.*

Racheal   Always rainin' here. Always fuckin' leatherin' it.

Chris   –

Racheal   Fuckin' hate it.

Chris (*laughs briefly*)   –

Racheal   Don't you, Chris?

Chris (*smiles*)   What?

Racheal   Don't you hate it here?

Chris (*thinks, sniffs*)   S'arright.

Racheal   S'fuckin' never. S'fucking cheap. Grotty. Shit buildings. Stinks. (*She belches hugely and then giggles.*)

Chris (*with a grin*)   Yer got a tab?

Racheal   No.

Chris   Liar.

Racheal   Am not.

Chris   Y'are. Fuckin' seen ya. Juss now.

Racheal   Finished 'em.

Chris   Yer didn't. Yer still got some.

Racheal   I ain't.

He reaches for her shirt pocket. Slight scuffle. Giggle.

Chris   Here.

Racheal   Get off.

Chris   In yer pocket.

Racheal   Get off us.

He pulls out a packet of cigarettes.

Chris   Told ya.

Racheal   'S me last one.

Chris   Yer cheeky little monkey. Knew y'ad one.

He puts it in his mouth. Goes to light it. She grabs for it. Misses.

Racheal   Don't.

He backs away from her, always watching her, grinning.

Chris   Stop me.

Racheal   Chris.

Chris   Come on.

Racheal   What are yer like?

Chris   If yer don't want me to smoke it come and gerrit off me.

Racheal   Yer mental.

Chris   Am not.

Racheal   Yer crackers.

Chris   Am not. Am well sane.

He lights the cigarette.

Racheal   Loony.

Chris   Look at yer. Yer all red. Yer look dead cute when yer all red.

Racheal (*affectionately*)   Cracked you.

Chris *takes a long draw on the cigarette. They stare at each other for a time.*

Racheal (*turning from him, out into space*)   Only good things around here are Man U. And Mr Everson.

Chris   Mr Everson?

Racheal   Yeah.

Chris   He's a fat fucking thick twat.

Racheal   He's not. He's fucking great.

Chris   Yer fancy him, don't yer? Fucking hell.

Racheal   No. I just think he's good.

Chris   You fucking fancy him and all.

Racheal   Teaches us new words.

Chris   New words?

Racheal   Catatonic. A state of schizophrenic unconsciousness.

Chris   New words? Are you eight?

Racheal   Philanthropy. Love of mankind. (*Suddenly turns to him.*) Yer know what else I love?

Chris   What?

Racheal   All mountains.

Chris   Yer what?

Racheal   Our mum went on about them all the time and all. Yer should've seen 'em this morning. Such a clear day. Yer could see 'em all really detailed. We should go. Shouldn't we? Me and you. Tek Luce and Danny.

Chris   Tek your kid.

Racheal   Fuck off.

Chris   I like him.

Racheal   Yer can have him.

Chris   He's a nutter. Nicks owt, don't he?

Racheal   What?

Chris   Billy. Nicks owt. 'S funny. Like 'avin' a lickle dog.

Silence.

'S not mountains. 'S fuckin' hills. 'S fuckin' Pennine Way that. 'S never fuckin' mountains.

Racheal   Yer ever noticed how many transport routes cut through this place?

Chris   Yer what?

Racheal   All the transport routes come through here. Every single fuckin' type.

Chris   What yer crackin' on about now, you?

She begins to circle away from him.

Racheal   Yer got yer A6 for yer cars. Yer got yer viaduct for yer trains. M62. River fuckin' Mersey. Flight paths down Ringway. 'S mental. Planes have still got the wheels down when they come over here. Every cunt's trying to get out.

Chris   Am not.

Racheal   Int yer?

Chris   Nah.

Racheal (*to him*)   Int yer, Chris? Really?

Chris   No.

Racheal (*turning away, staring out again*)   Fuckin' should.

Chris   I like it.

Racheal   Why?

Chris   'S a laugh, innit? Yer can bunk off school. Go home. Watch telly. Brother's all right. Mum and Dad and that. Phone yer mates. Come down here. Ride buses. Go down Manchester. Go cinema. Gerr up to all sorts.

Racheal (*turning to him, seriously*)   I hate my family.

Chris   No yer don't.

Racheal   The only person in my family who's any cop was my grandad and he's been dead two year. Most significant person in my life and he's fucking snuffed it.

Chris   Yer brother's all right.

Pause. **Racheal** *stares out.*

Racheal   I hate death. Scares the shit out of us.

Pause.

Remember Paul Castle?

Chris   Yeah.

Racheal   Remember his brother?

Chris   His brother?

Racheal   In third year. When we was in first year. Threw himself off bridge over M62. Remember that?

Chris   Oh yeah.

Racheal   I remember thinkin' it were funny. And that he were stupid. That he were a thick cunt. I mean, as if yer do that. We're older than he was now. Paul Castle's older than his older brother. Nuts that, int it?

Chris (*disinterested*)   Yeah.

Racheal   It is though, Chris, int it?

Chris   I used to like Paul Castle. He were all right. How come he never comes to school any more?

She looks at him for three seconds. Looks away.

Racheal   I don't know.

Pause. She looks back to him. He begins to lift his own weight up off the bar. And then stops.

Chris   Yer know one thing I like about you?

Racheal   What?

Chris   You've got really lovely tits.

Racheal   Yer what?

Chris   Y'ave. They look lovely.

Racheal   Do they?

Chris   Yeah.

Racheal   Right.

Chris   Don't panic. It's a good thing.

Racheal   Thanks.

Chris   'S all right.

He turns away again, grinning.

Racheal   Where are they?

Chris   Don't know.

Pause.

Racheal   Chris.

Chris   Yeah.

Racheal   What are you scared of?

Chris   How do yer mean?

Racheal   Like I'm scared of death. And when I were a nipper I were scared of me mum when she used to thump us with her hairbrush and me dad because he was fucking weird. What are you scared of?

Chris   Nothing.

Racheal   Nothing?

Chris   No.

She touches his face with her finger. Pulls it away.

Racheal (*seriously*)   Liar.

Chris   Am not.

Racheal   Yer are.

Long pause. Neither shakes eye contact.

Racheal   Y'ever get like yer just want to go fucking ape?

Chris   Yer what?

Racheal   Don't matter.

She turns away from him. The two stare out. **Billy** *runs on. He is ten years old.*

Billy   That was fuckin' magic!

Racheal   Billy.

Billy   That was fuckin' brilliant!

Racheal   What?

Billy   That!

Racheal   What?

Billy   We just went down Merseyway. Fuckin' robbin' and everything! It were top!

Racheal   Yer what?

Billy   Just down Boots and that.

Racheal   Boots's closed.

Billy   Smashed the window.

Chris *bursts out laughing.* **Racheal** *is appalled.*

Racheal   You what?!?

Billy   Me and Luce and Danny.

Racheal   Billy.

Billy   Threw a big fuckin' brick through the window. Grabbed a load of films for cameras. And skin cream. And pegged it. Alarms going. (*Imitating the sound of the alarm.*) BLAH BLAH BLAH BLAH!!

As **Billy** *talks he moves like a monkey. Swinging on the queue divider. Circling the stage. He hardly stops moving at all.*

Racheal   Billy, I am going to fucking kill you.

Billy   It were magic. It were mighty!

Chris   Where's Luce now, Billy? And Danny?

Billy   They're coming. Slow fuckers. Am a dead fast runner, me. Fuckin' slaughtered 'em.

Racheal   What the fuck did you do that for, Billy? Christ!

Billy   For a laugh.

Racheal   Yer don't need skin cream!

Billy   I nicked it for you. Lucy's got some and all.

He gives her six bottles of skin cream that he pulls out of his pockets.

Racheal   I don't want this!

Billy   Why not?

Racheal   Fuckin' handling stolen, int it?

She refuses to take them.

Billy   But I nicked it for you. And look at these. Fuckin' top these are. Fuckin' quality.

He pulls out a handful of boxes of film.

Racheal   Billy. You haven't even got a camera. What do yer want film for, yer monghead?

Billy   Fuck off.

Racheal   No, Billy –

Billy   Am not a monghead.

Racheal   It's not on.

Billy   Don't call me a monghead, Rache, because I'm fucking not one, arright?

Racheal   Billy.

Billy   What?

Racheal   Dad'll kill you.

Billy   He won't.

Racheal   He fucking will.

Billy   Don't need to tell him.

Racheal   I *know*.

Billy   Don't need to tell him nothing. Gissa fag.

Racheal   Fuck off.

Billy   Go on. Am gasping.

Racheal   Billy. You do my head in.

Billy   Anyways. What's all this?

Racheal   All what?

Billy   All you two. What's all this about?

Racheal   Shut it.

Billy   Give 'im one, did ya?

Racheal   Billy.

Billy   Honestly, Chris. You should hear her going on about you. She really fancies yer. She'd definitely give yer one. If yer wanted. Just ask her.

Racheal   Right, Billy.

Billy   She's always going with lads and all. She's a right slapper.

Racheal *gives* **Billy** *a Chinese burn. He buckles in pain.*

Racheal   Take that back.

Billy   I was joking.

Racheal   I don't care. Take it back.

Billy   It was a joke, Rache.

Racheal   It wasn't a fucking funny one. Take it fucking back.

Billy   I'm sorry.

Racheal   Take it back.

Chris (*amused*)   You should take it back, Billy.

Racheal   Keep out of this, you!

Billy   Arright. I take it back. I'm sorry. I take it back.

Racheal (*letting* **Billy** *go*)   Nothing to do with you. To do with me and him.

Chris (*slight laugh*)   Sorry. I was just trying to help.

Racheal   Yeah. Well, just don't.

Lucy and **Danny** *enter running.* **Lucy** *is fifteen. School uniform worn like* **Racheal**'s. *Pretty. Slightly softer than* **Racheal**. **Danny** *is in messy school uniform too.* **Lucy** *is laughing.* **Danny** *fretting slightly.*

Lucy   Oh my fucking lord!

Danny   I can't breathe.

Lucy   Racheal. Your brother is a fucking lunatic.

Danny   I've never known anything like it.

Racheal   What did he do?

Lucy   He is off his head. I swear.

Racheal   What did he do, Lucy?

Lucy   He wants to go up Dollis Hill. He wants to go in' fuckin loony bin.

Racheal   Lucy, what did he fucking do?

Lucy   Only threw a brick in window of fucking Boots is all. Only did that, didn't he?

Danny   Racheal. He's cracked. Am telling yer.

As **Lucy** *talks,* **Billy**'s *movements calm. He is very proud of himself.* **Lucy** *cracks into laughter as she speaks.*

Lucy   Juss walking down Merseyway. Went into McDonald's and going down Merseyway. Just having us chips. And he just turns round with this fucking great brick and he just lobs it into window of fucking Boots. Grabs all these, all these, all these fucking films and skin cream and that and just fucking pegs it. He's off his fucking head. He wants to go to fucking hospital. What does he want fucking skin cream for? I swear. It were brilliant.

Billy   I gave you some.

Racheal   Lucy.

Lucy   Yeah. You did, love. It were very sweet of you. I nearly pissed myself.

Danny   Alarms going and everything.

Billy (*going to* **Lucy**)   It were good though, weren't it?

Danny   Cops coming now, I reckon, probly.

Billy   Lucy, weren't it good though?

Lucy   Eh?

Billy   Doing that. It were good, weren't it?

Lucy *strokes his face. He beams.*

Lucy   Yeah. Yes, love. It were fucking cracking.

Racheal   You mean it wasn't your idea?

Lucy   Yer what?

Billy   Am gonna do it again.

Racheal   Robbing shop. Robbing Boots. It wasn't your idea to do that?

Lucy   No. First I heard about it he's got the brick in his hands and he's going, 'Watch this!'

Billy   What you reckon, Danny, should we do it again?

Danny   What?

Billy   Go and do JD Sports. Get some trainers.

Racheal   Billy, I need a word with you.

Billy   Get us a football.

Danny   Are you mental?

Racheal   Billy. Now.

Billy   Fuck off.

Danny   Cops'll be fucking crawling all over this place. They'll be after yer. Get yer on camera and that.

Billy   Will they fuck!

Danny   They will, Billy.

Billy   Be the last thing they expect then, eh? Go back and nick stuff from right in front of 'em. Fucking thick coppers.

Lucy   He's a lunatic.

Chris (*grinning, watchful*)   I'll go.

Billy   Excellent!

Racheal (*staring at* **Chris**)   I don't believe this.

Chris   You coming, Danny?

Danny   What?

Chris   You coming with us or what?

Danny   No chance.

Racheal   Chris, don't.

Chris (*big grin, loving it*)   Chicken.

Danny   Fuck off.

Chris   Fucking ten-year-old got more balls than you do.

Danny   I was fucking there just then, weren't I? Don't know where you were.

Chris   Fucking coward. Int he, Rache? He's a fucking coward.

Danny   I just done fucking Boots me, mate.

Chris   Yer never. Billy did fucking Boots. You just stood there. That's not doing it. That's just fucking coincidence is what that is. Yer a fucking pussy.

Danny   Fuck off.

Chris   Fucking pussy. You coming, Lucy?

Lucy   Me?

Chris   Aye.

Pause.

Lucy   Just let us get me breath back.

Chris   Good girl.

Billy   You coming, Rache?

Racheal (*looks at* **Chris**, *appalled, and then addresses* **Billy**)
You're not going anywhere.

Billy   Yeah I am. Me and Chris and Lucy are going
robbing JD Sports. We're going getting trainers. You
coming too, Danny?

Danny   I don't know, mate.

Chris   He's fucking chicken. 'S what he is.

Danny   'S not chicken. 'S never chicken, arright? 'S
fucking mental is what it is!

Racheal   Chris, please.

Chris   What? Rache? Yer never going mard-arsed on us
and all, are yer?

Lucy   She fucking is, int she? What's she fucking like?

Billy *goes to leave.*

Racheal   Billy. Wait here.

Billy   No. Am going. You coming or what?

Racheal   This is doing my nut in.

Billy   Rache?

Racheal   You can't take him, Chris. He's my brother.
He's only ten.

Billy   So?!

Chris (*with real relish*)   Mard arse.

Lucy *laughs at* **Racheal**.

Billy   God, Racheal.

Danny   Yer shouldn't, Chris.

Chris   Shut it, chicken shit.

The two face off. Brief time. **Danny** *looks away.*

Billy *drops the face cream on the floor as he starts to go.*

Racheal   This int right.

Billy (*turning to her as he goes*)   Am not a fucking kid any more.

Racheal   Yes you are.

Billy (*stops, stares at her briefly, sniffs once*)   Am going.

He turns and leaves.

Chris   Me too. (*Goes to leave.*) Coming, Danny?

Danny (*after a brief beat, and with great reluctance*)   Aye. Yeah. Am coming. Fuck.

Chris   You wanna sort your head, Rache. Yer wiv me? It's turning fucking yellow, mate.

Leaves. **Danny** *follows* **Billy** *and* **Chris** *off.* **Racheal** *watches them go. Turns away. Looks out. Wraps her arms around herself. Brief time.* **Lucy** *goes right up to her.*

Lucy   So?

Racheal   What?

Lucy   Did you?

Racheal   What?

Lucy   You and Chris? Did yer do it with him?

Racheal *simply stares at her for a few seconds.*

Lucy   Yer did, didn't yer? I knew it!

Pause. She stares at **Racheal** *with a wonder that edges on to disgust.*
Racheal *turns away from her.*

You coming?

Racheal   I don't believe this.

Lucy   You coming or what?

Racheal   I hate this.

Lucy   Racheal, are you coming with us or fucking what?

No response.

Used to be arright you and all, I thought.

Lucy *leaves.* **Racheal** *watches her go and then stands.*

Lights dim.

Racheal *takes off her tie. Tucks in her shirt. Takes off her shoes and socks. Puts on a light, summer cardigan, maybe some sunglasses.*

Scene Four

1994. The garden of a nursing home in Offerton, Stockport.
    A wrought-iron bench. Some flowerpots. It is a beautiful day. There is golden sunshine. A bright, warm, open light.
    Racheal Keats, *seventeen, tends the plants in the pots. Afterwards she walks, relaxed, around the bench. Her nana,* **Anne Dickinson**, *sits still on the bench.*
    Anne *is seventy-four years old. She is blind. She wears a powder-blue cardigan over a white dress. Her ankles are thick and rolled in brown tights and bandages.* **Anne** *is recovering from a stroke. Her temperament is resolutely cheery. Sometimes the tone of her voice is inappropriately, confusingly cheery.*
    They are drinking tea from china cups and eating a huge block of Dairy Milk chocolate.
    We can hear birdsong. Perhaps cars. And offstage we can hear the sound of an old **Man** *howling from an open window.*

Man   What am I doing here? What am I here for? I've never done nothing. I've not done owt. Please. Please. Please. Please. Please. Please. Please. Please. Please. Please don't. Please don't do that. Please stop doing that. Please stop.

They stop to listen. After a short while the window is slammed closed. They both stare out.

Racheal   Who was that?

Anne   Who?

Racheal   That man. Him shouting.

Anne   What man?

Racheal   Did you not hear him. That fellah. Shouting on he was. Going crackers and everything?

Anne   No.

Racheal   He was shouting like mad.

Anne   Oh. I don't know.

Pause. They look out. **Racheal** *checks her watch.*

Racheal   It's a beautiful day, Nana.

Anne   Yes. It feels it.

Racheal (*looking at the sky*)   The sky's very blue.

Anne   Is it?

Racheal   It looks amazing.

Anne   Does it?

Racheal   Sun's out. Couple of clouds and that. All white. Very little.

Anne   I love it when there's a little breeze.

Racheal   Yeah. Me too.

Anne   It smells like artichokes.

Racheal   Artichokes?

Anne   And tea. The air. From when I was a little girl and everything.

Pause.

Racheal   Do yer want some more chocolate?

Anne   Yes. I do please.

Racheal *cracks off a large chunk and passes it to her. Her nana starts biting on the large chunk.*

Racheal   Nana, there was something I wanted to ask you.

Anne   Does it no good.

Racheal   What?

Anne   My teeth.

Racheal   No. (*Beat.*) Nana.

Anne   How are you, love?

Racheal   You what?

Anne   How are you? Are you all right? Is everything all right? With you?

Racheal   Yes. It's fine. I'm good. I'm all right. It's all right.

Anne   How's your brother?

Racheal   Billy?

Anne   Yes. Billy. How is he?

Racheal   He's not bad. Have you been to see him?

Anne   Have I what?

Racheal   Have you been to see him? Billy?

Anne   No. No I've not.

Racheal   You should go.

Anne   I've not.

Beat. **Racheal** *turns to her.*

Racheal   Have yer seen Mum, Nana?

Anne   Have I what?

Racheal   Mum. Have you seen her?

Anne   No. I haven't.

Racheal   Do you know where she's gone?

Anne   No, I don't. Do you?

Racheal   No. I've no idea.

Anne   Yer what?

Racheal   I said I've no idea.

Anne   No.

Racheal (*moves to sit on the arm of the bench*)   Can I ask you something, Nana?

Anne   What, love?

Racheal   Don't you miss her?

Anne   Who?

Racheal   Mum.

Anne (*smiling*)   Yes. I do.

Racheal   Doesn't it make you sad? That she's gone away and she never even said goodbye or nothing. She just left.

Anne (*smiling*)   Yes it does.

Racheal   I always wondered. It's been ages now. I always wondered if she wrote to you. Or spoke to you on the telephone. Or come to see you.

Anne (*smiling*)   No she didn't.

Pause. **Racheal** *stares at her.*

Racheal   Do you miss Grandad ever?

Anne   What did you say, love?

Racheal   I asked you if you ever missed Grandad?

Anne   No. No I don't. No.

Racheal   I miss him all the time.

Pause. **Racheal** *stands, moves away.*

Anne   Have you got a boyfriend yet?

Racheal   No. Nana. I haven't.

Long pause. She tends the plants again. Then stops. Stares at her nana.

Racheal   Nana. I'm going to get a flat.

Anne   Are you, love?

Racheal   Up Edgely.

Anne   That's nice.

Racheal   I'm dead excited.

Anne   Are you?

Racheal   I am. It's really smart. It's got a bathroom. Kitchen. Got a shower.

Anne   Has it?

Racheal   It's cracking. Rent's thirty quid a week. I can afford that. It's all right.

Anne   Good girl.

Racheal   Nana. I need some money. For the deposit. I need two hundred and forty pound. For the deposit, which is a month's rent, and for a month's rent in advance. Nana, I've not got it. I can't afford the deposit. I was going to ask you. If you had it. If I could borrow it from you. If you could lend it to us.

Anne   Were you?

Racheal   Yeah.

Pause.

Can you, Nana?

Anne   Can I what?

Racheal   Can you lend us the deposit? The two hundred and forty pound?

Anne (*smiling*)   No, love, I don't think so.

Racheal   Yer what?

Anne   I don't think I can love, no.

Racheal   Nana? Did you hear what I said? I've not got it. If I don't get the deposit and the rent then I'll lose the flat. I'll pay you back. I will, Nana, I swear. On my life. I'll pay you back. Every month. I could pay you like twenty quid a month or summit. I could do that. I could afford that. Nana. On my life.

Anne (*smiling*)   I don't think so, love. No.

Racheal   What do you mean you don't think so?

Anne   I don't think I could lend you the money, love, not really.

Racheal   Why not?

Anne   I haven't really got enough, love.

Racheal   Yer what?

Anne   I haven't. I can't really afford to do that.

Silence. **Racheal** *stares at her nana, disbelieving. She eats some more chocolate.*

I've not got the money.

Racheal   I thought, Mum always said you were . . . didn't Grandad leave you any?

Anne   I'm sorry, love?

Racheal   Didn't Grandad, I thought – Grandad always said there was some money . . .

Anne   No, love.

Racheal   He always said, he told me, Grandad told me that there was some money and if that, if I ever needed some money badly that he would find it for me and he would lend it to me. He told me. He promised. (*Beat.*) Yer must have it.

Anne   Love, I don't.

Racheal   How do you, how do you, how do yer afford to pay for this place if you've not got any money, Nana?

Anne   Yer what?

Racheal   How can you afford to pay for this place if you've not got any money to lend us?

Anne   It's not easy, love.

Racheal   Not easy?

Anne   No, love.

Racheal   Grandad promised me.

Anne   It's not, love.

Racheal   I need that flat, Nana. I need it. Dad's, Dad's, Dad's, Dad's . . . I'll crack up. If I don't get that flat, Nana, I will go mental. I swear.

Anne   You won't.

Racheal   I will, Nana. I really will.

Anne   Is there any more chocolate, love?

Racheal   Grandad said.

Anne   Is there? Could you pass me some?

Racheal   I could pay you back thirty a month. If that's what's bothering you. Nana, please. I need this so much.

Anne   You wouldn't.

Racheal   What?

Anne   You wouldn't, love. Would you? Not really. You never would.

Racheal   You what?

Anne   Would you?

Racheal   I don't believe this.

Anne   Would you though, love? You wouldn't. Would you?

Racheal   I don't believe this one bit. I swear.

Anne   Racheal, sweetheart, is there any more chocolate?

Racheal   Don't call me sweetheart. You're not. I'm not your sweetheart.

Anne   Is there, love?

Racheal   You have no idea. Do you?

Anne   Yer what, love?

Racheal   Yer lying.

Anne   Yer what, love?

Racheal   You heard me. You can hear me perfectly well. Yer lying. Yer lying about yer ears and yer lying about yer money. Yer a lickle liar.

Anne   Racheal, love. I'm not, I swear.

Racheal   I'll give yer some more chocolate. Here y'are.

Passes her a chunk of chocolate that she puts in her mouth.

Here, Nana, have some more.

Gives her some more chocolate, which she holds in her hand.

Have some more.

Anne   I can't hold any more, love. I can't fit it in my mouth.

Racheal   Have some more chocolate, you skinny fucking tramp.

Anne   Racheal, please.

Racheal   Have it. Have it. Have it. Have it. Have it. I'll kick your teeth in.

Anne *takes some more. Puts some more in her mouth. Her mouth is full. Dribbles of chocolate on her chin.*

Racheal   Have some more.

The same. **Anne** *can't talk. She's crying.*

Is it good being you, Nana? Is it good being a cripple? What about pissing all the time, is that good? Does it hurt? Do your legs hurt when you piss on them? Do they? Do you think –

Anne   Christine?

Racheal   Do you think, Nana – I'm not Christine, you blind – Nana, do you think you're going to die soon? Do you, Nana? Do you think you are?

Anne   Where's Christine gone? Where is she?

Racheal   She's not here. She's gone. She left you. She left you because she couldn't stand you.

Anne   Christine?

Racheal   Her and Grandad. Both of them. Yer blind fuck.

Racheal *picks up her nana's handbag. Pulls things out from it. Tissues. Sweets. Pills. A make-up compact. Her purse. She opens the purse and pulls out two or three ten-pound notes and a handful of change and holds them in her hand.*

Anne   Christine? What are you doing, love?

Racheal *stares at her nana for some time. Appalled by the chocolate, the spittle, the tears, the money. Appalled by what she has done perhaps.*

Racheal (*gulping her breath*)   Nana. What's the saddest thing that ever happened to you? What is it? Do you think?

Anne   My daughter's gone. She went. She's gone.

Racheal   Can yer blame her though, really, can yer?

Anne   I feel sick.

Racheal   Stick yer fingers down yer throat. Make yer feel better.

Anne   I don't know who you are.

Racheal   Yer what?

Anne   I don't know who you are.

Racheal *drops the handbag on the floor. Stares at the money and at her nana for three seconds.*

Lights dim.

Racheal *takes off her sunglasses. Watches her nana leave. Waits.*

Scene Five

1996. The staffroom of the Gateway's supermarket, Heaton Moor Road, Heaton Moor, Stockport.
    Early-evening autumn light coming in from a small window.
    There are two sets of lockers at opposite sides of the stage. Each have a clipboard hanging from them with timesheets and a pen attached.
    In the centre of the stage there is a double-sided bench divided by a row of hooks. Normally the coats on these hooks would divide the staffroom more obviously into a girls' changing area and a boys' changing area but now there are no coats. The demeanour of the characters should still, however, delineate the gender of the areas.
    *Before the lights rise, **Racheal** puts her cardigan in her locker and puts on a green Gateway's uniform. She is getting changed*

*out of her uniform. She will take trainers and socks from out of the
locker.*

Lights rise. **Danny Miller**, *aged nineteen, stands perfectly still,
quite rigid, in the boys' half. He has just been punched by a shoplifter.
His eye is bruised. His contact lens has become dislodged.* **Racheal
Keats**, *also nineteen, holds his eye open and is trying to prise the lens
from underneath his eyelid.*

Danny *has nurtured and developed the combination of boyish
charm and guarded caution that we saw in Scene Three. He is a
handsome boy now. He too is wearing a Gateway's uniform.*

Danny   Careful.

Racheal   I'm being careful.

Danny   It kills that.

Racheal   Shut up. Keep still.

Danny   I'm keeping still, aren't I?

Racheal   Danny.

Danny   How fucking still do you want me to be?

Racheal   You keep blinking. Don't swear.

Danny   You're sticking your fingers in my eye. Of course
I keep blinking. Fuck's sake.

Racheal   Danny!

She spots the lens and starts to move it out of the eyelid.

Hold on. I see it. Steady. Steady. Steady.

Danny   Rache.

Racheal (*succeeding*)   Got it.

Danny (*folding back*)   Arrrgghh.

Racheal *hands him the lens, which he takes.*

Racheal   Say thank you, Racheal.

Danny   Jesus. That was sore.

Racheal   Danny.

Danny   Thank you, Racheal.

Racheal   Wash that. Before you put it back in.

Danny *looks around. Finds nothing to wash it with.* **Racheal** *returns to the girls' side.* **Danny** *spits on the contact lens. Puts the lens back in his eye.* **Racheal** *takes off her overall and puts it in the locker, folding it while she talks. Takes out socks and trainers, which she puts on, and a coat. Checks her hair in a mirror in her locker door. Maybe brushes it. Maybe applies some deodorant. All while she talks to* **Danny**.

Racheal   That was weird. Touching your eyeball. It felt much harder than you'd have thought.

Danny   Thank you for getting it out.

Racheal   That's all right. Did he hurt you?

Danny   No. Just caught us. Right on the lens and that. Couldn't get to it. It does your head in a bit.

Racheal   He was a poor bastard, wa'n't he?

Danny   Police come yet?

Racheal   Just now. He were crying. Did you see?

Danny   Serves him right.

Racheal   Reckoned they'd send him down. Done it before, he said.

Danny   Fucking tuna fish. Brainy fella, eh?

Racheal *(grinning)*   You looked very funny running after him.

Danny *(grinning back)*   Fuck off.

Racheal   Your legs were all mad. Flapping out behind you.

Danny   Fuck off.

Racheal   Run like a girl.

Danny   Rache.

Racheal   What?

Danny   Shut it.

Racheal (*with a giggle, interrupting her changing, going to peer round into his side*)   Or what?

Danny   Or . . . just . . .

They hold each other's eyes for a long moment. Smiling. Both of them on the point of saying something. Neither speaking. Eventually:

You look beautiful. Even in uniform and that. You do.

Racheal   Thank you.

Danny   Uniform's hanging. Makes most people look like spastics. But it don't bother me on you.

Racheal   That's good. You look like a knob in yours.

Danny *takes his shoes off and wipes dirt from them. Breathes on them. Polishes them. While he talks to **Racheal** he hardly looks at her. Concentrating deeply on the cleaning of the shoes. She goes back to her side, continues to change. He starts to talk quite quietly. As though he is afraid somebody might overhear him. Nobody would.*

Danny   Last night. (*Beat.*) It was good, wasn't it? It was all right. I liked it.

Racheal   Me too.

Danny   I was worried when I got up this morning. Just looking at you and that. I was worried that you might have thought that you'd made a big mistake or summit. Y'know what I mean?

Racheal   I didn't.

Danny   I was trying to figure out if you were really asleep or if you were just pretending to be asleep so that I'd leave.

Racheal   I wasn't.

Danny   No. I know. You started snoring.

Racheal   I never.

Danny   Yer did. Like a little baby pig.

Racheal *sticks her tongue out at him.*

Danny   I like your flat.

Racheal   Thanks.

Danny   It's smart. Yer lucky.

Racheal   I know.

Danny   Good area Edgely. I reckon.

Racheal   It's all right.

Danny   How much you paying?

Racheal   Thirty quid a week.

Danny   'S all right that, int it?

Racheal   Working here. It's easy.

Danny   How d'yer get the deposit?

Racheal   Saved up.

Danny   Do you like it? Living on your own?

Racheal   I love it.

Danny   Don't you miss your Billy? Or your dad or nothing.

Racheal   No. I see Billy most days. I never saw much of Dad anyway.

Beat. Looks at **Danny** *before she speaks.*

You know when you think of somebody?

Danny   Yer what?

Racheal   Like if you had a mental picture of somebody. When you close your eyes and you think of them just off the top of yer head.

Danny   Yeah?

Racheal   When I do that with my dad I can only ever see him down the pub. I can't imagine him in our flat. At all. I can't get it in my head. In the pub. Or in hospital.

Danny   In hospital?

Racheal   In the café there. Don't matter. It got to the point when I couldn't actually stand the way they smelled. The way the flat smelled. The way our dad ate apples. Did my head in.

Danny   How's your Billy doing?

Racheal   He's all right. Glad to be home. Reckons he's going to keep himself out of bother and that now. We'll see, eh?

Danny   You reckon he'd remember us?

Racheal   Course. He used to like you.

Danny   Say hello to him for us, eh?

Racheal   I will do, yeah.

She comes round to the boys' side and sits on the bench and looks at him.

Can I ask you a question?

Danny   Go on.

Racheal   Does it bother you that we didn't have sex last night?

Danny   No.

Racheal   Are you sure?

Danny   Course I am.

Racheal   Yer not lying?

Danny   Rache, I had, it was, I thought, it was one of the best nights I'd ever had. In my life, Rache. In my whole life, mate. Honestly.

Racheal (*with a huge smile*)   Right. Good. I just wanted to check.

She smiles at him for a few seconds. Stands up and, as she speaks, moves around exploring the boys' changing room. Trying to open **Danny***'s and even other men's lockers. Pacing the size of the side.*

What star sign are you?

Danny   Yer what?

Racheal   What's your star sign?

Danny   Gemini, why?

Racheal   I'm trying to think of things I don't know about you.

Danny   Why?

Racheal   I just think it would be good. To know them. I'm Aquarius. That's good. Gemini and Aquarius.

Danny   Do you believe all that?

Racheal   No. Not really. Sometimes. What's your favourite colour?

Danny   (You're) Mental.

Racheal   Go on, Danny, tell us.

Danny   Why?

Racheal   Because I want to know. What is it?

Danny   Blue. What's yours?

Racheal   Indigo.

Danny   Indigo?

Racheal   What's your favourite taste?

Danny   Steak.

Racheal   Steak?

Danny   Yeah. A really nice steak. Juicy. All the blood. I love that.

Racheal   You ever had ice cream and lemonade?

Danny   Course.

Racheal   That's better. Than steak.

Danny   No it isn't

Racheal   Fucking is.

Danny (*mocking, with a gentle snort*)   Girl.

Racheal   What about clothes? What are your favourite clothes? This is good this.

She stands on the bench and walks up and down it. Kicking him out of the way when she arrives at him.

Danny   I've got a Pringle jumper that my brother got me. 'S top.

Racheal   I like shoes better than almost anything in the world.

Danny   Even better than ice cream and lemonade?

Racheal   Miles. What's your favourite smell?

Danny   Oil paint.

Racheal   You what?

Danny   Oil paint.

Racheal   You some kind of glue sniffer, are you?

Danny   No. Always reminds me of primary school. Used to love it there.

Racheal   I love the way swimming pools smell. All the chlorine. And the fans on the walls outside. The way they're really warm.

Danny (*simply*)   I love the way your hair smells.

Racheal   Thank you.

Danny   That's all right.

Racheal (*watches him, jumps down, and then, after a beat*)   I really want to kiss you.

Danny   Do you?

Racheal   Like mental. Like nothing you'd ever believe.

The shop manager, **Jake Moran***, walks in. He is a short, bespectacled man. Forty-eight years old. He has short, wispy hair and wears a suit. He is agitated. He distracts himself from the frankness of his apology by constantly rifling through the timesheets, attached to a clipboard which he takes down from their place hanging on the lockers, and neatening his tie as he talks. He is surprised to find* **Racheal** *in the boys' side of the changing rooms.*

Moran   Beirut. That's what it's getting like in here. It's like a war zone. It's like Beirut. All these little monkeys coming in here. Do you know, Racheal? Do you know how many, how many, how many incidents of shoplifting we've reported in the last month?

Racheal   I'm not really sure, Mr Moran, no.

Moran   Have a guess. Go on. I bet you never get it.

Racheal   Twelve.

Moran   Twenty-three. Twenty-three thieving fucking shoplifters in one fucking month. And they're just the ones we see. And report. It's not, what it's not, is, it's not reasonable. These aren't reasonable conditions under which my staff should be expected to work. Are you all right, Danny?

Danny   I'm fine, Mr Moran, honestly. I'm all right, yeah.

Moran (*concentrating on the timesheets*)   I tell Mr Ridgely. I tell him. I tell him. He makes sympathetic, well, noises. Sympathetic little noises is what he makes. But I don't think that's enough. I really, I, I really, actually, I really don't. I don't. Any more. I just don't. (*Looking straight at* **Danny**.) He could have hurt you. Couldn't he?

Danny   He wouldn't have done.

Moran   But he might have done. People get, these people, they, well, they get desperate is what they get. I'm really very sorry that this had to happen to you, Danny. I'm very grateful to you for what you did. If you want to take the rest of the afternoon off then you can do and I'll fill out your hours as normal. I'll do that. Because you shouldn't expect to deal with what you had to deal with just now. It's not . . . (*large inhalation of breath as he finds the right word*) . . . reasonable.

Danny   No. Honestly. I'll be fine.

Moran (*polishes his glasses on his shirt*)   When the police came to get him. He started whimpering. Stamped his feet. Before they got here he begged me to actually, what he did is, he begged me to let him go. Actually. Had a, a, a, a tantrum. He must have been thirty. Thirty-two. If you need anything, Danny, I'll be in my office. It leaves you breathless. Doesn't it? Sometimes?

Danny   It does, yes.

Moran   Just. Breathless. Danny. Racheal. I'll be in my office.

He leaves. They laugh affectionately. Smile at each other. Vaguely bewildered.

Racheal   Are you all right? Really?

Danny   I'm fine. Honestly.

Racheal   I wasn't worried or nothing. Watching you. My heart didn't beat any faster. It was just like watching TV. Is that bad do you think?

Danny   No. Course not. (*Having tied his laces he stands.*) I should get back.

Racheal   Do you have to?

Danny   Got to finish stuff. Before the shift finishes. You done now?

Racheal   Yeah. What time do you finish?

Danny   Six.

Racheal   Should I wait for you?

Danny   Four hours. Don't be soft.

Racheal   You could take the afternoon off. He said. Tell him you've got an headache.

Danny   He wouldn't finish the work for us though, would he? It's not fair to leave it for night staff. I hate night shift. Keep yer for hours if you don't get stuff done.

Racheal   I'd like to see you.

Danny   Would you?

Racheal   Yeah. Will you ring us?

Danny   Yeah. Course.

Racheal   Will you?

Danny   I told you I would, didn't I?

Racheal   You promise?

Danny   What's the matter with you, eh?

Racheal   I don't know. I just. I just get. I'd just like to see you. There's nothing the matter with me.

Danny   Rache.

Racheal   What?

Danny   I bought you a present.

Racheal   Yer what?

Danny   This morning. On way in. I got you a present.

Racheal (*not delighted*)   Did yer?

Danny   It's a bit shit.

Racheal   Is it?

Danny   I'm bollocks at buying presents, me. I'm shit at it. But. I just wanted to get you something.

Racheal   Right.

Danny   I never had time to wrap it.

Racheal   That's all right.

Danny *passes her a paper bag. From the bag she takes out a small jewellery box. Inside the box there is a gold bracelet. He watches her, anxious.*

Racheal (*doesn't look at him*)   It's . . . Danny. This is a bit mad.

Danny   Does it fit you?

Racheal (*trying it on*)   Course. Look. (*Beat.*) I can't take this.

Danny   Course you can –

Racheal   Danny –

Danny   I just wanted to. Last night, y'know.

Racheal   I know.

She looks at him only now. Goes towards him. Goes as though to kiss him. But doesn't.

Thank you. Go back to work now.

Danny   I'll ring you when I'm done.

Racheal   All right.

Danny   We could go Savoy or summit.

Racheal   We could do, yes.

Danny   You coming down with us?

Racheal   No. Give us a minute. Gotta sort me timesheets out and that. I'm a bit all over the place.

Danny   Say goodbye to us before you go, won't you?

Racheal   Soft bugger.

Danny   I'll see you later.

Racheal   Yeah. See you in a bit.

He leaves. She watches him go smiling.

She moves into the girls' room and pulls out timesheets from the clipboard. Sits on the bench. Starts filling one out. Clips it back and hangs the clipboard up. Stops. Stares at her bracelet. Takes it off. Stares some more. Hits her head against the locker, gently, five times. Rests her head against it. Whispers 'Danny Danny Danny Danny Danny. You . . .' Stands up straight. Goes to leave. Pauses. Gathers her breath as though screwing up her courage to face something inexorable. Leaves.

Should it be decided not to have an interval here, then the lights should dim and **Racheal** *should change according to the convention that has been established.*

Scene Six

1999. A hotel room. The Fir Tree Hotel, Edale, Derbyshire. New Year's Eve. The last night of the millennium. Pitch black outside. The room is a warm bubble of light around a bed and a dressing table. There is a large mirror. And a small fridge.

Racheal Keats *sits at the dressing table. She wears a short black dress. Her hair is tied up. She is applying make-up. She is twenty-two years old.*

Her husband, **Kevin Brake**, *a wiry man, tied up like a knot, stands behind her. He is twenty-eight years old. He wears black jeans*

*and no shoes, socks or shirt. He is drinking from a bottle of Corona. He
is watchful. Slightly drunk.*

Racheal   Funny looking in the mirror and seeing this
room, Kevin.

He looks at her.

Yer get used to seeing rooms in mirrors. When you're doing
your make-up. Your hair and that. When you see a new
room. It looks odd.

He puts on his shirt. Smiles at her.

Been ages since I've stayed in a hotel. Years.

*Puts his shoes and socks on, ties his laces. She drinks from a glass of
wine by her side. Turns to him.*

It's a beautiful part of the world this.

He goes over to the window and stares out.

I love it, all the hills. The smell of the air. You go for walks
round here and you don't see anybody for miles. Only
sheep. Come right up to you. Eat your butties. Find little
pubs. Have a pint. By the fire sometimes. Get a nice packet
of crisps. My mum used to come up here. She told us. When
she were little. Yer can see this place from our dad's flat
sometimes. On a clear day and that. Not this hotel. But
round about here.

*He looks at her for a long time while she continues her make-up.
Finishes his bottle.*

Kevin   You're funny.

Racheal   What?

Kevin   You.

Racheal   What?

Kevin   Nothing.

She drinks some wine. Sprays perfume on to her wrists and applies it to her neck.

Racheal   So. You excited?

Kevin   Excited?

Racheal   About tonight?

Kevin   I am, yeah.

Racheal   Big night, innit?

Kevin   It's the biggest, Racheal.

Racheal   Amazing when you think about it. (*Beat.*) Do you think of it, Kev, as the last night of this millennium or the first night of the next one?

Kevin   I don't know.

Racheal   'Cause when you think about it it could be either, couldn't it?

Kevin   It could be, yeah.

Racheal   I think about it as a beginning. The beginning of something.

Kevin   I hope so.

They smile at each other.

How late's the bar on until?

Racheal   Four o'clock. I think.

Kevin   It better have Jack Daniel's.

Racheal   It will.

Kevin (*patting her back*)   I'm telling you, Rache, it better fucking had do. You go to some of these places, don't you, though? Some of these fucking old country places and they don't have anything fucking any good. All fucking bald bastards with brandy and real ale and cigars and wank like that. I'm just drinking Jack Daniel's, me. Tonight. And champagne.

Racheal (*smiling at his description*)   Yer want another bottle?

Kevin   Yeah. Go on.

She goes to fridge. Pulls out another bottle of Corona and the opened bottle of wine. Tops up her glass. Gives him the bottle. Goes back to the dressing table. Sprays herself with a touch more perfume.

We just got to keep it together.

Racheal   Yer what?

Kevin   Us two.

Racheal   What are you like?

Kevin   That's what matters.

Racheal   Get you.

Kevin   What?

Racheal (*imitating*)   'We just gott akeep it together. That's what matters.'

Kevin   What?

Racheal   Nothing.

Kevin   What, Racheal?

Racheal   Nothing. Honest.

Some time.

Kevin (*honestly, as though gently scared*)   I hate the countryside. It's too quiet.

Racheal   I like that.

Kevin (*the same*)   At night-time. You open your window. You can't hear nothing. Scares the shit out of us.

Racheal   You can hear foxes. Owls and that.

Kevin   And it's so fucking dark. Can't fucking see anything. Yer need, yer need, yer need, yer need. I don't know. Something.

Racheal   I think that's nice. Makes me feel cosy. Safe.

He looks at her for some time.

Kevin   You smell nice.

Racheal   Thank you.

Kevin   Is that a new perfume?

Racheal   It is, yes.

Kevin   It's nice.

Racheal   Billy got it for us.

Kevin   Did he?

Racheal   For Christmas.

Kevin   That's nice.

Some time.

Did he nick it?

Racheal   Kevin!

Kevin   What?

Racheal   No.

Kevin   You sure?

Racheal   He bought it. He's got a job and everything.

Kevin   Has he?

Racheal   He's working in Bull's Head.

Kevin   He all right, is he?

Racheal   He is. Yeah. Been six month now.

Kevin   Good lad. Six month, eh? Fuck me. How's yer old man?

Racheal   He's all right. Bit. Yer know.

Kevin   What?

Racheal   Bit moody.

Kevin   Is he?

Racheal   Strops about. Like a big kid.

Kevin   You nearly finished.

Racheal   Just do my hair.

He watches her as she lets her hair down and starts to comb it.

Kevin   Tell you one good thing about hotel.

Racheal   What's that?

Kevin   It's very tidy, int it? (*He grins, squeezes his eyes tight. Opens them again and breathes out a sigh of relief.*) Not like our fucking dump. Eh, Racheal?

No response. He coughs once.

Sometimes wonder, honestly, sometimes I wonder what the fuck you actually do all day.

Racheal   Yer what? Kevin?

Kevin   So, your kid, he still hanging round all Chris Bennett? That lot. Lucy Moore?

Racheal   Yeah.

Kevin   He see much of Danny Miller?

Racheal   Don't know. A bit.

Kevin   What do you mean?

Racheal   Yer what?

Kevin   You said you don't know and then you said 'a bit'. Which is it?

Racheal   I think he sees him every so often.

Kevin   Yer know that, do yer?

Racheal   Yeah.

Kevin (*quietly, grinning*)   So, if you know that, if you know that, Rache, how come you said you didn't know when I first asked you?

Racheal   You what?

Kevin (*still*)   You heard. Bit fucking weird that, int it?

Racheal   Kev –

Kevin (*louder*)   No it is though, a bit fucking weird. Int it though? It fucking is. Why did you lie to us, Racheal?

Racheal   I wasn't lying, Kevin. I just wasn't thinking. I was just, y'know.

Kevin   No. I don't know, Rache. I don't know at all. What were you just doing? You were just – what?

Racheal   I was talking without really thinking about what I was saying. That's not lying. That's different from lying. Kev, are you all right?

Kevin   Me? I'm fine. Fucking great, yeah. Cracking. Never better. Yer just . . .

Racheal   What?

Kevin   You look lovely, Racheal. You know that. You do, sweetheart.

Racheal   Thank you.

Kevin   You look . . .

Racheal   What?

Kevin   When was the last time you saw him?

Racheal   Who?

Kevin   Danny Miller.

Racheal   Two years ago.

Kevin Was it?

Racheal Just before we got married.

Kevin (*looking at her first*) Are you sure?

Racheal Yes.

Kevin You're not just talking without really thinking what you're saying now, are you, Rache?

Racheal No. Just after I left Gateway's. Down White Lion. I remember it.

Kevin I bet you do.

Racheal Yer what?

Kevin I said I bet you remember seeing him. I fucking bet you do.

Racheal Kev, please, don't.

Kevin Don't what?

Racheal Just . . .

Kevin Don't what, Racheal? I don't *believe* you. So. Can I ask you a question? Rache? Can I? Rache, look at us. Rache, if your perfume is a Christmas present, Racheal, if your perfume is a Christmas present, how come the bottle's not full?

Racheal Yer what?

Kevin It's not though, is it? Look. There's some gone out of that.

Racheal There's never –

Kevin Rache, there fucking is. Of course there fucking is. I can see there fucking is just by fucking looking at the cunt.

Racheal Kev.

Kevin (*picking the bottle up*) Now. If this was a Christmas present from your brother that you got last Saturday yes?

And this is the first time I have seen you wear it yes? Then how come there is some taken out of the bottle?

Racheal   Kev, I swear –

Kevin   That must mean, Rache, when you think about it and everything, that must mean that either a) your brother gave you a half-full bottle of perfume for your Christmas present, which is a bit fucking mard-arsed of him in my opinion, or b) you've worn it before somewhere else when you went out with someone else, you've worn it for someone else, without letting me know. It must do, Rache, mustn't it?

Racheal   No, Kev –

Kevin   It must do. Really. Come on, Rache. I'm not a fucking thick cunt. Which is it?

Racheal   What?

Kevin   Which is it? Did your skinny-arsed fucking rat of a brother give you some dodgy cheap shitty bottle of half-filled fucking perfume or have you worn it before? This week? When I've been out? Which is it?

Racheal   Kev, neither – it's not half –

Kevin   Which is it?

Racheal   I can't do this.

Kevin   Do what?

Racheal   I haven't got the energy any more, Kevin.

Kevin   Which is it, Racheal?

Racheal   It's not half opened.

Kevin   Racheal, which is it?

Racheal   Kev.

Kevin   Don't you fucking lie to me. I'll break your fucking teeth. Which is it?

Racheal   Kevin, don't.

Kevin   Which is it, Racheal?

Racheal   It's neither, I swear.

Kevin   Why are you lying to me? Racheal? Why?

Racheal   I'm not.

Kevin (*perhaps punches his chest with each beat*)   Why? Why? Why? Why? Why?

Throws the perfume against the floor. It smashes. He pulls back. Finishes his can. Stares at her while she talks. Nodding his head. Chewing frantically.

Racheal   I thought we could have a night out. Just tonight. Just for the millennium. Just us two. Be nice, wouldn't it? If just for one night, if just one night. It would be nice. I hate this. You're just like fucking Dad. Stinks in here now.

Kevin (*very quietly*)   Where's your phone?

Racheal   You what?

Kevin (*still*)   Where's your phone? Racheal? Your mobile phone.

Racheal   What do you want my phone for?

Kevin (*still, he turns to her*)   Where's your fucking phone, Racheal?

Racheal   I'm not telling you. It's my fucking phone.

Kevin (*shouts suddenly*)   Fuck.

Goes to her. Grabs a handful of her hair.

Where's your fucking phone, Racheal?

Racheal   Get off me.

Kevin   Tell me. Where is it?

Racheal   It's in me bag.

He lets her go. She falls to the floor.

That hurt me. You little fuckwad.

Flashes a glare at her. Raises his fist suddenly. She cowers back. He goes over to her bag. Pulls the stuff out of her bag randomly, wantonly, throwing it around. Pulls her phone out. Finds her phone-book function on it. Lists through the names kept on the phone.

Kevin   Where are we? Where are we? Come on? Where are we?

Racheal   What are you doing?

Kevin   C, C, C, C, C – D. Danny. Fuck. You lying fucking cunt.

Racheal   Kev, I swear.

Kevin   Who's Danny, Racheal? Heh? Who's that? Fucking Danny? Who's fucking Danny, Racheal? Is it Danny Miller? Is it?

Racheal   Kev, please, don't.

Kevin   You fucking slag.

Gets her by her hair. Lifts her up. Throws her across the bed. Presses dial on the phone.

It's engaged. It's fucking engaged. C'mon, Danny. You fucking cheap cunt fucker.

Dials redial. It is still engaged.

Fuck. Fuck. Fuck. Fuck. Fuck.

He smashes his head into the mirror. Three times. It cracks around him. He slumps down on to the floor. Starts sobbing. Huge big sobs. Wails as he inhales. His shoulders heave. **Racheal** *doesn't move. Stares at him.*

Kevin (*tiny broken-hearted voice*)   You're my wife. You're supposed to be my wife. See, you know what your problem is? Don't you? You're a fucking tart. Is your problem.

Racheal (*simply*)   I'm not.

Kevin Just a slapper. Just a slag. Worst day of my life day I married you. Hated it. Had to get drunk just to get through it. Manky old slag.

Racheal (*again, simply*) I'm not, Kev. Don't say that.

Kevin Don't you fucking dare even think about telling me what to do.

He stares at her for a while. And then stands.

I'm going out now. I don't know when I'm coming back. I hope you die soon.

He leaves. She watches him go.

Stands up after a while. It hurts. She goes to pick up her wine glass. Drains it. Gets the wine bottle from the fridge and refills her glass. She goes to where **Kevin** *has dropped her phone and picks it up. Sits back on the bed. Drinks from her glass. Phones her brother.*

Racheal Billy? It's me, Racheal. How are you? Good lad. Are you? That'll be good, won't it? I'm OK, love. I'm fine. I don't know. I don't think so. Kevin's had a bit of a bad one, mate, you with me? No I'm fine. He's just. I hate him, Billy. I want to kill him. I think I might. I fucking could. I bet you. No. I won't. No, don't worry about that. I'll be fine. I will. I'll be magic. I just wanted to talk to you. I was thinking about yer. Got yer perfume on. I have and all. I like it. It's really nice. Oh, fuck him. I think it's lovely. I just wanted to wish you Happy New Year. I know, well. I'm doing it early, aren't I? Happy New Year. I know. Happy New Century. Happy New Millennium. It's mental, int it? Listen, mate, I'm gonna fuck off. I just wanted to, you know, I just wanted to talk to you. No. I'll be, I'm fine. I'm cracking. Yeah. I know. I love you, Bill. Well. I do. I'll see you later. Have a good one. You have a good night, mate. See you later.

She turns the phone off. Sits up on the bed. Staring out of the window.

Stands up after a while.

The lights fade. She walks right to the very edge of the stage. Puts on a small black cardigan.

Scene Seven

2002. The beer garden at the front of the Elizabethan Pub, Heaton Moor, Stockport.
    It is ten o'clock at night. Towards the end of summer. The first night when you notice that the temperature has begun to drop.
    There is a wooden table in the centre of the stage. Two wooden benches are attached, one either side.
    Racheal Keats, *twenty-four, enters. She has just walked out of the pub. Something about her demeanour, the way she holds herself, the way she glances back to where she came from suggests that something has happened inside the pub to upset her. She stands in the middle of the stage. As though on the cusp of leaving the beer garden. But stops herself. Wraps her arms around herself to keep her warm.*
    After a short while, **Danny Miller**, *also aged twenty-four, in a short-sleeved shirt and jeans, comes out to find her. He carries her vodka and lime, half drunk, and his half-drunk pint of lager. He expects her to have left the beer garden. When he realises she hasn't he pulls himself up short.*
    She becomes aware of his presence. Straightens. Doesn't look back at him.

Danny (*tentative*)   So. Did you miss us?

Racheal (*still not looking back, not smiling*)   Course.

Danny   Should have rung us. We could have come to see you.

Racheal (*still not*)   I know. I'm sorry.

Danny   Always wanted to go to York.

Racheal (*still not*)   It's very pretty.

Danny   Go t'races. Check out minster. All that.

Racheal   Good pubs and all.

Danny   Are there?

Racheal   Cracking, aye.

Danny   Are you all right?

Racheal   Yeah. Funny.

Danny   What?

Racheal (*with a nod back to the pub*)   In there. All them cunts. Look at yer. Like. Once you've left you can't ever go back. Who do they think they are?

Danny   I don't know.

She turns back to him.

How long were you there for?

Racheal   Ten month. Bit more.

Danny *pulls out a cigarette. Lights it, looking at her.*

Danny   Did you enjoy yourself, Racheal?

Racheal   Yeah. I did. It was all right.

Danny   Is it very different?

Racheal   What?

Danny (*putting the drinks down next to her*)   York. From Stockport?

Racheal   I don't know. It feels smaller. It's older. With the wall and that. Load of fucking students. Shops are all right.

Danny   Did you . . . ?

Racheal   What?

Danny   I don't know.

Racheal *smiles. Moves towards him.*

Danny (*puts drinks on table*)   You make any friends there?

Racheal   Couple. They were all right. Couple of girls from work. People were well friendly, mind you. Go into pubs and folk just talk to you.

Danny   What about fellas?

Racheal (*turns to face him briefly, with a smile*)   What about fellas?

Danny   Meet anybody?

Racheal   No one special. Not really. Couple of morons.

Danny   York City casuals?

Racheal   Yeah, right.

Danny   You not cold?

Racheal   No, I'm fine.

Danny   What's it like coming back?

Racheal   It's all right.

Danny   Notice anything different?

Racheal (*grins before she speaks*)   You've had your hair cut.

Danny   No. About Stockport.

Racheal   Only weird stuff.

Danny   What like?

Racheal   I noticed how short the clock tower in Merseyway was.

Danny   You what?

Racheal (*walks once around the table*)   When I was a kid I used to think it was massive. Fucking big skyscraper. I couldn't understand how come, when they had programmes about the tallest buildings in the world, I couldn't understand why they never mentioned the clock tower in Merseyway. I went back in there at the weekend. It's tiny.

Very squat. Really short. I was quite disappointed. Noticed
the viaduct.

Danny   The viaduct?

Racheal   I never really paid any attention to it before. I
never really noticed it. But I was looking at it, on my way
into town. It's actually, y'know, it's quite impressive. There's
something about it.

Danny   Single largest brick structure in the world.

Racheal   Oh aye?

Danny   It is actually.

Racheal   I noticed how many pubs there are. Pubs
fucking everywhere in this place. A lot of the shops have
changed. Smartened up a bit.

Danny   Still fucking grotty, mind you.

Racheal   I don't know. Some of them are all right. And I
was up at the station. Looking down. Noticed the way the
valley curves down.

Danny   Oh aye?

Racheal   When I was little, I used to love all geography.
All about continental drift. And the ice age. Stuff like that.
And looking at the town centre I could just have imagined
what it must have been like. All the ice and that. How it
would have settled. See all the curves of where the water
was. Imagine what it was like underneath the sea. That was
a bit mad.

Danny   Sounds it.

*She is on the point of sitting at the table. But then doesn't. Takes a
drink. Moves away again. Folds her arms again. He settles on the
bench.*

Racheal   Funny going back into Manchester. All the rain.
Went in with Billy. It were pissing down. Felt, kind of, it felt

all right. Felt like it was meant to be raining here. Felt OK.
You know what I mean?

Danny   Built on rain. Manchester. All towns round here.

Racheal   Yer what?

Danny (*follows her*)   Whole city only settled where it is
because the air was so moist. Made it all right for cotton
industry. All factories and that. If it hadn't rained so much it
wouldn't have even been here.

Racheal   Is that right?

Danny   Fucking dead right.

Racheal   Yer know a lot of funny stuff, you, don't you?

Danny   It's not funny. It's good.

Racheal   I did miss you. Funny that, int it? Mind you.
You little bugger. Yer could have rang us.

Danny   I couldn't find you.

Racheal   Could have told us.

Danny   Didn't know where you were.

Racheal   Could have asked our kid.

Danny   He was –

Racheal   Well, our dad then.

Danny   I . . .

Racheal (*moves away from him*)   Could have tried. I would
have loved to have come. I'd love to meet her, Sarah.

Danny (*stays where he is*)   You'd like her.

Racheal   You reckon?

Danny   She's very, I don't know, she's, she's tough. Is
what she is. She's not thick. You know? Don't take shit from
anybody. I, I, I really, yer know, I love her and that.

Racheal   I should hope so.

Danny   I do.

Racheal (*turns to face him*)   How old's Hazel?

Danny   She's two next September.

Racheal   Good age that, int it?

Danny   She's funny.

Racheal   With all the talking and that?

Danny   Yer should hear her.

Racheal   I can imagine. Would y'ave another one?

Danny   Maybe. One day. I hope so.

Racheal   I bet yer a great dad, you.

Danny   I don't know about that.

Racheal   I bet you are. I bet she loves you like mad.

Danny (*drinks*)   I wish I didn't have to work so much. So I could spend more time with her. All that.

Racheal   How is your work?

Danny   It's all right. Nice and quiet this time of year. Everybody's fucked off on holiday. Gets a bit mad around Christmas. All cards and that.

Racheal   You got a uniform?

Danny   Course.

Racheal   I bet you look dead cute in it.

Danny   Fuck off.

Racheal   Like yer dressing up or summit.

Danny   Sometimes think I'll jack it in.

Racheal   Why?

Danny   Sort something out. Set something up. Work for myself or summit. Sometimes I think I'd like to do that.

Racheal   Doing what?

While he talks he taps his fag packet.

Danny   Mate of mine's got a little company. Does panelling. Yer know, for people's houses. Pubs and that. Couple of months back he was having a bit of a rush on. Asked us if I could help him out. It were magic.

He takes a cigarette out.

Racheal   Was it?

He points with his cigarette to punctuate his observations.

Danny   It was quite, you know, it was creative. Yer had to think and that. But then after a bit, you get into it, get a rhythm going. And when you look at it all done. It looks quite, like, quite beautiful. You just, you just ended up thinking just – well, well, what the fuck? Why am I doing this? Why am I doing my job when I could be making panels? Be good, wouldn't it?

Lights cigarette.

Racheal   Be great.

Danny   Get a little van. Pop Hazel up in the passenger seat. Whizz all round. Doing panels. I'd love that. I think about it quite a lot.

Racheal   You should do it.

Danny   Yeah. Maybe.

Beat.

He looks down at his cigarette. Smokes from it. Embarrassed by giving himself away a little. **Racheal** *smiles at him.*

Rache.

Racheal   Yeah.

Danny   I was sorry to hear about Kevin.

Racheal (*turning away*)   Oh yeah.

Danny   He sounds like he was a fucking cunt.

Racheal   He was.

Danny   Yer seen him? Since you've come back?

Racheal   Fuck off.

Danny   Good. I'm glad. I don't think you should either. He don't deserve you.

Racheal   No. He don't.

Danny   I couldn't believe it. When I heard what he'd done.

Racheal (*turning back*)   It was just a big. Horrible. Mistake. I should never have even. I don't know what I was thinking about. Just with, just with, with Lucy and Chris and everybody seemed to be, and he was there. And he was quite, yer know, he still is, quite handsome. He asks us. I just think, well, Rache, yer may as well. It's convenient.

Looks straight at him.

How shit is that?

Danny   I know.

Racheal   Convenient. I hope you never do anything like that because it's convenient, Danny. I really hope you don't, love.

Beat.

She looks away only briefly. Goes to the table again. Stands by it, resting her weight on her knee against it.

You see much of Chris and Lucy?

Danny   Yeah. From time to time. You should give 'em a ring.

Racheal   I will.

Danny   Go out with Chris every so often. Have a bevvy.

Racheal   They happy?

Danny   Lucy's expecting.

Racheal   Is she?

Danny   Next February.

Racheal   Fucking hell. Are they excited?

Danny   Yeah. She is. She'll be great. Comes round to play with Hazel every now and then. Hazel loves her. I think Chris is a bit freaked out.

Racheal   Bless him.

Danny   Yer get like that. Most blokes. I think. And then when the baby's born. It's just, it's different. It changes. They live up in Moor.

Racheal   Do they?

Danny   Top of Dialstone Road.

Racheal   Oh aye.

Danny   Back behind of Elm's House.

Racheal   Ha!

She pushes herself away from the table again.

Danny   What?

Racheal   That's where our gran lived.

Danny   Is it?

Racheal   Yeah. She died last year. (*Beat.*) Weird.

Danny   What?

Racheal   How small things are.

Danny   Yeah.

Beat. He moves towards her slightly.

How's your dad?

Racheal   He's all right. Bit drunk. Can be a bit of a
fuckhead.

Danny   You staying with him?

Racheal   For the time being. It's all right. I don't see
much of him. He sleeps quite a lot of the time.

Danny   If you ever want a break, y'know, Rache? We've
got a spare room and that. Could come and crash with us.

Racheal   Thanks. I'll be all right. He's changed.

Danny   Has he?

Racheal   He seems much more gentle.

Danny   Right. That's good.

Racheal   In the morning and that he brings us a cup of
tea in bed, if he's up.

Danny   Well, we wouldn't do that for yer. That's certainly
fucking true. (*He moves closer.*) How's your Billy?

Racheal   He's Billy. Yer know. Not been run over for a
long time.

Danny   Yer what?

Racheal   Do yer not remember? He were always getting,
every week, for a while, he couldn't move without being hit
by a bloody car.

Danny   I don't remember.

Racheal   It was never serious. Years ago now.

Danny   When did he get out?

Racheal   February.

Danny   Is he getting any help or anything?

Racheal   Bits. He goes to see probation. He's trying to sort himself out with another job. It's not easy.

Danny   No.

She moves away from him.

Racheal (*talking out*)   But he's done well. Yer hear stories of people who go down. Getting all fucked up with all kinds of stuff. He don't. He don't do drugs. Nowt like that. He just. He really tries. I hope . . . (*Turns back.*) This is a very big chance for him. I hope he doesn't fuck things up this time. I hope he'll be all right.

Danny   I'm sure he will.

Racheal   You should go and see him. He'd love to, you know. He always really liked you.

Danny   Did he?

Racheal   He looked up to you.

Danny   Fucking hell.

Racheal   You know he did.

Beat.

She looks at **Danny** *before she speaks to him.*

Danny.

Danny   Yeah.

Racheal   Yer know you said you loved Sarah?

Danny   Yeah.

Racheal   Would you say you were in love with her as well?

Danny   I think so. Yeah. I would.

Racheal   That's good.

Danny   Yeah. I think it is.

Racheal   What do you think the difference is?

Danny   I don't know.

Racheal   Do you know what I think the difference is?

Danny   Go on.

Racheal   I think if you're in love with somebody then what you've got is a pure compatibility. There's something, it's just, it's pure. Is what it is. I think there's something pure about it.

Danny   Maybe.

Racheal   Just pure. (*Beat.*) I've never had that. Not with anybody. Never. You know what the closest I ever came was?

Danny   What?

Racheal   When I was with you. I thought . . . We did all right, didn't we? And you know what? You know what I was thinking, what I was going to? Actually. You know what I was going to ask you? You know what I was going to ask? Do you think, did you ever think, if I asked you to leave Sarah, and leave Hazel, and come and live somewhere with me, you'd say no, wouldn't you?

Long pause. The two don't shake eye contact from one another.

Danny (*very quietly*)   Yes. I would.

Racheal   I knew you would.

Danny   I'm sorry.

Racheal (*looking away from him*)   No. Don't be. Don't be sorry, Danny. Honestly. It was just something I was thinking. (*Looks back to him again.*) I think about you all the time.

Danny   I know.

Racheal   Sometimes I just sit down and I just think why the fuck did I do that?

Danny   I know.

Racheal   I, I, I . . .

Danny   It's hard. Int it?

She looks at him. And then turns away and can't look back.

After a pause.

Racheal   I keep having these nightmares.

Danny   Nightmares?

Racheal   Stupid ones. About our grandad. And our nana. About all these folk. Fucking Paul Castle's brother. Sarah Briard.

Danny   Who?

Racheal   Just this girl from our primary school. She died when I was ten. She wanted to play for Man U. I keep dreaming about people I know and who have died. It does my head in. Dream they're in the house with us. Watching us.

Long pause.

Danny   Yer know what I think?

Racheal   What?

Danny   What I think about ghosts?

Racheal   What?

Danny   I don't think they exist, Racheal.

Racheal (*turns to him and then away*)   Don't you?

Danny   I think you need to go somewhere.

Racheal   Yer what?

Danny   Somewhere, maybe, maybe, maybe somewhere you used to go with yer grandad or your brother or your mum –

Racheal   My mum?

Danny   Or summit. And just spend a night there. Watch the morning come up.

Racheal   What the fuck are you going on about, you, eh?

Danny   It's just something I think. It might help. I don't know. (*Pause.*) Rache. (*Pause.*) Rache, look at us. (*Pause.*) Yer know when yer have a mental image of somebody. When you close your eyes and think of somebody just off the top of your head. When I do that and think of you, yer know what I see? (*No response.*) I see you in the morning, on the first morning I stayed over at your house. Waking up. Watching you lying asleep next to me. You looked, you looked. It was like. I think about that more than you probably think I do. (*Pause.*) Rache, I'm really sorry. I can't. I just can't.

Racheal   I know. All right? I know.

She dries her eyes. Looks back at him.

Danny   You all right?

She laughs once. Gently. Smiles at him for a moment.

What? What are you smiling about?

Racheal   You.

Danny   What about me?

Racheal   It's just, it's good to see you. I'm glad you're doing all right. Yer know?

Danny   Yes. I do.

Beat. She walks over to him at the table.

You know you'll be all right, mate, don't you?

Racheal   Everybody keeps fucking saying that.

Danny   You will. You'll be, you'll be fucking great, Rache. I swear.

She touches his face with her hand. Lets it fall. Holds his hand. Squeezes it.

Lights dim.

Racheal *goes back to sit in the car.* **Danny** *exits.* **Billy** *joins* **Racheal**.

Scene Eight

2002. A parked Vauxhall Cavalier in the car park of the flats on Lancashire Hill in Stockport. We should see the interior of the car stripped bare towards the edge of the stage.
   Isolating light on the car.
   Racheal Keats, *aged twenty-four, and* **Billy Keats**, *nineteen, stare out looking up at the flats and around the hill into the town.*
   It is four o'clock in the morning.
   Racheal *is in the driver's seat.* **Billy** *in the passenger seat. He tries to lower it as far back as it will go. Tries to sleep. Can't. Raises it back up again. Lights a cigarette.*

Racheal   Shouldn't smoke. Knacker your lungs. Make you sterile. Give you cancer.

Billy *stares at her in utter disbelief.*

Racheal   'S true.

Billy (*about her audacity rather than her science*)   I don't believe you.

Racheal   Well, it is.

Billy   Do you know what time it is?

Racheal   Yeah.

Billy   Well then.

Racheal   What?

Billy   This is stupid.

Racheal   Yer don't have to stay here. I'll be all right on my own.

Billy   Racheal.

Racheal   I'm not a little baby, Bill.

Billy   I'm not leaving you sat out here on yer tod. You said you wanted me to come with you.

Racheal   I do.

Billy   Well, I'm here.

Racheal   Well, open the window.

He does. Yawns. Stretches. Flicks fag ash out of the window. Turns to her.

Billy   What were it you wanted to ask us?

Racheal   You what?

Billy   Before. Said you had summit to ask us. What were it?

Racheal   It can wait.

Billy   I'm knackered, me. Honestly. I'm fucked.

Long pause. Big, big, big yawn from **Billy***. His movements become agitated. Perhaps he starts tapping his feet under his chair. Drumming on his knees.*

Racheal   Billy.

Billy   Racheal.

Racheal   Do you remember when we came here with Mum? When Dad locked us out?

Billy   Yeah.

Racheal   Do you remember that?

Billy   Course I do.

Racheal   Mad that, weren't it?

Billy   She thumped us.

Racheal   I know. I remember.

Pause.

I knew then that she was gonna go. Y'know? I figured it out.

Pause.

I never told anybody that. You're the first person. Keep your feet still. Always fucking drumming. Like your wired up to the mains or summit.

Beat. He does.

Not changed that much really, has it?

Billy   No.

Racheal   Used to like it here. It were all right. Me and Leanne Macyntyre. Come down here. Look for Ronald Abbey. Smoke fags. Play near the river. Look at the motorway. Throw stones at it.

Billy   That's fucking dangerous. Yer can get sent down for that. I'm telling.

Racheal   Don't.

Billy   (*opens his car door, sits sideways, stretching his legs*) Fucking am.

Racheal   Wonder whatever happened to Leanne Macyntyre.

Billy   (*lighting another cigarette*)   She fucked off.

Racheal   Did she?

Billy   Ages back. Her and her mum. Went up Sheffield, I think. You remember her mum? I used to fancy her summit rotten.

Racheal   Fucking hell.

Billy What?

Racheal Just . . . I wonder what she's doing. Right now. Right this second.

Billy Probably fucking sleeping, I expect. In a fucking bed.

Racheal Wonder what Ronald Abbey's doing.

Billy Having a fucking wank, knowing him. Thinking about you and Leanne Macyntyre. Happiest days of his life, they were. Never been the same since.

Racheal Sometimes I get quite sad.

Billy You what?

Racheal Thinking about people like Leanne Macyntyre. Ronald Abbey.

Billy What the fuck are you going on about, Rache?

Racheal Thinking about what they're doing. Dad.

Billy Yer live with Dad. You fucking live in the room next door to him.

Racheal Chris and Lucy. Danny. Kevin. Mum. That's the worst one. I get scared about people who've died. And sad about people who I don't really see much any more.

Billy You're fucking weird.

Racheal But I'm not sad just now.

Billy Thank fuck for that.

Racheal I'm all right. Just, y'know, thinking. (*Beat.*) I saw Danny last week.

Billy Did ya?

Racheal He told me to say hello to you.

Billy Right. Hello, Danny. How's he doing?

Racheal   He's doing all right. He's doing great. Got married. Got a little girl. Hazel. She's two.

Billy   That's good, int it? I always used to like him. He was all right.

Racheal   Yeah. He was.

Billy   Bit chicken, like. But he was all right. *(Beat.)* Yer know what I think's mental.

Racheal   What?

Billy *(gesturing out)*   Thinking about all t'athletes. Down Manchester.

Racheal   Yer what?

Billy   All gathered together, like, in one place. Getting ready to compete. I think that's a bit mad. Can y'imagine?

Racheal   What?

Billy   Being them.

Racheal   Yer what?

Billy   Being an athlete. Fucking off all over the world. Running and jumping. Being the best in the world and going all over the place doing your stuff. That'd be mental, wouldn't it?

Racheal   Yeah.

Billy   It would though, wouldn't it, Rache? I'd love that. I used to be a right cracking little runner, me.

Racheal   Shoulda stuck at it.

Billy   Shoulda done.

Climbs back in the car. Lowers his seat slightly. Leans back.

Racheal   Billy.

Billy   Rache.

Racheal   What are you gonna do?

Billy You what?

Racheal What are you gonna do? It's been five month now.

Billy I know. Is this what you wanted to ask us about?

Racheal Yer not . . .

Billy What?

Racheal Yer not gonna start nicking stuff again, are you?

Billy Is this what you wanted to ask us about, Rache?

Racheal Not only this. You're not though, are you?

Billy No. No way, mate.

Racheal I really don't want you to go back down.

Billy Yer fucking telling me.

Racheal I worry about you.

Billy Do you?

Racheal Because I know it's difficult. Getting a job and that.

Billy Difficult int the fucking word, Rache, you with me?

Racheal Billy, what was it like?

Billy What was what like?

Racheal Inside.

Billy It was horrible.

Racheal Why?

Billy Just . . .

Racheal What was horrible about it, Billy?

Billy I don't really want to talk about this, Racheal.

Racheal Was it different to young offenders'?

Billy   Yes.

Racheal   How?

Billy   Look, Rache, I told you. . . Can we just fucking drop it?

Racheal   You should talk about it.

Billy *rolls over in the car seat, away from* **Racheal**. *Covers his head with his coat.*

Billy   Fucking hell.

Racheal   It might help.

Billy   Fuck's sake.

Racheal   Sorry. (*Pause.*) I worry about yer.

Billy   Yer said. Don't bother.

Racheal   It's 'cause I like yer.

Pause. He looks at her very briefly, still lying down. Uncovers his head.

Billy   It was nasty. (*Pause.*) Does your head in. Gets me thinking odd stuff.

Racheal   What like? What like, Billy? What kind of stuff do yer think about?

Long pause.

Billy   Y'know, at times I imagine myself getting fucking smacked up something rotten or summit.

Racheal   Like what?

Billy   Like heading a flying concrete football. Getting smacked in the face by a metal girder. Having an iron spike cutting right through my brain. Yer know what I mean?

Racheal   I'm not sure.

Billy   I think about that stuff when I think about going down.

Racheal   I see.

Long pause. **Billy** *props himself up. Looks out of the window.*

Billy   Do you know how old the world is?

Racheal   No.

Billy   Five hundred million years old. They reckon.

Racheal   How do you know that?

Billy   I read it. In nick. And scientists are starting to think that it might be even older.

Racheal   Are they?

Billy   Do you know how long human beings have been around on it?

Racheal   How long?

Billy   Fifty thousand years. It's fucking nothing. We don't matter a jot. Not one jot.

Racheal   I don't think that's true.

Billy   It fucking is.

Racheal   Did you cry ever?

Billy   Yer what?

Racheal   When you were in prison did you used to cry? (*No response.*) What's your favourite colour?

Billy   I'm not playing this.

Racheal   Go on.

Billy   No. I'm too tired. I'm all –

Racheal   Yer know what I reckon?

Billy   What?

Racheal   You know what I think. I think that nobody or nothing should make you cry. Ever. And I'm sorry because I know that there are some things that I just don't know about prison and about what it was like and what happened and all that. But I do get you now. I do get you. And I didn't always but I do now. And I love yer. And I do think that you will be all right.

Billy   You don't know what you're talking about.

Racheal   You know I said that there was something I was going to ask you.

Billy   Yeah.

Racheal   Billy, I think I might go away again.

Billy   Right.

Racheal   But for a long time this time. Not just a few months. For years. And maybe, go, maybe even leave the country even. Go and live somewhere else completely. I wanted to talk to you about it. I wanted to know what you thought about it.

Billy   What I thought about it? What's it got to do with me?

Racheal   I wanted to check that you'd be all right. If I went away.

Billy   If I'd be all right?

Racheal   I'm still not sure. I still, I haven't really decided if I should go now or if I should go at all of if I should –

Billy   I think you should. I think you should go. I think you should go now. I think you should just fuck off.

Racheal   Yer what?

Billy   I think you should.

Racheal   Right.

Billy   I mean, people should. You know? It's not enough to just stay somewhere. You can't do, all your life, you can't do things just for me. Or for Dad. Or any of that. It'd fucking kill your head, mate, you with me?

Racheal   I am. Yeah.

Billy   This place is just, it's odd. You should go and look at stuff. You might come back, mightn't you?

Racheal   I might do. Yeah.

Pause. He looks at her. She looks up at the flat.

I want to go to college.

Billy   That's a top idea.

Racheal   Go and get trained up. Get some qualifications.

Billy   Qualifications?

Racheal   I want to work as a nursery nurse. Do it properly. Get certificates and that.

Billy   You'd be very good at that.

Racheal   And I really want to get a dog.

Billy   A dog?

Racheal   I couldn't get a dog in the flats and Stockport isn't a very good place for a dog anyway.

Billy   What are you talking about? Loads of people have dogs in Stockport. Fucking hundreds. Anyway. Dogs stink.

Racheal   They don't.

Billy   They fucking do. (*Beat.*) I hope it works.

Racheal   What?

Billy   This. (*Beat.*) Or going away. Or whatever.

Long pause. The two of them look out.

I think about Mum all the time.

Racheal   So do I.

Billy   I hope she's all right.

Racheal   So do I.

Billy   She broke my heart though.

Racheal   Mine and all.

Billy   I'm going to go to sleep now.

Racheal   All right.

Billy   If I can get fucking comfy.

Racheal   Good luck.

Billy   G'night.

Racheal   Goodnight.

Long pause.

Sun's coming up.

Billy   Yer what?

Racheal   Look. Up over hills. Sun's coming up.

She points out of car window. He moves his head to look but doesn't move out of his reclined position. Settles his head back down. She looks straight ahead for a while.

Blackout.